BATTLES
OF THE ANCIENT WORLD
1285 BC ~ AD 451

Paul Hollow

June 2010.

BATTLES
OF THE ANCIENT WORLD
WORLD
1285 BC ~ AD 451

FROM KADESH TO CATALAUNIAN FIELD

KELLY DEVRIES MARTIN DOUGHERTY IAIN DICKIE PHYLLIS G. JESTICE ROB S. RICE

amber
BOOKS

First published in 2007 by Amber Books Ltd
Bradley's Close
74–77 White Lion Street
London N1 9PF
United Kingdom
www.amberbooks.co.uk

ISBN: 978-1-905704-23-1

Produced by
Amber Books Ltd
Bradley's Close
74–77 White Lion Street
London N1 9PF
United Kingdom
www.amberbooks.co.uk

Project Editor: Michael Spilling
Design: Joe Conneally
Illustrations: JB Illustrations
Picture Reseach: Terry Forshaw

All map and linework illustrations © Amber Books Ltd.

Printed in Dubai

CONTENTS

INTRODUCTION

THE ORIGINS OF WAR ARE PREHISTORIC. BY THE TIME THE MESOPOTAMIAN AND EGYPTIAN CIVILIZATIONS WERE FOUNDED, WAR HAD BECOME AN ESTABLISHED BEHAVIOURAL PRACTICE. IT WAS THIS PERIOD THAT SAW THE DEVELOPMENT OF SIMPLE FORMATIONS, INVENTION OF STRATEGY AND TACTICS, USE OF DEFENSIVE FORTIFICATIONS AND DEPLOYMENT OF WEAPONS WITH LONG- (THROWN STONES), INTERMEDIATE- (JAVELINS), AND SHORT- (SPEARS, AXES AND CLUBS) RANGE CAPABILITIES. SOME OF THE FIRST FEATURES OF WAR CAN BE TRACED TO THE EARLY STONE AGE (C. 35,000–10,000 BC). THE USE OF WEAPONS FOR HUNTING IS WELL ATTESTED TO IN CAVE PAINTINGS, BUT SO TOO IS THE USE OF SIMILAR WEAPONS BY MEN FIGHTING MEN. SKELETONS CONFIRM THIS: SOME SHOW WOUNDS THAT COULD ONLY HAVE BEEN MADE BY THESE WEAPONS, WHILE OTHERS HAVE SPEAR AND ARROW POINTS LODGED IN JOINTS AND BONES.

During the later part of the Stone Age (c. 10,000–4,000 BC), there was a great improvement in military technology. New weapons began to appear – bows, slings, daggers and maces/hammers – as did armour. The invention of the bow and arrow was important as they both increased the range of firepower and allowed their user to conceal himself. Warriors could also carry a larger number of arrows than javelins. Of equal, if not greater, importance was the invention of armour. Cave paintings from this period show defensive attachments – possibly made of bark, wood or leather – tied to the person's torso and loins that can only be described as armour or proto-armour. Extensions to the arm in some of these paintings also indicate the invention of shields.

A Sumerian warrior armed with a bronze-headed spear and simple wooden shield made from planks. A bronze helmet was his only other protection.

Cave paintings also show groups of men organized under the command of a leader and the use of formation – column and line – for the stampeding of animals over cliffs as well as combat. One cave painting even shows a flank attack, the envelopment by wings of soldiers closing in on a victim, perhaps the first recorded battlefield tactic. But it was in the Bronze Age where ancient warfare really began to change. This period saw the rise of two civilizations which would dominate their parts of the Middle East: Egypt and Mesopotamia.

EGYPT

The older of these two civilizations, in military historical terms at least, was Egypt. Some historians believe that the first large Egyptian civilization (c. 3100–2150 BC) was isolationist. However, it appears more likely that the earliest dynasties of the Egyptian kingdom were fashioned in war and maintained by military force. The first pharaoh, Narmer or Menes, united the

This relief from the vast temple of Ramses II at Thebes shows the pharaoh at the battle of Kadesh leading his massed chariots. Chariots were an expression of power and authority.

centred on Anatolia, had been extending into lands in the Middle East also desired by Egypt. Frequently armies from the two lands clashed, but it was at the battle of Kadesh, fought in *c.* 1285 BC, where the two met in all-out battle and, as happened in most of their other dealings with each other, little was concluded.

MESOPOTAMIA

The rise of Mesopotamia was also militaristic and as historically enduring as Egypt. The first Mesopotamian kingdom began sometime in the fourth or third millennium BC on the fertile lands watered by the Tigris and Euphrates rivers. After building and fortifying cities that were famous for their monumental architecture, Mesopotamian rulers recruited large armies to defend those cities and to increase the size of their kingdoms. However, soon internal conflicts between the cities – having far more independence than their Egyptian counterparts – began to develop. Alliances were often made between one group of city-states against another group of city-states only to be broken and refashioned within a very short time. The city-state that found itself unaligned also found itself quickly conquered.

Out of this, in the twenty-third century BC Akkad came to power under its king, Sargon I. He led his armies against several neighbours until virtually the whole of Mesopotamia had been re-formed into the Akkadian Empire. Still, the empire did not last long. Within 40 years Mesopotamia again fell into a civil war which would last until *c.* 1900 BC when another city-state, Babylon, was able to reunite most of the land. Its military history gained Babylon a mythic reputation, the 'walls of Babylon' especially becoming a symbol of defensive strength. But it was the offensive power of that city-state that was most impressive. Babylonian armies were disciplined, trained and technologically strong, as well as being

Upper and Lower Nile lands by warfare, as portrayed in a contemporary pallette showing the pharaoh killing his opposing leader in battle, reviewing the banners and headless bodies of the defeated, and 'symbolically' uniting Egypt. Fortified sites and warships are also depicted.

However, the main concern of the early pharaohs was defensive. Archaeology has established that Egypt was strongly defended by a system of fortifications that could and did withstand lengthy sieges. Royally led standing armies existed, but rarely functioned outside the borders of the Old Kingdom. They were, however, well led, well trained, well organized and well armed, and they could be reinforced when needed by local militias.

The Old Kingdom of Egypt collapsed *c.* 2150 BC when numerous smaller entities fought each other for more than a century. Out of this emerged the Middle Kingdom (*c.* 2050–1640 BC). There is no doubt as to the Middle Kingdom's use of offensive warfare. Pharaohs led large armies, strong enough to protect their kingdom from any threat, internal or external.

These armies were also organized into companies, regiments, and garrisons backed by a large military bureaucracy, clerks there producing some of the earliest muster, recruitment and logistical records, and an organized espionage unit. The defence of

the borders continued to be of primary importance, but Egyptian armies also marched into Nubia to the south and Palestine to the east. These raids brought booty, allowing the Middle Kingdom to become extremely prosperous.

The Middle Kingdom of Egypt was toppled by the Hyksos, whose origin has not entirely been determined, although it is thought that they came from the Semitic or Southwest Asian lands to the east. They ruled for nearly a century (1640–1550 BC), during which time they introduced the chariot to Egyptian warfare – perhaps the most important feature of their reign.

Rebellions were frequent during the reign of the Hyksos, but it was not until the beginning of the sixteenth century BC, that an Egyptian general, Ahmose, led his soldiers in a coup that made him the first pharaoh of the New Kingdom. The Egyptians, especially under Ahmose (1550–1525 BC), Thutmose III (1479–1423 BC), and Ramses II (1279–1213 BC), were active in offensive campaigns which reached into the Middle East and Ethiopia. Part of this was due to the rise of enemy principalities which potentially threatened the security of Egypt but also had wealth which could be plundered. Of these, it was the Hittites who became the Egyptians' most powerful opponents. From the eighteenth century BC, the Hittite Empire,

This detail of a relief sculpture from the sixth century BC depicts Persian nobles and dignitaries bearing gifts to the king at Persepolis, in today's Iran. Persia was the superpower of its time, dominating the Near East and threatening Greece.

numerous, and conquered lands as far as the Mediterranean.

Yet, it is perhaps Assyria that is historically recognized as the strongest Mesopotamian power. Beginning in the twelfth century BC, Assyrian armies frequently defeated the Babylonian forces they encountered as the two kingdoms began vying for control over the Middle East. Although Babylon itself never fell, the Assyrians dominated the region from around 1120 BC. Assyria ultimately even conquered the Hittite and Phoenician Empires. Assyrian armies were famed for their ruthlessness. They boasted of the destruction they caused and plunder they acquired. This led to the rise of leagues of city-states which attempted to end this brutality, but on each occasion these revolts were crushed by even more violence. One of

the most renowned of these was ended at the siege of Lachish in 701 BC. Combining battering rams with siege towers, the Assyrians breached the walls and conquered the city. Those captured were tortured and slain. However, less than 80 years later, Assyria fell, as enemies overran the borders and conquered the empire.

BRONZE AGE WEAPONRY

As its name implies, the Bronze Age added metal to tools and weapons. As early as 6000 BC people in Anatolia began to experiment with copper, but it was not until around 4000 BC that this metal, alloyed with other elements, yielded bronze, which offered greater strength than weapons previously made of wood and stone.

In the Bronze Age, fighting was still mostly done with short-range weaponry – spears, axes and daggers – although longer-range weapons – javelins, slings and bows – began to appear on the battlefield. Bronze meant far more to the shorter-range weapons, giving them a sharpened edge, and to protective armour and helmets to defend soldiers against these weapons. It

also led to the invention of the sword. However, the most important addition to Bronze Age warfare was undoubtedly the chariot. This first appeared in Mesopotamia c. 3000 BC and in Egypt c. 2000 BC, although it may have appeared earlier in Anatolia. The Mesopotamian chariot was large and heavy, usually with four solid wheels and used beasts of burden to pull it. The Egyptian chariot was smaller and lighter with two spoked wheels and was a horse-drawn vehicle. (The Mesopotamians began copying Egyptian chariots after observing their speed and efficiency in conflicts between the two.) At their height chariots became the elite force of ancient armies which used them primarily as mobile archery platforms.

MYCENAEAN GREECE

The earliest settlement in the Aegean was Knossos on Crete in c. 6100 BC. Flint dagger blades were found in excavations there, but no other evidence of military activity until a millennium later when the settlement was surrounded by its first wall. By the early Bronze Age the Cretan population had become the Minoan civilization which hit its peak between 2000 and 1600 BC. There is little evidence of war in the Minoan civilization. Some weapon remains have been found, with few sites fortified. However, one fresco does show several warships carrying men armed with spears and shields.

This may be why in 1450 BC armies from a rival Aegean kingdom, Mycenae, may have had such an easy time defeating and nearly destroying the Minoan civilization. Mycenae, unlike the Minoans completely defined by war, became dominant in the region. The Mycenaeans had intricately organized armies, but they were not innovative ones. Even into the Iron Age, Mycenaean warriors preferred using bronze weapons, although they did use light chariots but solely as means of transportation to take elite warriors to the battlefield where they dismounted and engaged in single combat with their enemy counterparts. The Mycenaeans also maintained extensive fleets which they used for conquest and piracy.

Undoubtedly, the most well known of these conquests was the western Anatolian city-state known in ancient literature as Troy. Excavations have shown that Troy did exist, was economically powerful and well fortified, all claimed accurately in Homer's epic, the *Iliad*. Excavations have also shown that Troy fell to a siege around 1200–1180 BC, but how long this siege took is impossible to ascertain.

Mycenaean warriors pull their ships ashore and prepare for battle in the fifteenth century BC. As seafaring became more common and shipbuilding skills became more advanced, ships began to be built for combat. They were unstable platforms balanced by the oars of their rowers.

INTRODUCTION

This colourful engraving from a book by the German historian Karl von Rotteck (1775–1840) depicts the Persians being driven back into the sea by Greek cavalry at the battle of Marathon (490 BC).

ruin, trade virtually ceased, peace was replaced by violence and crime, and even written language was lost (it was later relearned from the Phoenicians). Around 800 BC the Greeks began to rebuild their civilization, and being fairly isolated from other parts of the world, especially the very militaristic Middle East, no doubt allowed this recovery.

The Greeks found that chariots and individual combats, like those celebrated in the *Iliad*, had been replaced by the horse and the phalanx. Horses had been in armies before 800 BC, but they were used mostly for pulling chariots or wagons. It may have been the Hittites who introduced the horse as a cavalry mount, having learned it from fighting steppe warriors. They passed it to the Assyrians, who used cavalry to great advantage against slower-moving foes, and perhaps to the Greeks, who also seem to have quickly adopted cavalry as a companion force to the infantry.

Sometime between 750 and 650 BC Greek city-states introduced the hoplite phalanx. This is confirmed by a number of artistic sources which portray a unit of soldiers armoured with breastplate, greaves, helmet, and a large round shield – known as a *hoplon* – and carrying a 1.8–2.4m (6–8ft) long thrusting spear. More important than these armaments, however, was the solidly packed formation in which the soldiers appeared in these portrayals. This was the phalanx, where several lines of soldiers stood tightly formed in a square. On the battlefield these ranks moved together in a slow and disciplined march, the shock of their weight and power quickly causing the defeat or flight of all non-phalanx infantries. It was both a defensive and an offensive formation, necessitating strong leadership and strict training to keep everyone together, as the solidarity of the phalanx was what brought it victory.

Homer's ten years is plausible, though, as Mycenaean Greece did not last much longer itself, defeated not by military force but by economic collapse, as if a large number of men were away for a lengthy period of time and could not recover their financial losses.

THE PHALANX

For the 400 years following the fall of Mycenae, Greece fell into civil war that ushered in the 'Dark Ages' of Ancient Greece. All of the great centres fell into

THE GREEK WARS

In the fifth century BC Greek hoplite armies fought two of the most famous wars in ancient history: the Persian Wars and the Peloponnesian War. Succeeding the Assyrians in the Middle East were the Achaemenid Persians, who under King Cyrus the Great built a strong empire north

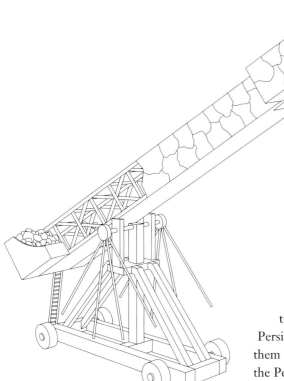

The sambuca, or 'harp', was developed in the late fourth century BC. It was a siege ladder that allowed attackers to gain access to the top of a wall in relative safety. Men inserted themselves at the top of the ladder and operators then placed stones at the opposite end; this acted as a counterweight and raised the device. It had several advantages: attackers did not have to estimate the height of enemy walls; it could be placed across moats and ditches; defenders could not immediately push it away; and it was covered in hides to protect against fire.

of Mesopotamia which quickly spread into the Middle East and Anatolia. By 545 BC Cyrus reached the Bosphorus, conquering several cities in western Anatolia populated by Greeks, and in 514 BC a successor, Darius I, crossed the Bosphorus over the borders of the Greek city-states.

In 499 BC, Greeks living under Persian control decided to break away. Athens and Eretria came to their aid. In 494 BC Darius responded by reconquering Ionia and in 490 BC by attacking Athens and Eretria. Eretria fell in seven days, but the Athenian army defended its city by defeating the Persians at the battle of Marathon. The defeat of the Persians was far from decisive, however, as Darius' son, Xerxes I, again invaded Greece in 480 BC. On this occasion, the Athenians baulked at mounting a defence, but the Spartans did respond, at least 300 did – the others being involved in a religious festival – and together with a similar number of Thespians, withstood the entire Persian army at the battle of Thermopylae until most of the Greek city-states could respond to the threat. Athens was sacked, but the rest of the Greeks banded together and after defeating the Persians at Plataea later in the year drove them out of the Balkans. In the meantime, the Persian fleet was also active but avoided direct battle with the Greek navy until lured into the battle of Salamis where more than 200 Persian ships were sunk and several hundred more were captured. The Persian Wars had ended.

Recovering from the Persian Wars, Athens controlled the Aegean and eastern Mediterranean Seas. At the same time, Sparta controlled the land. In 431 BC jealousy between the two culminated in a plan by the Athenian leader, Pericles, to destroy Spartan power which led to the first phase of the Peloponnesian War. For ten years the two powers sparred in Greece, although few engagements were fought. Pericles, it seems, believed that the Athenians could not contend against the Spartans on the battlefield but should allow their fleet to wreak havoc along the Spartan coast. Eventually the two sides simply wore each other out, signing the Peace of Nicias in 421 BC.

But peace did not hold for long, as war broke out once more in 416 BC, although not in Greece itself but in Sicily. A civil war on the island brought the two Greek city-states into conflict again when one side, Syracuse, asked Sparta to intervene and the other, Segusta, approached Athens. However, little went right for Athens in this phase of the Peloponnesian War, for despite landing first with a large force, the Athenians spent months vainly besieging Syracuse until being forced from the island in 415 BC.

The failure of Athens in Sicily encouraged Sparta to reopen war in Greece itself. The Spartan navy had improved and Athens was no longer dominant at sea. Several naval battles were won by the Spartan fleet. Eventually, in 405 BC Athens was besieged by both land and sea, leading to its surrender in the spring of 404 BC, and giving Sparta complete control of Greece. But keeping this control was difficult, with frequent uprisings of Greek city-states – especially Thebes, Athens, Corinth and Argos – necessitating military responses. Finally, at the battle of Leuctra in 371 BC an army from Thebes turned the tables on the Spartans, defeating them soundly. Sparta ceased to play a major role in Ancient Greek military history.

ALEXANDER THE GREAT

Following the defeats of Athens in the Peloponnesian War and Sparta in the Corinthian War, there was a void of leadership and power. Fortunately, at the same time Persia was suffering through a similar political disunity. Nevertheless another state on the borders of Greece was about to bring an end to Ancient Greek military power: Macedonia.

Before 359 BC the Greeks considered Macedonians to be barbarians, capable of little more than cross-border raids, which nevertheless kept them in a military posture. That year Philip II took over the Macedonian kingship, but because his assumption of the throne was disputed, he also immediately went to war. In a very short time he had built an army of disciplined and well-trained infantry and cavalry which soon defeated much larger armies.

By 356 BC he had conquered all neighbouring lands and moved into Greece. Over the next few years his territory increased substantially, and by 337 BC he had defeated all the major city-states. Philip's next target was Anatolia, but despite crossing the Bosphorus that year he would not see the completion of this campaign as he was assassinated the following year while walking in a triumphal procession. His son, Alexander, succeeded him.

INTRODUCTION

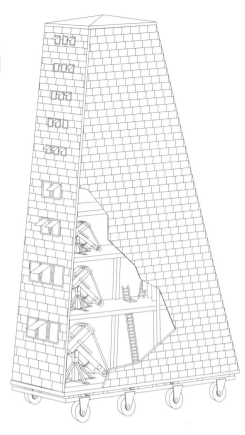

Above: The helepolis *or 'city-taker' used by Demetrios Poliorketes against Rhodes from 305 to 304 BC. The* helepolis *measured 43m (141ft) in height. On the bottom was the propulsion system, where 200 men operated a capstan turning eight wheels. The first floor housed large* lithoboloi, *capable of launching huge stones. The entire outer structure was iron-plated and each floor had equipment for fighting fires.*

Alexander had served as one of Philip's generals in several campaigns. His disputes with his father were well known, but one thing they agreed on was Macedonian expansionism. He quickly put down any threats to his rule and in 334 BC crossed into Asia to face the old enemy of Greece: Persia. As a military power, Persia was far from what it had been under Cyrus the Great, Darius I or Xerxes. The kingdom had been ravaged by almost a century of civil war; indeed, the new king, Darius III, had only seized the throne in the year that he faced Alexander. At the battle of the Granicus, fought in 334 BC, the Macedonians gained their first victory over the Persians, with the second, at the battle of Issus, the following year.

After Issus many of the Macedonian generals thought that they should pursue the fleeing Persians, but Alexander had different plans. He turned south, along the Mediterranean coast, and in 332 BC he besieged the island city of Tyre, before conquering Egypt, where he was to establish his capital, calling it after himself, Alexandria.

Then he turned towards Persia. In 331 BC Darius III gathered his army, a much larger force than Alexander's, at Gaugamela. But in the battle that was fought there, Alexander again proved his leadership,

soundly defeating the Persians. The large Persian cities of Babylon, Susa and Persepolis fell quickly to him, and Darius, who was trying to rebuild an army, was instead killed by his own men.

But Alexander's campaigns did not end with the capture of Persia. He then turned towards the mountains of Afghanistan, where he found little organized opposition, but more difficult terrain. His troops slogged on, and in 327 BC entered what he felt was the farthest extent of the earth, India. Here he gained one of his most impressive victories, at the battle of the Hydaspes, fought in 326 BC, again defeating a much larger army – including 200 war elephants – but his men refused to go further. Alexander decided to return to Persia, but did not want to face the mountains of the north and turned to the south, only to discover an equally treacherous terrain in the desert of southern Persia. Alexander made it as far as Babylon where in June 323 BC he died, his body wrecked by fever, excess, and the many wounds he had suffered. He was only 33 years old.

The death of Alexander meant the end of the Macedonian Empire. He had no heirs other than an unborn son, and chaos soon followed. Alexander's top generals decided to divide his lands into Macedonia (including Greece); Egypt (and the Middle East); and Asia (including Persia). These three kingdoms continued throughout the following few centuries, but they would eventually meet a power that even Alexander probably could not have defeated, Rome.

EARLY ROME

The first Roman rulers, from 754 to 510 BC, were kings. Of these, the only one of memorable military significance was Servius Tullius (578–535 BC) who, among other things, first fortified Rome. The earliest

The death of the scientist and philosopher Archimedes at the hands of a Roman centurion, following the capture of Syracuse by the Romans, 212 BC. The city had held out against the besieging Romans for three years, aided by various military engines built to Archimedes' designs.

Roman army consisted of a general levy raised from the propertied classes. These soldiers were equipped with a helmet, body armour, greaves, a long shield (the infantry only), and a throwing spear. By the early sixth century BC, the number of Roman soldiers had risen to 6000 and became known as the levy (or *legio*), which established the standard size of what became known as the legion.

The rule of the Roman kings came to an end in 510 BC with the expulsion of the last king, Tarquinius Superbus; in his place two consuls and a number of senators were elected. Initially, Republican Rome feared attacks by outsiders more than it thought about conquest of them. The first threat came from the Etruscans of nearby Clusium. They even captured Rome for a while but were defeated at the battle of Aricia (*c*. 506 BC), with Rome ten years later, *c*. 496 BC, defeating them again at the battle of Lake Regillus. Throughout the remainder of the fifth century BC the rest of the Etruscan tribes were also defeated: the Sabines, the Aequis, the Volscians (whose leader, the exiled Roman Coriolanus, was later made famous by Shakespeare), and the Veii.

More formidable opponents were the Cisalpine Gauls (Gaul on the Italian side of the Alps was Cisalpine Gaul, Transalpine Gaul being on the other side of the Alps). In 391 BC an army of Gauls attacked the Etruscan lands north of Rome. An attack on Rome ensued, with the defeat of a Roman army at the battle of Allia and the seven-month siege of Rome following. Rome fell, but, instead of being sacked and destroyed, the citizens offered to buy off the Gauls who accepted the bribe and left. (The Gauls would, however, remain a threat to the Romans until forced to the other side of the Alps a century later.)

The defeat of Rome led to a refortification of the city and the levying of a larger and better trained army. The previously practised Greek-style of warfare

– which had been defeated easily in battle once the phalanx was penetrated by Gallic soldiers wielding long swords – was replaced by a legion formed into two ranks, the first armed with javelins (*pila*) and swords, and the second using *pila* as thrusting spears. Eventually all soldiers would be armed as the front rank. They also exchanged their round shields for long, slightly cylindrical ones. Thus the tactical expertise of the Roman legion, the military unit that would dominate the rest of the Ancient World, was born.

In recovering from the Gallic invasions, the Romans became increasingly more offence-minded in their military activities. Roman armies began to secure the city against other Italians by waging campaigns against them. First they struck at the others living nearby in Latium which were not already under their control, and by 350 BC central Italy was secure. Following the completion of this war, the Romans campaigned against the Samnites, who occupied the lands southeast of Rome. Three wars between the two followed: the first from 343 to 341 BC; the second from 326 to 304 BC; and the third from 298 to

At an ancient battle re-enactment in Britain, Roman legionaries establish a tortoise formation, using their shields to render the squad impenetrable. Roman infantry tactics and organization proved to be superior to all other armies of the period.

290 BC. Several battles were fought, with a large number of casualties resulting from them and other military conflicts. Finally, the Samnites accepted their defeat and Roman governance.

Southern Italy had now fallen almost completely under the control of the Romans. Only the wealthy trading city of Tarentum held out, but the citizens there felt threatened by Roman expansion, and in 280 BC they petitioned Pyrrhus, the king of Macedonia, for assistance. He responded with a large force, estimated to be 25,000 men, and that same year at the battle of Heraclea they faced an equally large Roman army. This is thought to have been the first time a phalanx army met a legion army, with the legions completely dominating the battlefield. Pyrrhus retreated to Greece, but returned the following year with an even larger army – estimated at 40,000–50,000

Legionary training using a wicker shield and wooden sword. A variety of strokes were practised against the wooden post, but the short, thick gladius *was primarily used as a stabbing weapon in battle.*

troops, plus elephants. Again the Macedonians met the Romans in battle, at Asculum; this time the Macedonians were victorious, but the fight was not decisive and Pyrrhus' losses were heavy. This prompted Carthage – which held Sicily and seemed to worry about the Mediterranean threat of the Greeks more than the Romans – to offer aid to the latter, and in 276 BC all the armies met at the battle of Beneventum. Pyrrhus was defeated and retreated to Greece, leaving Tarentum to Rome.

THE PUNIC WARS

The Carthaginians, allies with Rome during the Pyrrhic Wars, became bitter enemies almost as soon as the wars were completed.

Beginning as a Phoenician trading colony, by the third century BC Carthage was the most powerful state in the central and western Mediterranean, holding North Africa, Spain, southern France, Sardinia, and Sicily. Once Romans took control of Italy their immediate concern became the Carthaginians.

Taking advantage of a local conflict on Sicily, the Romans invaded the island and the Carthaginians responded. The first Punic War had begun. The two armies fought to a stalemate on land, but on the water the Romans dominated. This was unexpected, as Carthage had controlled the Mediterranean without opposition for a very long time. At naval battles fought off

holding out against the Carthaginians, and following the successful siege of that city, Hannibal Barca, son of Hamilcar, invaded Italy by crossing the Alps. Hannibal's crossing was unprecedented, so that when he entered Italy he caught the Romans unprepared for his invasion. Still, they were able to assemble an army larger than the Carthaginians, with both meeting at the battle of the Trebia in December 218 BC. Hannibal won and followed that victory by meeting and defeating another Roman force at the battle of Lake Trasimene in June 217 BC. But it was at the battle of Cannae, fought in August 216, where Hannibal's leadership skill was most evident, as he virtually annihilated the Romans who faced him. But his own army – newly reinforced by the addition of his brother Hasdrubal's force from Spain – still lost 6000 men, leaving him unable to take on the fortifications of Rome.

For the next 14 years Hannibal and his army roamed Italy. Ultimately the Romans rebuilt their depleted forces and actually began to defeat their foes in small engagements, such as at the battle of Metaurus in 207 BC where Hasdrubal was also killed. But it was in their strategy away from Italy where the Romans were to make the most impressive military gains. By 211 BC a Roman army, led by the two Scipios, father and son, crossed into Spain and recaptured Saguntum, and in 209 BC Scipio the Younger – his father having died – took

New Carthage, the Carthaginian capital there, with the remainder of Spain falling within the next two years. In 204 BC he crossed into and fought across North Africa, prompting the Carthaginians to recall Hannibal to defend the city. At the battle of Zama, fought in 202 BC, outside the walls of Carthage, the two famous generals finally fought each other, deciding the second Punic War in favour of Rome. Hannibal did escape, however, and would continue to fight against Rome from Syria and Anatolia, although he never defeated them again. (Carthage rose up later, in 149–146 BC, constituting what was essentially the third Punic War, although what is most notable about this war is that at its conclusion the Roman Senate declared that 'Carthage must be destroyed'.)

REPUBLICAN ROME

After their victory in the second Punic War, nothing seemed to hold Rome back from conquering the eastern Mediterranean and between 200 and 49 BC the Republic achieved its largest territorial gains. The Macedonians gave Rome some trouble, but a series of wars ending in 168 BC at the battle of Pydna saw the fall of Greece to Rome. But, other lands were captured with relatively less opposition – the Seleucid Empire in 192–189 BC, North Africa in 111–105 BC, and Pontus in 90–63 BC – and some decided rather than contending against Roman armies that they would

the coast of Mylae in 260 BC and Cape Ecnomus in 256 BC the Romans easily defeated the Carthaginians, but they could not defeat the weather and storms decimated their fleet by the end of this Punic War in 241 BC.

Perhaps the most important feature of the first Punic War for the defeated Carthaginians was the appointment of Hamilcar Barca as leader of the forces in Sicily in 247 BC. Although he eventually lost on that island, once he returned to Carthage he completely reorganized the military forces there. By 221 BC they were ready to take on the Romans again. Using as an impetus for attack an alliance made by Rome with Saguntum, a Spanish city

The foredeck of a Carthaginian pentecontor, showing the thick keel and frame giving the vessel enough strength to survive ramming an enemy vessel. The rowers' deck was immediately below the top deck, although their benches are not shown.

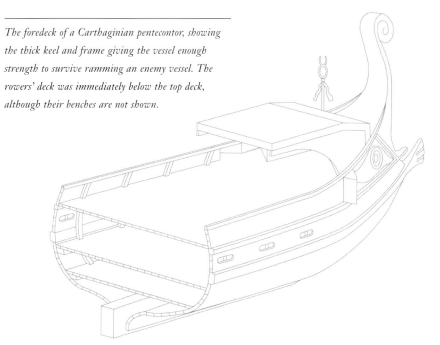

INTRODUCTION

This neoclassical-style statue of Julius Caesar in the Louvre Museum, Paris, was completed by sculptor Nicolas Coustou (1658–1733) in 1696.

become client-states, such as Egypt, Judea and Armenia. Only the Parthian Empire seemed to be able to constantly keep out of Rome's imperialistic orbit. Despite frequent attempts at conquering this Middle Eastern state (historical and territorial descendants of ancient Mesopotamia and Persia), as at the battle of Carrhae fought in 53 BC, the Parthians were more often victorious than defeated. Despite these setbacks, by the middle of the first century BC the Mediterranean Sea had become, as contemporary Romans called it, *Mare Nostrum* (Our Sea).

Meanwhile, the Republic was also extending its frontiers to the north of its heartland in Italy. Migrations of Germanic peoples from across the Danube river had diluted the early Gallic power that had caused so many previous problems to Roman security. But they had replaced this threat with their own, and there arose a need from around 113 BC on for Rome to provide troops to protect its territory north of Italy. Rome was successful in almost all conflicts with these peoples, with only a few minor defeats – such as at the battle of Arausio in 105 BC – that were quickly reversed by victories at battles fought at Aquae Sextae in 102 BC and Vercellae in 101 BC.

Nevertheless, raids and migrations continued, although as the Romans were then actively defending the Danube these pushed north to cross the southern Rhine river. The Gauls living there applied to Rome for assistance. A Roman general who saw an expedition into Gaul as a means to build political power, Julius Caesar, answered their petition. By crossing the Rhine himself, he quickly stopped the raids but just as quickly turned on the Gauls who had asked for Roman assistance. They tried to defend themselves, with one leader, Vercingetorix, even repulsing a Roman army at Gergovia in 52 BC. This led to one

of the most impressive victories in the history of ancient warfare, when later that year Caesar besieged Vercingetorix at Alesia, while at the same time anticipating an extremely large Gallic relief army which nevertheless could not find a way through Caesar's defences before Vercingetorix was forced to surrender.

Gaul had fallen to Rome and became an important part of the Republic. Still, from this time until the fall of the Roman Empire five centuries later, Rome was often forced to fight against Germans who crossed into their territory. Most of the time Rome was victorious but one engagement stands as the largest defeat the Romans ever suffered, at Teutoberger Wald in AD 9, when a recorded 20,000 Roman soldiers were slain by a coalition of German tribes.

During the time that Rome was making its greatest expansion, the Republic began to fall apart. Individual politicians, like the two Gracchi brothers – Tiberius and Gaius – Gaius Marius, Pompey, and Caesar, all sought to increase their own power at the expense of the more representative Senate. When these politicians were also military leaders, as Marius, Pompey and Caesar were, this meant the use of military force against the Roman people.

Finally it was Pompey and Caesar who faced off against each other at the battle of Pharsalus in 48 BC, with Caesar victorious but then murdered four years later. For the ensuing two decades a civil war followed between those who murdered Caesar and his heir, Octavian, and his lieutenant, Mark Antony, and eventually between Octavian and Antony. Octavian and Antony's victory at the battle of Philippi (42 BC) and Octavian's victory over Antony at the battle of Actium (31 BC) followed by the suspension of the Senate led to the establishment of the Roman Empire.

THE ROMAN EMPIRE

For the next four centuries of Roman history the empire's chief military characteristic was civil war. Emperors came and went with tremendous speed. Many also had to assert their power using military force against other would-be emperors and their armies. Only rarely was there governmental stability, such as during the reigns of the five 'good emperors' – Nerva, Trajan, Hadrian, Antoninus Pius and Marcus Aurelius – (AD 96–180). Moreover, the empire expanded very little after the time it was established. Numidia was conquered in AD 24, Mauretania in AD 41–42, Britain in AD 43, Thrace in AD 46, Dacia in AD 105, Parthia in AD 113, and Mesopotamia in AD 115, but some of these were client-kingdoms which needed to be brought in line.

Rebellions there and elsewhere were frequent. One of the most well-known of these, and one that was put down with an especially violent ruthlessness, was that in Judea in AD 66–73 (although most of the province was subdued in a single year). There the siege of Masada, a fortress occupied by a group of Zealots which almost alone held out until AD 73, shows not only the determination of some of the Jews but also that of the Roman troops who were not about to let any enemy rebel survive.

By the third century AD the Roman civil wars had so depleted military manpower along the borders that barbarian raids plundered the riches of the empire. In AD 249, Goths crossed the Danube river into the Balkans. In AD 256, Franks crossed the Rhine to attack Gaul, and Saxons, also from the Rhineland, crossed the English Channel to raid Britain.

Elsewhere, the Borani raided the eastern Black Sea coast in AD 256, and that same year the Sassanid Persians from Mesopotamia overran Armenia and Syria and even captured and imprisoned the inept Emperor Valerian. By AD 262, Goths had taken over Greece as far south as Athens, although they were eventually driven back, and in AD 268 the Heruli, another Germanic people, repeated this campaign.

THE FALL OF ROME

The fall of Rome had begun. Despite a reorganization of the military and a division of political power by Emperor Diocletian at the end of the third century AD, disagreements among his co-emperors and successors led to years of civil war, resulting in the removal of most Roman frontier troops. At the battle of Milvian Bridge in AD 312 Constantine ended these wars with a victory and in AD 330 he tried to bolster the

weakened empire by moving its capital away from Italy to a city in the East, which he named Constantinople, after himself.

In AD 376, however, the Emperor Valens let the Visigoths enter the empire after they had petitioned him for leave to cross over the Danube river and farm the wastelands of Thrace, and to become 'confederates'. It is estimated that 200,000 Visigoths crossed into the Roman Empire only to find that they could not be fed. Within two years, the Visigoths had turned into a military threat. At the battle of Adrianople in AD 378 the Visigoths utterly defeated the Romans under the Emperor Valens.

For the next century the Roman Empire foundered. Further barbarian tribes followed the Visigoths across the Danube and Rhine rivers – notably the Alans, Suevi, Burgundians, Vandals, Huns, Ostrogoths, Alemanni, Franks, Angles and Saxons – while the Sassanid Persian Empire continued to expand in the Middle East. There were some Roman successes, as at the battle of Catalaunian Fields in AD 451 where the Huns led by Attila were defeated by a Romano-Visigothic army, but these victories only postponed the inevitable.

In AD 410, the Ostrogoths sacked Rome after a decade-long siege, and by AD 476, after a series of weak and inept 'puppet-emperors' had quickly risen and just as quickly fallen, Romulus Augustulus, the last Western Roman Emperor, was deposed. The Ancient World had become the Middle Ages.

Cataphract heavy cavalry were known to the Romans as clibanarii *(literally 'oven men') after the temperatures endured by these riders when wearing their armour in Asia Minor. They became increasingly important on the ancient battlefield from the second century AD onwards.*

KADESH
1285 BC

ARMOURED VEHICLES, DECAPITATION STRIKES, HIDDEN FORCES AND AN ADVANCED CHAIN OF COMMAND PLAYED DECISIVE ROLES IN A CONFLICT OF CULTURES IN THE MIDDLE EAST. DISINFORMATION AND PERSONAL LEADERSHIP DROVE THOUSANDS INTO AN EPIC BATTLE LOST IN THE MISTS OF TIME.

WHY DID IT HAPPEN?

WHO The rich and powerful kingdom of Egypt under Pharaoh Ramses II (d. 1213 BC) clashed in northern Syria with the militarily innovative Hittite Empire under their king Muwatallis.

WHAT Egyptian chariots and light-armed infantry played a sanguinary game of hide-and-seek around the walls of a fortified city until finally an all-out clash resulted.

WHERE Kadesh was a rich and powerful fortified city that offered an excellent outpost to defend an empire, or to expand one from.

WHEN 1285 BC.

WHY Kadesh was a Hittite obstacle to Ramses' efforts to make Egypt's claims of world supremacy more than empty boasting.

OUTCOME Hittite cunning and technology were almost too much for Egyptian numbers and organization. A tactical victory for the Egyptians, a strategic one for the Hittites, and in the end – a draw.

When empires expand, there is resistance – from native peoples, established smaller states; and in the case of another expanding empire, resistance takes its strongest form. Ramses II's great battle of 1285 BC was the product of a young king's desire to surpass the achievements of an illustrious ancestor – and the success of the Hittite Empire's ongoing expansion southwards from Asia Minor. The two competing imperial tides clashed around the walls of a fortified city in one of the most fought-over regions on earth.

For a long time Ramses' own account of the battle of Kadesh – carved with loving care onto temple after temple – provided the only account of the action. Predictably, the Pharaoh portrayed the struggle as his personal victory over treachery in the face of overwhelming odds. Recently, however, cuneiform tablets unearthed at Boghazköy, Turkey, provide some of the other side's perspective, and the results of the battle do not quite match up with the account the ruler of Egypt left for posterity.

BACKGROUND

By the New Kingdom epoch (1539–1075 BC), Egypt had an established, and better documented, history of military activity in lands far distant from the Nile. Egypt was a rich strip of land on either side of the desert, but there were wider vistas to the north. There was a long and wide vein of racial supremacy in the character of Egyptian foreign policy – their art depicted foreign nations as helpless captives, bound to await the will of Pharaoh.

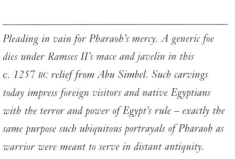

Pleading in vain for Pharaoh's mercy. A generic foe dies under Ramses II's mace and javelin in this c. 1257 BC relief from Abu Simbel. Such carvings today impress foreign visitors and native Egyptians with the terror and power of Egypt's rule – exactly the same purpose such ubiquitous portrayals of Pharaoh as warrior were meant to serve in distant antiquity.

SUMERIAN CHARIOT
Combined traditions at Kadesh led to the development of this later Sumerian chariot that combined the best traits of the two differing varieties of fighting vehicles hurled into the fray by Egyptian and Hittite builders. This later chariot is four-wheeled, like the more heavily armoured and stable vehicles of the Hittite warriors. The extra horse power of two extra asses gave the heavier vehicle greater speed, in an effort to equal the velocity of the lighter horse-drawn Egyptian chariots at Kadesh.

Imperialism came as naturally to Egypt's rulers as did their belief in themselves as the children of the Sun-God on earth. That military impulse endured and often prompted the rulers of Egypt to aggressive war. After thousands of years of experience, the pharaohs had come to be in possession of proven ways of projecting force abroad. Centuries of experimentation was a large part of Egyptian military prowess, that which the ages had taught being left for future generations to learn in texts, sculpture and monuments.

On the walls of his ancestors' temples, Ramses himself could read and benefit from the experiences of Egypt's former warrior pharaohs, including the inscription modern scholars study today detailing Thutmose III's great battle at Megiddo in 1458 BC, two centuries before. So epic were the achievements of that warrior pharaoh that even the Christian Bible's prophecy of

Armageddon, 'the hill at Megiddo', may be an echo of Thutmose's titanic struggle with the King of Kadesh and his allies the Mitanni, forerunners of the Hittites. Ramses would win his own glory – or try to – from the same source.

Some things had changed in 200 years, however. The Hittites were Egypt's most formidable opponents yet. Starting in the central regions of what is now Turkey, the smaller city-states and kingdoms of the northern Middle East had come under the centralized dominion of the Hittite Empire. With the resources of the north behind them, they were a far more formidable foe than the Mitanni – but they had taken Kadesh from Egypt, and Ramses wanted both it back and the glory of recapturing the site of Thutmose's triumph.

The Hittite king Muwatallis had no inclination to yield to the dictates of Ramses' perceived destiny, and, possessing

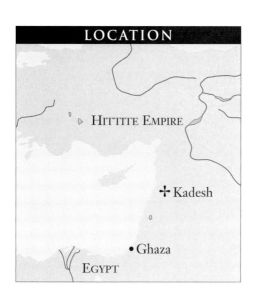

LOCATION

Ramses' campaign was an attempt to win back territory that had been Egypt's a few centuries before. Although he failed to regain all of the lost lands, he nonetheless secured a lasting peace.

KADESH

the advantages of the defender, made his own preparations to exploit them.

RAMSES' ARMY

The understanding in Egypt that peasants had to be levied, trained and fed for great undertakings went back to the Old Kingdom's massive construction projects, some of which still survive in the pyramids looming over Cairo. Ramses would once more employ the vast human resources of Ancient Egypt.

While the Nile flooded and the crops grew, the wealth of Egypt could take idle fellahin and mobilize them into armies, as well as the construction gangs that had left the glories of the past. The richness of Egyptian agriculture could equip these levies for war, but training and controlling them in battle would prove a very difficult task. War was more complicated an affair than dragging one more stone up onto the sides of a pyramid. With king fighting king on the chessboard of battle, both sides enjoyed a unified supreme command

Terror on the battlefield – and hopefully in international relations – was the objective behind the gruesome images portrayed in this relief from the vast temple of Ramses II at Thebes. For the education of his subjects and the intimidation of his enemies, Pharaoh's exploits needed and received the florid magnification of skilled artists to leave a lasting impression.

structure, but the simple limitations on the abilities of a single man to control an army nonetheless required compensatory measures.

The Egyptian solution, which is the one Ramses recorded on his own inscription describing the battle, was a fairly effective one. Ramses divided his army of approximately 20,000 men into four divisions of equal size under trusted subordinates, men with positions and possessions back in Egypt and hence a stake in victory. Ramses hit upon a useful combination of divine patronage and unit identity by naming each of his divisions

THE OPPOSED FORCES

EGYPTIANS (estimated)
Chariots:	2000
Infantry:	18,000
Total:	**20,000**

HITTITES (estimated)
Chariots:	3000
Infantry:	20,000
Total:	**23,000**

The prototypical armoured fighting vehicle. Chariots such as these offered a degree of stability and protection to the Hittite archers stationed within them. The sturdy wild asses pulling them offered endurance, as their top speed was no more than the primitive construction of the chariots could endure.

The wealthier Egyptians favoured a faster, lighter – and less stable – horse-drawn version of the chariot.

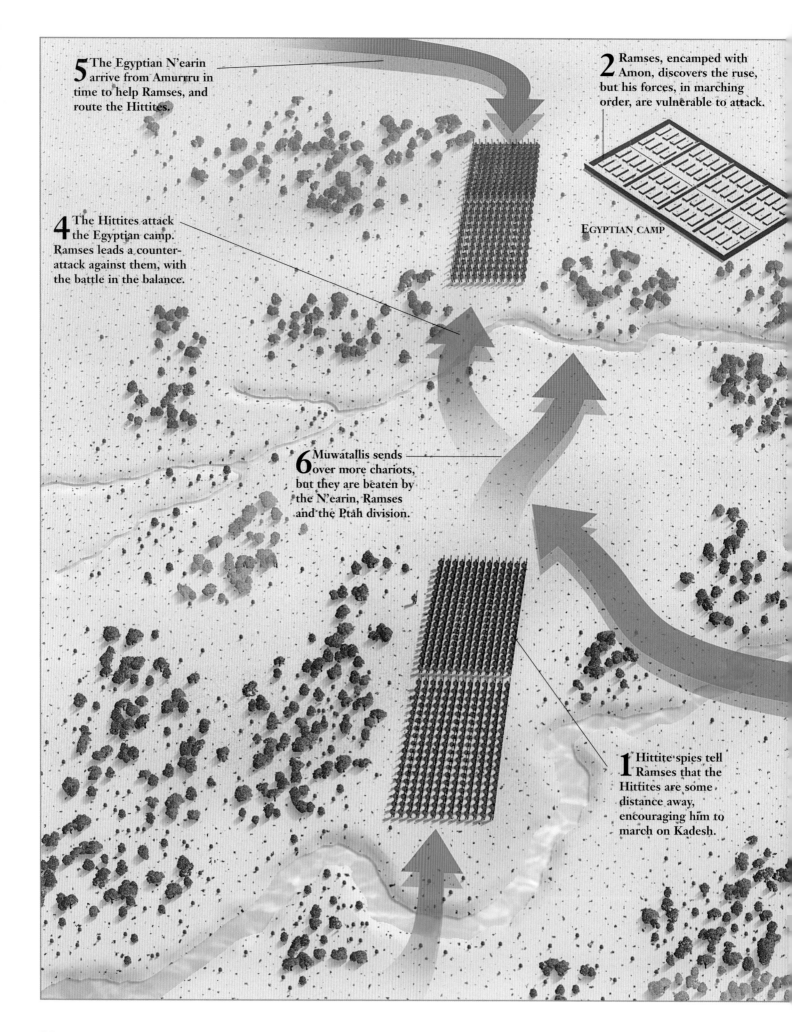

5 The Egyptian N'earin arrive from Amurrru in time to help Ramses, and route the Hittites.

2 Ramses, encamped with Amon, discovers the ruse, but his forces, in marching order, are vulnerable to attack.

EGYPTIAN CAMP

4 The Hittites attack the Egyptian camp. Ramses leads a counter-attack against them, with the battle in the balance.

6 Muwatallis sends over more chariots, but they are beaten by the N'earin, Ramses and the Ptah division.

1 Hittite spies tell Ramses that the Hittites are some distance away, encouraging him to march on Kadesh.

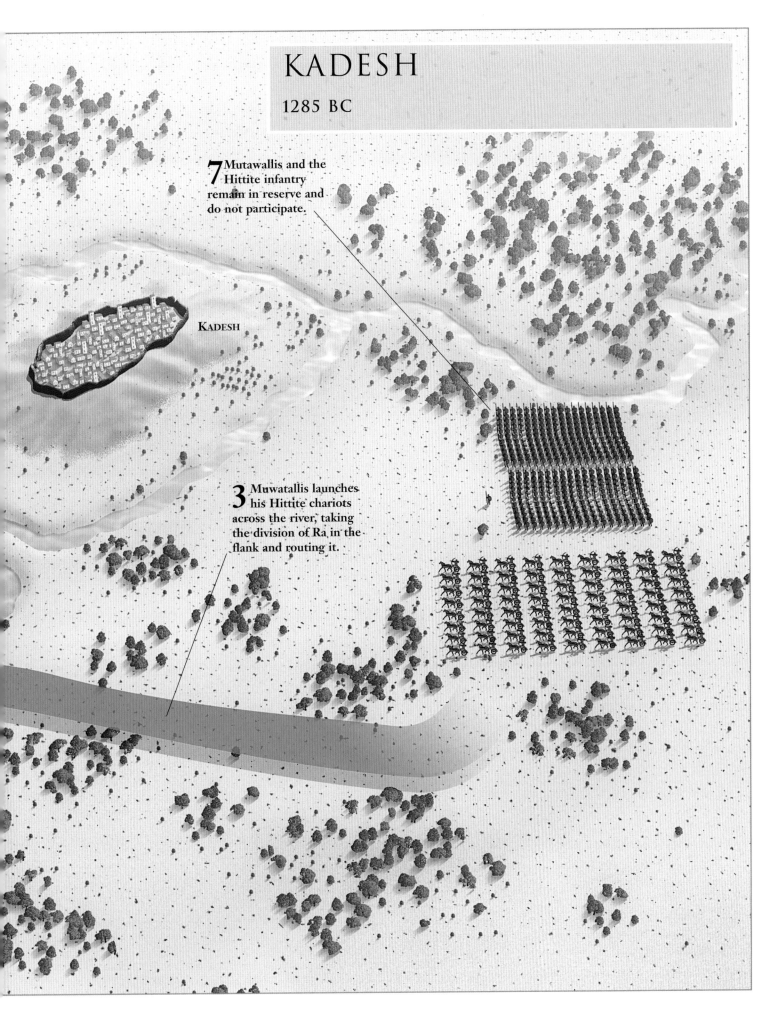

KADESH
1285 BC

7 Mutawallis and the Hittite infantry remain in reserve and do not participate.

KADESH

3 Muwatallis launches his Hittite chariots across the river, taking the division of Ra in the flank and routing it.

KADESH

In this mural depicting Ramses II's carefully propagandized exploits at Kadesh, the exaggerated sizes of Pharaoh and the targeted city emphasize the respective importance of each in the mental picture the image is intended to create. The terror of the defenders and the absolute order of the Egyptian ranks were more the products of wishful thinking by Ramses than historical reality.

after a divine patron, those being Amon, Ra, Ptah and Sutekh, while at the same time keeping his own person, bodyguard and immediate subordinates outside of that structure in a separate, mobile unit. The Egyptian officer corps' task would be to get the most out of their mostly raw troops by localized supervision.

THE CAMPAIGN

During Ramses' march toward Kadesh, these four divisions moved at some distance apart, a tactical trade-off between access to such roads as there were and the need for time to let assorted water sources and reservoirs be refilled or replenished, and the considerable, and in this case realized, risk of the army's component parts encountering the enemy while still separated and being destroyed in detail. Still, the Egyptians were successfully moving huge numbers of men a great distance, the very essence of aggressive war. The Hittites were facing no minor threat.

Some details in text do survive of exactly what an Egyptian called up for the wars could expect, in addition to 'no clothes, no sandals ... a march uphill through the mountains ... water every third day ... body ravaged by illness'. Pharaoh's wealth provided the infantry with orders, a short linen skirt, a leather helmet and a cowhide shield with the pelt turned outwards. But at least there were a lot of their fellows about them to share the burden of war, if they could be fed, if they could be given water.

Organization and wealth allowed Ramses both to employ mercenaries to support his native levies and to make a very rapid march from Egypt to the north of Syria where the battle took place. The speed of the Egyptian march risked causing problems in supply and sudden attack, but the advantage was very great in terms of surprise and preparation. The expertise of the mercenaries was a definite asset to the Egyptians, and drained the pool of talent available to the Hittites.

The wealth of Egypt found expression in the copper and bronze heads of the knife, mace, sword and spear shown here. As much a soldier's tool as a weapon, the knife would have been of greatest value at close quarters or at mealtimes. The mace was at its best against the skull of an unhelmeted enemy, being the first weapon specifically designed to slaughter humankind, while as a lance, pike or throwing weapon, the humble spear made up the classic mainstay of any ancient soldier's fighting gear.

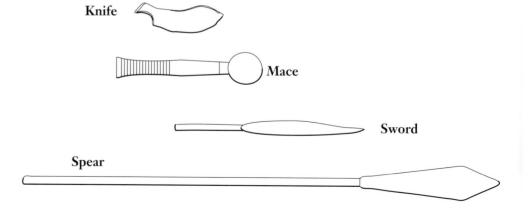

Knife

Mace

Sword

Spear

Muwatallis, however, was no supine foe. The Hittite king managed, at what the Egyptian account notes as considerable expense and disruption, to produce a matching army of his own by the time the Egyptian forces approached the walled city of Kadesh.

THE BATTLE

Always involved in any exercise of command and control is the flow of information to and from the commander. Muwatallis cannily fed some 'disinformation' into Ramses' control apparatus by planting two spies in the path of Ramses' army. The captured pair informed Ramses that the Hittite army was still some distance off, prompting Ramses to make another tactical gamble and take his foremost division, that of Ra, and his own command and bodyguard to Kadesh with the hope of seizing the city before the Hittites arrived. Ramses and his bodyguard encamped to the north of the city while the division of Amon rendezvoused with them the following morning.

The Hittite army, probably smaller than the Egyptian army, accordingly had two great advantages besides the simple, greatest one of more battle experience. Ramses was unaware of their actual position, and they themselves were unified, in a position to annihilate the division of Ra and win perhaps the war by capturing or killing Ramses himself.

For all the advantage having the king as commander gave ancient armies, like the chess game that reflects them, struggles in which the king was the cause could be lost with the neutralization of one man.

With visual reconnaissance being the only sort Ramses apparently saw need to employ, the Hittite army's simple strategy of using Kadesh itself as cover worked quite well against the Egyptians. As the Amon and Ra divisions approached from the south and west of the city, the Hittites moved to the east, poised to move across the Egyptian line of march.

Muwatallis' decision to hold his army outside of the city was a very sound one. The difficulties of controlling an army in an urban environment are very serious even today, and in those days, using his complete force for a tactical offensive within the city would have been impossible for Muwatallis as walls and streets would have blocked audible and visual signals and disrupted his unit formations.

The Hittites struck the second of Ramses' divisions – Ra – as it approached their new positions and hit it in the flank. The Egyptians, surprised, panicked and fled for safety to the division of Amon and threw that formation into disorder and confusion as well, just as the victorious Hittites

'Shield high, stay in ranks,' were basic commands that could be taught and under ideal conditions adhered to by fellahin levied into the Egyptian infantry by Ramses' officers. In equipment, bare, in training, poor, such chariot-fodder as these lacked everything but numbers and a desire for loot and glory. In those Egypt was wealthy enough to pose a sizeable threat to even so sophisticated and skilled an opponent as the expanding Hittite Empire.

attacked again from the south directly across the Egyptians' escape route. Disaster loomed.

At that point of the battle Ramses and Muwatallis each faced differing problems in controlling their armies. The panic and disorder of fully half of his forces left Ramses physically unable to transmit countering orders to his own troops, and no message could be sent that would dramatically hasten the impending arrival of the divisions of Ptah and Sutekh to the battlefield where they were desperately needed. Muwatallis, for that matter, found his own ability to command his forces disintegrating as his men stopped to plunder the Egyptians' camp, including the tents of the Pharaoh, as the disorganized Egyptian forces gave ground.

Moreover, Muwatallis himself apparently made a lapse of reconnaissance and intelligence-gathering and remained unaware that the other half of the Egyptian army was marching directly into his rear, while a formation of mercenaries hired by Ramses was moving in from the Mediterranean coast and about to take him squarely in his eastern flank with more trained ferocity than the raw Egyptians could achieve.

Ramses and his army would live or die upon his ability to regain control of his forces, and the Pharaoh took the only, therefore the best, means of doing it, by very visibly leading his own bodyguard into a headlong counter-attack against the advancing Hittites. Instantly, every Egyptian on the field knew where his commander was and where his own duty lay, and a general movement against the Hittites allowed the division of Ptah to strike the

Hittites in the rear just as the mercenaries pitched into them from the flank.

Muwatallis withdrew in some confusion. It is worth noting that in even the most autocratic of armies retreat is a decision democratically arrived upon, when the majority of soldiers 'vote with their feet', and force even the officer corps to retire with them. Moving into Kadesh, the Hittites were sheltered against any further Egyptian surprises but did forfeit the substantial psychological advantage of holding the battlefield.

AFTERMATH

Ramses' reverses prompted him to withdraw his remaining forces from the vicinity of Kadesh, while the Hittites had seen enough of Egypt's military resources to agree to a lasting peace after the battle. Both sides had shown good and bad exercises of central command, both sides had had their failures of communication, and the result was a tactical win for the Egyptians, a strategic victory for the Hittites, and, in the light of the treaty, an international 'draw'.

At Kadesh, Ramses did inflict a great deal of damage on the Hittite army, at a considerable, and inadvertent, risk of losing his crown and life due to his own belief in the information planted by the two captured spies. At considerable cost in time, treasure and the blood of both armies, Ramses did secure a peace treaty and security on his northern frontier, not to mention a stele of his own to rival the enduring military glory of Thutmose III and the other warrior pharaohs. In his own view – and no one else's mattered – the battle was a success, whatever else shows up under the glaring spotlight of modern analysis.

Opposite: The massive statue of Ramses II fronting the temple of Ramses II at Abu Simbel, near Lake Nasser in modern Egypt, was built to mark the ancient kingdom's southern border and is testament to the Pharaoh's power.

LACHISH
701 BC

THE ASSYRIAN EMPIRE WAS THE DOMINANT MILITARY POWER OF THE REGION. ITS ARMIES WERE SO CAPABLE THAT ITS ENEMIES WOULD NOT FACE THEM ON THE FIELD OF BATTLE, AND SO THE EMPIRE WAS FORCED TO DEVELOP ADVANCED SIEGE TECHNIQUES.

WHY DID IT HAPPEN?

WHO An Assyrian army under King Sennacherib (705–682 BC) versus the defenders of the town of Lachish.

WHAT After a request to surrender upon the promise of clemency was refused, the town was assaulted and the population massacred.

WHERE The town of Lachish in Judah.

WHEN 701 BC.

WHY King Sennacherib of Assyria launched a campaign to conquer the Kingdom of Judah and make it part of his empire.

OUTCOME The town was stormed, looted and its inhabitants put to the sword. The Assyrian Empire then pushed on into Judah, and much later captured Jerusalem.

The Assyrian Empire was founded along the Tigris river in what today is northern Iraq, with its capital at Ashur. At first a minor kingdom located close to Babylonia and the kingdom of the Hittites, Assyria gradually became more important. Although the kingdom had existed for a long time before, King Ashur-uballit (1366–1331 BC) is considered to be the founder of the Assyrian Empire as such. He dealt with Egypt as an equal and defended his kingdom against the Kassites. His son fought against Babylonia and his grandson expanded to the west where the empire first encountered the Semitic tribes.

Over time the empire grew, largely through conquest, and for a while it included all of Mesopotamia, though areas were lost to the Hittites. The fortunes of the empire ebbed and flowed, and through these troubled times the Assyrians amassed an enormous body of experience on the subject of making war.

The economy of the empire was based on agriculture, though it was fortunate to have more fertile land than Babylon and therefore needed less artificial irrigation. Agricultural endeavour included the breeding of horses. Trade was also important: Assyria imported many necessary items such as timber and metals, and traded them beyond its borders. Some of the empire's many wars were over trade; either to prevent interference, to remove competition or to open up new routes.

THE ASSYRIAN ARMY
These many wars led to the Assyrians becoming masters of the art of armed conflict. They understood that success in

In this relief sculpture taken from Sennacherib's palace, the uniformity of equipment, spacing and posture of these Assyrian soldiers suggests an organized body of well-trained troops. This was one factor in Assyrian invincibility.

ASSYRIAN ARCHERS
(C. 700 BC)

The bow was an important weapon in Assyrian warfare. It was used from chariots or on foot, and was of a powerful design allowing enemies to be defeated at long range.

While some armies considered archers to be light skirmishing troops, Assyrian archers were front-line fighters, well protected by long coats of iron scales and a conical helmet. If threatened, they could take to their swords and fight it out, but would more normally rely on the protection of a shield-bearer and supporting infantry.

Assyrian tactics were sufficiently well developed (and their commanders well enough trained) that infantry could be moved forward to protect the archers, then pulled back out of the way once its protection was no longer needed.

war is all about the accrual of advantages, and they set about gaining as many of these as possible.

One of the key advantages enjoyed by the Assyrian army was the use of iron for weapons and armour. Compared with bronze, iron had many advantages. It afforded better protection for the same weight (or the same protection at less weight), it took an edge better and kept it for longer, and weapons made of iron were more durable. Soldiers armed with bronze were more likely to find themselves holding a bent, blunted weapon than their iron-equipped opponents.

The arrival of iron on the battlefield was a shock to the enemies of Assyria, whose equipment was thus outclassed. This gave the Assyrians a second advantage, a psychological one. The empire was never averse to using psychological warfare, and often used its reputation for invincibility to dishearten foes and dissuade potential enemies. Deliberate atrocities such as the blinding of thousands of defeated enemy soldiers were also used to spread fear among the enemy.

The Assyrian approach to warfare was aggressive but no need was perceived to take excessive risks. If a battle could be won by other means, then bloodshed was not necessary. For this reason the Assyrians used a system whereby their enemies were offered a chance to surrender and treated leniently if they did, but made to suffer terribly if they offered resistance. This led to many potential enemies deciding that the risk was not worth it, and many actual foes surrendering without a fight. This was particularly useful when facing an enemy ensconced inside a fortified city. Where a siege or storming attempt might be possible, it would be expensive and/or time-consuming. However, many cities simply surrendered rather than risk the terrible reprisals that would inevitably follow defeat.

The third great advantage of the empire lay in organization. The Assyrians were the first to establish military colleges where critical skills such as sapping and mining were taught, enabling sieges to be conducted more efficiently. Specialist troops conducted siege works as well as road-building, bridging operations and

other military construction, all in a highly organized fashion.

The backbone of the Assyrian army was the infantry. Men were armed with spears, swords, javelins and slings, but most notably the bow. Archers shot their iron-tipped arrows over impressive distances and were

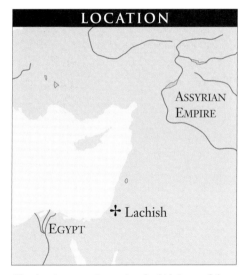

LOCATION

The Assyrian operation against Lachish is one of the earliest recorded sieges, and was part of a campaign by Sennacherib to wrest the rich kingdom of Judah from the Egyptians.

LACHISH

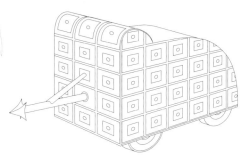

Assyrian battering ram from the reign of King Sargon II (722–705 BC). Later rams had towers built on top of them for archers to give covering fire. The beam was tipped with a sharp metal point to make it more effective. The rear of the ram was open.

This painting shows Assyrian forces attacking Kadesh. The use of rams and an assault ramp are clearly shown in the foreground, along with archers giving covering fire.

protected from counter-fire by shield-bearers. The bow also went to war aboard chariots. Initially these vehicles had a crew of two, but this was later increased to three. Cavalry were deployed by the Assyrian Empire, though not in the early years. Later on they became a feared combat arm and gradually supplanted chariots in the mobile-strike role.

SIEGE WARFARE

The result of all these factors was a period in which no enemy would fight the Assyrians in the field at all. It became axiomatic that to try to fight a field battle against the armies of Assyria was to invite utter defeat. No one ever beat them in open battle, so what was the point of trying? The usual pattern was that as soon as hostilities broke out between Assyria and any given foe, the enemy's forces scurried into the nearest fortresses and refused to come out. Strong walls might give the advantage they needed to offset Assyrian invincibility.

Of course, all this meant was that the Assyrians became masters of siege warfare. Their genius for logistics and organization was turned to the development of

techniques and weapons designed to pry their foes out of their strong places and destroy them. The usual Assyrian approach to a city assault was to first create a secure base of operations in the form of a fortified camp, much as the Romans would do centuries later. The city was then surrounded in order to cut it off from reinforcements and supplies, and the slow process of siege would begin. If other means did not work, the defenders could eventually be starved out.

Assault was used where appropriate. The Assyrians had available a range of siege engines including iron-tipped battering rams and siege towers. They also had units of specially trained miners who would tunnel under the enemy defences and collapse parts of them. Tactics were also a critical part of an assault, and the Assyrians had well-trained officers who could draw on an impressive body of experience. As more and more cities fell to them, so their skills grew and lessons learned from each conquest were passed on through the efficient training programmes maintained by the empire. In many ways the Assyrian empire was well ahead of its time.

The ruins of Lachish are located in modern Israel and are visited by thousands each year. The remains of the city's fortress-mound can still be seen.

THE CONQUEST OF ISRAEL

The Assyrian Empire was a major power, dominating the region and enjoying massive military advantages over its rivals. It destroyed those who rose up against it and used harsh reprisals to discourage others from rebellion.

One of the border states of Assyria was the ancient Kingdom of David, now divided into two smaller states, Israel and Judah. Both were Jewish kingdoms, but they were rather different. Israel was larger and more prosperous and lay on the major trade routes, while Judah was more sparsely populated, less accessible and poorer. Judah was something of a poor relation, following in the footsteps of Israel in the development of pottery and wine-making industries but always later and on a smaller scale. In 732 BC, Ahaz was recognized as king of Judah. He had fought for Assyria and was probably given the throne as a reward for his service. Judah itself was recently independent of Israel, and while both Israel and Judah paid tribute to Assyria, Judah in particular was an Assyrian client state whose king was little more than a puppet.

As Judah was becoming an independent state – independent from Israel at least – Israel itself was about to suffer catastrophe at the hands of the Assyrians. It was taken in conquest by an army under Sargon II (722–705 BC). Its capital, Samaria, was destroyed and the people enslaved. Many were deported and became the Ten Lost Tribes of Israel mentioned in the Bible. After the destruction of Israel in 722 BC, Judah was the only remaining kingdom of the Jews, such as it was.

King Ahaz and his successor Hezekiah (715–687 BC) knew that they were living on borrowed time. Sooner or later Assyria would finish the conquest of the Jewish kingdoms. The end was staved off by paying tribute the kingdom could scarcely afford and by avoiding any hint of rebellion that might invite the displeasure and intervention of the mighty Assyrians. Thus

when an alliance arose against Assyria around 720 BC, Judah stayed well out of it.

INVASION

But in 713–711 BC King Hezekiah decided to take a chance. This decision was not made lightly, for the penalties for rebellion were severe, but it seemed that the time was right. Not only did holy men, including the Prophet Isaiah, think that this was the right move, but there was a powerful alliance forming. Egyptian, Phoenician and Philistine armies were on the march. It seemed that the Jews under Hezekiah had a real chance to strike back at the enemy that had destroyed the other great Jewish kingdom and scattered its inhabitants. The rebellion was not a success. The Assyrians quickly defeated the Egyptians, leaders of

THE OPPOSED FORCES

ASSYRIANS (estimated)

Total:	**10,000**

LACHISH TOWNSPEOPLE (estimated)

Total:	**8,000**

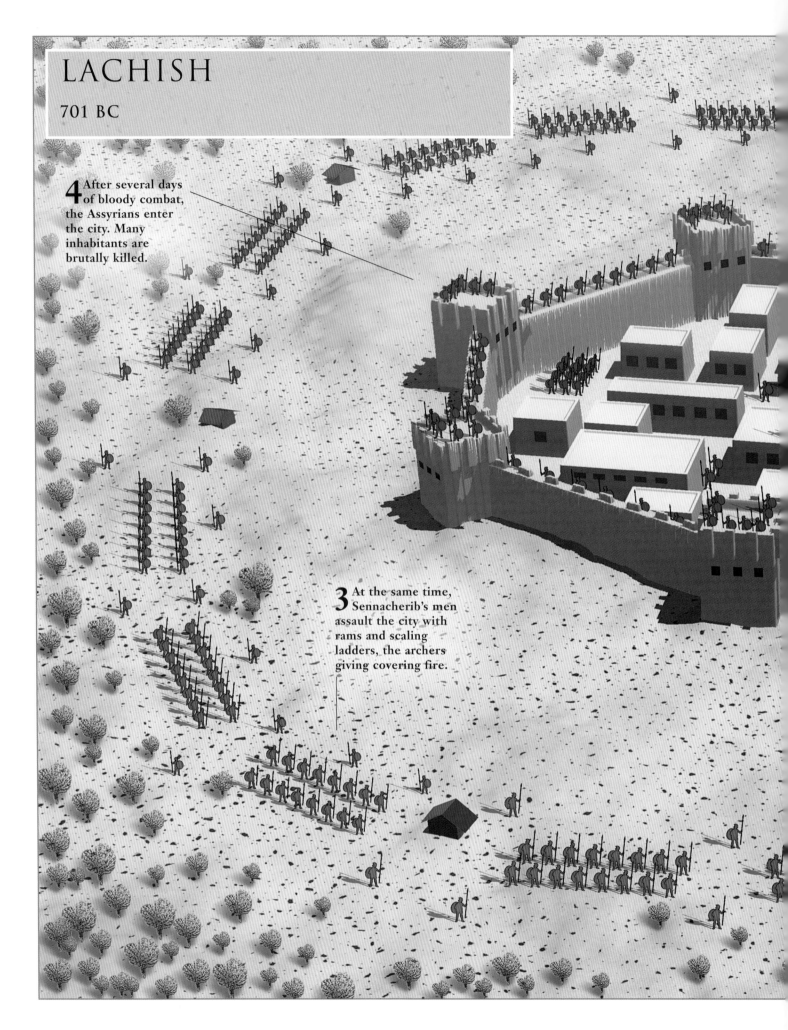

LACHISH

701 BC

4 After several days of bloody combat, the Assyrians enter the city. Many inhabitants are brutally killed.

3 At the same time, Sennacherib's men assault the city with rams and scaling ladders, the archers giving covering fire.

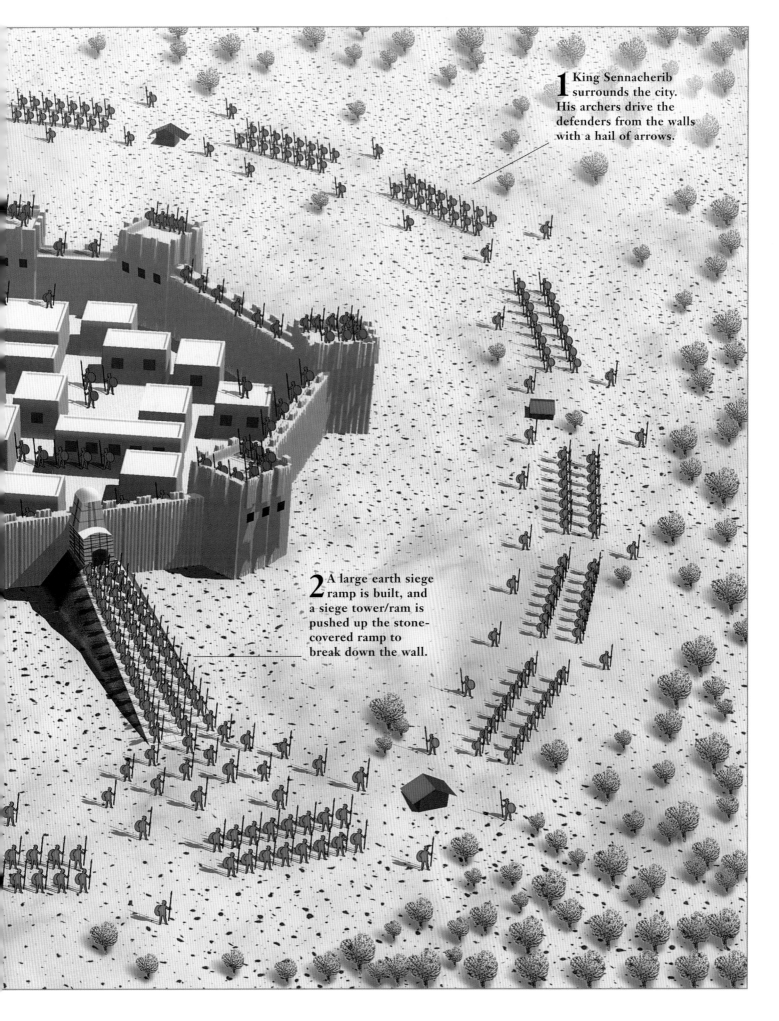

1 King Sennacherib surrounds the city. His archers drive the defenders from the walls with a hail of arrows.

2 A large earth siege ramp is built, and a siege tower/ram is pushed up the stone-covered ramp to break down the wall.

LACHISH

A chariot from a drawing of the Assyrian monuments of Assurnasirpal II (884–859 BC). Assyrian chariots in this period had three horses, but only two were attached to the yoke, implying that the third was used as a spare, or to encourage the other horses to run faster.

the alliance, and Hezekiah sued for peace. Perhaps surprisingly, Judah escaped Assyrian retribution and continued to be a vassal state.

MARCHING ON JUDAH

In 705 BC Sargon II was murdered by his own troops and was succeeded by Sennacherib. Hezekiah tried to take advantage of the situation by forging an alliance and attacking Assyria before the inexperienced new king could find his feet, but Sennacherib proved to be a capable leader, and smashed the Babylonians before marching to confront Assyria's traditional enemies, the Egyptians. The army of Egypt was defeated at the battle of Eltequeh and once again Judah sued for peace. The Assyrians agreed to accept a large tribute and Judah survived its indiscretion – for the time being.

Then in 701 BC, perhaps tiring of the rebellious nature of Judah, Sennacherib decided to squash the problem in the usual Assyrian manner. His intentions were announced beforehand, and Hezekiah was dismayed. However, the religious leaders of Judah, including Isaiah, told him that God was with the people of Judah and that they would prevail.

Despite the promise of godly aid, things went badly for Judah at first, and the Assyrians captured no less than 46 fortresses and towns before finally failing in their attempt to capture Jerusalem. The deliverance of the final strong place of the last Jewish kingdom certainly seems miraculous, and it is possible that if Jerusalem had fallen, the Jewish religion might have been destroyed by the inevitable reprisals. Because Jerusalem survived, Judaism also endured. And from Judaism came both Christianity and Islam. However, Lachish was not so fortunate.

SENNACHERIB AT LACHISH

As already noted, it was well known that to fight Assyria in the field was to invite disaster, so Hezekiah prepared to defend his cities from siege. The defences of Jerusalem were improved, as well as those at other strong places. At Jerusalem Hezekiah had a new wall built to surround the western hill, and, critically, the water supply was improved. Lachish and the neighbouring town of Azekah received improvements to their fortifications. As matters turned out, it was not enough.

Sennacherib followed a similar path to Sargon II, advancing down the coastal highway and subduing the towns along the way. He then turned his attention on the fortified town of Lachish. Like many similar towns, Lachish had good walls. Taking them would be a costly affair. Sennacherib tried to avoid the necessity of an assault by asking for the town to surrender. This followed the typical Assyrian pattern; a display of the power of the army outside, intended to awe the defenders into thinking they could not possibly hold out, was followed by an oration which promised clemency if they surrendered and drew attention to the horrible penalties awaiting those who resisted.

Although the official language of the Assyrian Empire was 'Imperial Aramaic', and this would have been understood by the town's leaders, the oration was delivered in Hebrew so that the common people and

Opposite: King Sennacherib followed a similar route to Sargon II in his conquest of Judah and Israel. He had under his hand the finest military instrument of his era, and he used it ruthlessly.

LACHISH

This relief shows an Assyrian archer at his work. He is protected by armour and well supported by his shield-bearer, a group of infantry and men bringing him a fresh supply of arrows.

ordinary soldiers would know what was going on.

The intent was obvious – to sow discord and reduce morale. There was also a chance that someone would decide that his best chance to save himself would be to surrender or give the besiegers entry to the town. In this case, the ploy failed and the gates remained closed. Sennacherib was faced with the daunting prospect of storming Lachish or the equally difficult prospect of starving the defenders out.

THE RAMP

As with any defended place, the gates of Lachish were a potential weak spot. Walls can be made of stone but gates cannot. An iron-tipped ram could smash any gate

sooner or later. The problem was, the defenders knew that. Protecting gates was part of the art of fortification, and cities of the Middle East had some formidable defences.

Heavy, reinforced gates protected by stout gatehouses and swept by arrows from archers stationed on nearby towers made an assault a hazardous business that would cost many casualties just to reach the gates. The whole time troops were trying to break down the gates they would be being shot at from the flanks and assailed by objects dropped from above.

Even if a gate could be breached, it still presented a 'choke point' through which the attackers had to move. An unsubdued gatehouse or tower could rake the attackers mercilessly as they struggled through the wreckage of the gate and the bodies of the attackers. A counter-attack might drive them out, allowing the gate to be barricaded and thus require a second assault. Gates did indeed offer a way into a city, but it was an expensive option. Sennacherib knew

enough about siege warfare to seek an alternative, and he had one to hand.

After throwing a ring of troops around the town to cut it off from relief and replenishment, Sennacherib ordered the construction of an earth ramp to enable his great siege tower to approach the walls. Ramps were used in many assaults throughout the Ancient World. The cost in lives of building a huge ramp up to the walls was high, but once it was complete it offered easy access to the walls and negated much of the advantage enjoyed by the defenders. Sennacherib's ramp at Lachish was constructed mainly by forced labour. The workers were people captured during the campaign in Judah, meaning that the defenders had to make an agonizing choice whether or not to shoot at their countrymen as they worked. Undoubtedly they were forced to do so, as the alternative was to stand and watch the ramp coming towards the walls, bearing their doom. The construction work was covered by armoured Assyrian archers who were

the Persian squadrons guarding Psyttáleia. The ships had their sails up, while the usual custom for trireme combat was to leave both sails and mast on shore, so it seemed clear that they were in fact running rather than intending to fight. Soon the Athenian and Peloponnesian squadrons followed the Corinthian lead. It appeared that the Persian ambush had been set up perfectly: the Greek triremes would encounter the Egyptian ships stationed at the mouth of the western channel, and if Xerxes committed

the eastern parts of his fleet to chase them, the Greeks would be caught, with an overwhelming force both before and behind them. Therefore, Xerxes ordered squadron after squadron into the narrow channel to give chase.

There was indeed a trap, but it caught the Persians rather than the Greeks. The flight had been a ruse and once the Persian fleet had entered the channel, the 'fleeing' ships turned to face them, redeploying into three lines abreast. The Persians had rushed

into the strait in disorder due to overconfidence, and as squadrons were added they found their ships too tightly bunched together to manoeuvre. Disarray and disorientation must have followed rapidly, as the Greek squadrons from Aegina and Megara, hidden in a side channel, burst out and hit the exposed Persian left flank, the position held by Xerxes' Ionian Greek subjects.

Matters rapidly grew worse for the Persians. The Salamis Strait had indeed been well chosen for a Greek stand, as the Athenians, who would have known the local waters, were well aware. Sailors could depend on a rising swell in the morning, and it duly appeared at about 9.00 a.m. The weather conditions gave a decided advantage to triremes of mainland Greek design over those constructed by Persia's subject allies, whether Phoenicians, Egyptians or Ionian Greeks. The triremes used by the Greek League were heavier than their counterparts, with a centre of gravity much closer to the waterline. They were not even completely decked, and the small complements of marines were trained to sit or even lie down while throwing javelins. The Persian triremes, by contrast, were constructed to give a much larger role to marines. They had full decks, high prows and sterns, and each had at least twice as many marines as a Greek ship. All this weight above the waterline made the Persian ships top-heavy in bad weather. As the swell increased, the Persian ships pitched, disrupting the rowers' stroke and even slewing the vessels around so they presented their sides to the Greek rams.

The Persian ships were largely unable to manoeuvre, and even those with open water around them had no clear idea what to do; the Phoenician admiral Ariabignes was killed very early in the action, there was no recognized second-in-command, and Xerxes from his distant observation point could not convey orders rapidly enough in

A woodcut of Xerxes watching the battle from the hill called Xerxes' Throne. Depicted here as a leisurely spectator, in reality Xerxes needed a full view of the strait to give effective commands.

an age before modern communications systems. The Phoenician squadron, which formed the Persian right wing, was the first to break and flee. Their flight left a gap for the Athenians to exploit: they advanced and hit yet another Persian squadron. Some of the Phoenician triremes ran aground on the mainland, only to have their commanders beheaded on the orders of a furious Xerxes. The last of the Persian forces to continue to fight in the strait were the Ionian Greeks, who held their own for some time. But the Athenians stopped their pursuit and came back to hit the Ionians from the flank and rear until they, too, broke and ran. The Greeks then harried the retreating Persians relentlessly until night fell. Among those retreating was Queen Artemisia of Halicarnassus, one of Persia's subject allies. Hotly pursued by a Greek ship, she rammed a ship of her own side to make the Greek pursuer think that she was in fact an ally rather than an enemy. Her trick worked and she escaped to safety. Xerxes saw her dashing action and thought she had brought down a Greek ship; he is reported to have said, seeing it: 'My men have turned into women, my women into men.'

AFTERMATH

Persian losses were very heavy. At least 200 ships of the Persian fleet were sunk, and many more were captured, while the Greeks lost 40 ships. Casualties were also disproportionately high for the Persians, since many Greek oarsmen and marines swam safely to Salamis, while few of the Persian marines could swim. Many more of Xerxes' ships were damaged and had suffered serious losses during the day's fight. In a final action of the day, Greek marines landed on the isle of Psyttáleia, where 400 Persian infantrymen had been posted, and massacred them.

The Greeks spent 21 September frantically labouring to make their ships seaworthy, clearly expecting another attack and not realizing how much damage they had done. After Salamis, though, the Persian fleet was no longer capable of fighting. Many of the surviving ships were disabled and morale was extremely low. The number of battleworthy ships the king had at his command was now no longer even equal to that of the Greeks. Xerxes accepted the inevitable. He removed the marines from his surviving ships, placing them among the army. Then on the night of 21/22 September, the Persian fleet set out for the Hellespont, its mission to guard the Persian army's retreat. For without the fleet, the army had to withdraw. It could not be supplied, and it could not hope to carry the war on to the Peloponnese successfully. Although a sizeable Persian land army remained in Attica, to be defeated at Plataea the following year, Salamis marks the true end of the Persian dream to dominate the Greek world.

An engraving of an ancient marble bust of the Athenian statesman and admiral Themistocles (525–460 BC). The bust is an idealized image, meant to emphasize Themistocles' military valour.

SYRACUSE
415 BC

ATHENS' ATTEMPT TO CONQUER THE CORINITHIAN COLONY OF SYRACUSE IN SICILY DURING THE PELOPONNESIAN WAR WAS A DISASTER. THE DRAIN ON MANPOWER AND RESOURCES AS THE CAMPAIGN ESCALATED INTO A PROLONGED SIEGE CRIPPLED THE CITY, AND THE FINAL DEFEAT, WITH THOUSANDS OF ATHENIAN HOPLITES ENSLAVED, BROUGHT TO AN END ATHENS' HOPES OF DOMINATING THE GREEK WORLD.

WHY DID IT HAPPEN?

WHO An Athenian expedition attacked the Corinthian colony of Syracuse.

WHAT An Athenian feint to the north of the city allowed their main force to land unopposed in the harbour and bottle up the surprised garrison in the inner city.

WHERE Syracuse in Sicily.

WHEN 415 BC.

WHY To restrict the flow of grain to the Peloponnesian League and complete Athens' domination.

OUTCOME Although the Athenians had limited initial success, further land and naval reinforcements were sucked in and destroyed by the Syracusans, reversing Athens' earlier successes in the war.

In the fifth century BC Greece was split into a number of city-states, some large and some small. Some had prosperous colonies abroad like the Corinthian colony of Syracuse on the island of Sicily. When they were not forced into collective action by successive Persian invasions, the states fought each other, frequently forming extensive alliances or leagues with other states to achieve an advantage in numbers.

The early success of Athens, heading the Delian League, against Sparta, leading the Peloponnesian League (which included Corinth), in the Peloponnesian War of 431–404 BC left her dominant but not in control. For total control Athens needed to also dominate the colonies of her adversaries, for these would otherwise provide vital resources and a springboard for retaliatory action.

This map shows the complex state of Greek politics in the early fifth century BC, during the full term of the Peloponnesian War (431–404 BC), in which Sparta and her allies fought against Athens and hers.

KEY

	Athens and Delian League
	Thessaly (Athenian ally)
⚔	Athenian victory
	Sparta, Spartan allies (Macedonia)
✕	Spartan victory
✶	Revolt against the Athenians
	Persian Empire
	Epirus (neutral state)

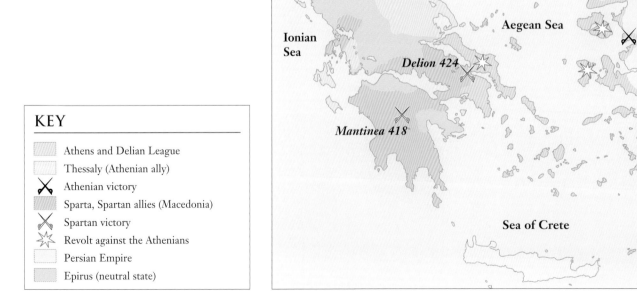

INITIAL SUCCESS

So, in the summer of 415 BC the Athenians invaded Syracuse. They sent a small army, 1500 Athenian hoplites, 2900 allied hoplites, 700 marines, 480 archers, 700 slingers, 120 light javelinmen and 30 cavalry, and a large fleet of 134 triremes, 40 oared transports, 30 merchant ships and 100 smaller craft. This was the first time such a large expedition had been sent such a long distance. In the days before offshore navigation, the fleet coast-hopped, beaching the ships each night for the large crews to eat and sleep ashore. Most of the cities en route gave them at best a suspicious reception, forcing the men to sleep outside the walls.

Thus the fleet made slow progress, and rumours of their approach reached Syracuse long before they did. At first they were not believed, but when the fleet arrived at the toe of Italy the truth struck home and defensive measures were put into place: weapons were checked and foodstuffs brought in from the countryside. The Athenians had sent three generals in command, Alkibiades, Lamachos and Nikias. Nikias was by nature very cautious and had a long history of political rivalry with Alkibiades. Alkibiades was then accused of sacrilege and defected to the Peloponnesian League, seeking shelter with the Spartans.

After a naval reconnaissance in force the army was landed unopposed at Catana, north of Syracuse, intimidating the assembly there into accepting them. From here they sailed anti-clockwise around Sicily towards Egesta and were joined by some of their cavalry and returned to camp at Catana. This delay and some false information encouraged the Syracusans to attempt a dawn attack on the Athenian camp. However, it was a trick. When they heard the Syracusan army was on the march, the Athenians embarked the army onto the ships and sailed south to assault Syracuse itself. Having caught their enemy off-guard, the Athenian infantry stormed ashore opposite the Olympieium and commenced building a fortified camp. Meanwhile the Syracusan cavalry had reported the Athenians gone and the army started a long and worried march home. The morning after their arrival both sides drew up for battle.

Athens

Syracuse

Sparta

Seeking to break the deadlock in the war against Sparta, the Athenians decided to attack Syracuse, hoping to deprive the Spartans of a vital source of supply and force them to sue for peace on terms advantageous to Athens.

GREEK HOPLITES (C. 400 BC)

The equipment of Greek hoplites – leg and chest armour, shield, helmet, spear and sword – varied little from one city-state to another. The training, however, did vary enormously. Male Spartan children were bred to be warriors from a very young age. They ate sparingly but well, exercised and trained daily. Just as important was the attitude engendered. They, and the rest of Greece, knew they were the best. Confidence in victory gives a man a huge advantage in a fight. Unfortunately for Syracuse, Sparta was only able to spare a general to help them. But that was enough.

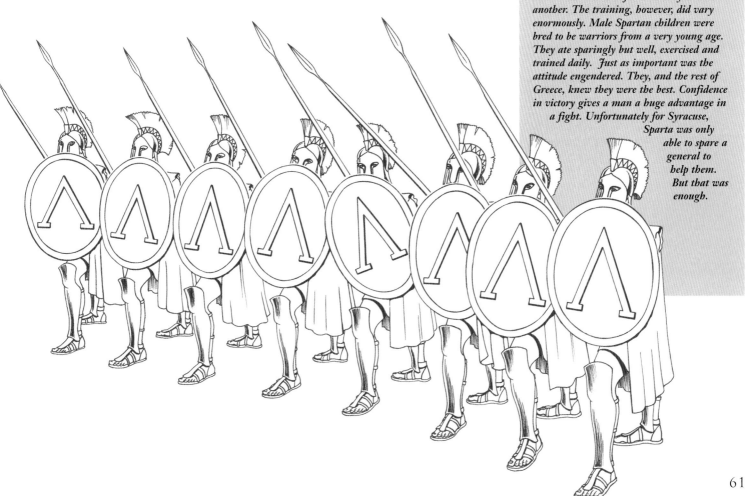

SYRACUSE

The trireme was the basic warship of the period and was propelled by sails or oars. The oarsmen were seated on tiers of benches inside the ship with each oarsman manning a single oar. Only the upper tier of oarsmen is shown here. A trireme had three tiers of benches on each side.

THE OPPOSED FORCES

SYRACUSANS

Hoplites:	12,000
Cavalry:	1500
Light troops:	2600
Local tribesmen:	1000
Sailors:	20,200
Triremes:	101
Total:	**37,300**

ATHENIANS

Hoplites:	12,000
Cavalry:	650
Light troops:	3250
Local tribesmen:	1000
Sailors:	52,800
Triremes:	264
Total:	**69,700**

The Athenians formed up between the cliff tops and a built-up area with a marsh, so the frontage was restricted negating the Syracusan superior numbers, particularly in cavalry of which they had 1200. The Athenians deployed a line of skirmishing light infantry armed with javelins, slings and bows followed by their hoplites, eight ranks deep, and a hollow square behind them also eight deep containing the non-combatants. The Syracusans also deployed a skirmish screen but had their hoplites 16 ranks deep with a mass of light javelinmen on their right and the cavalry beyond. The battle was fought during a thunderstorm, adding to the fear of the less experienced Syracusan force. The Athenian allies from Argive and Mantinea next to the cliffs forced the Syracusan infantry back, then the Athenian centre broke through and split the home side in two, proving the value of experience in a head-on clash. The Syracusan cavalry prevented a complete disaster by blocking any significant pursuit. The Syracusans lost 260 men, the Athenians just 50.

Winter loomed and despite this victory the Athenians could see the size of the task ahead of them and sailed back to over-winter at Catana and Naxos, sending to Athens for reinforcements, particularly of cavalry. The Syracusans also took stock and extended their fortifications with a new wall and forts at Megara and the Olympieium plus beach obstacles consisting of wooden stakes at all the likely landing places. They also sent to their allies, Sparta and Corinth. Both sides embarked on political efforts to recruit more Sicilian cities to their cause. Although the Mediterranean winter can be bitter, both sides carried out raids on each other and the country villages to bring in food and money. Sparta, hard-pressed in the recent wars by Athens and with her own manpower problems, sent instead one of her best generals, Gylippus.

SIEGE WARFARE

In this period, siege techniques were limited. There were no missile-throwing machines, siege towers or any means to breach or scale the walls other than ladders. Besiegers were therefore limited to cutting off the supplies to a city and starving it into submission. The normal method was to construct a defensive wall around the city, which the defenders would be equally unable to breach. In hostile territory or when a relief attempt was likely a second wall facing outwards would be built so the besiegers would also be secure to their rear. Athens opened the campaign of 414 BC by acting against the corn-growing areas that supplied the city, burning crops and villages and attacking Syracusan outposts where they found them. They also received 250 cavalrymen and 30 horse archers from Athens, which presumed that they would be able to find horses locally. Syracuse was dominated by the plateau known as Epipolae and although the Syracusans did not build a fort here they were establishing a garrison of 600 picked hoplites when the Athenians launched a surprise attack. They had moved their army by sea and marched at the double unseen up a gully to arrive on the heights. Although the Syracusans counter-attacked they were beaten back, losing 300 men. The Athenians established a fort here known as Labdalum. They were further reinforced by 300 cavalry from their Egestan allies plus another 100 from the native tribes, the Sikels, and from Naxos.

Having garrisoned the new fort at Labdalum, the Athenians shifted to Syca

and rapidly built another fort there called the Circle. This activity prompted the Syracusans to sally out of the city to give battle again. But the commanders could not get the inexperienced hoplites into a proper battle line and so withdrew, again covered by their cavalry. These were charged and routed by the Athenian cavalry supported by some of their hoplites.

The Athenians then started building double lines of circumvallation from the Great Harbour around the city to the coast to the north. The Syracusans attempted to block this by building their own double walls out from the city like the spoke of a wheel, forcing the Athenians to build an ever longer wall. This bizarre construction race is reminiscent of nineteenth-century railroad barons trying to block each other's routes across the country.

Inevitably the Athenians attacked the 'spoke' at midday when any sensible Greek would normally be sheltering from the sun. They used just 300 chosen hoplites and some armoured skirmishers. The rest of their force was split into two parts. One

approached the city in case of counter-attack, the other stood to arms by their own wall as a reserve. The Syracusans on the 'spoke' routed back inside the city and the Athenians dismantled the wooden wall and carried the materials off to help with their own construction works. Undeterred, the Syracusans began again, this time on the southern side, taking their walls through the marsh by the harbour, this time with an additional ditch.

Again the Athenians attacked the new wall, bringing their fleet around from its base at Thapsus. This time the Syracusans sallied out from the city and gave battle, but unfortunately they routed, with their right wing going back to the city and their left towards the river. Here a small band of Athenian hoplites attempted to cut them off from the bridge but they were attacked by

---

This engraving depicts the battle of Potidaea (431 BC), where the famous Greek philosopher Socrates (470– 399 BC) is reputed to have fought for his home city of Athens against the Corinthians.

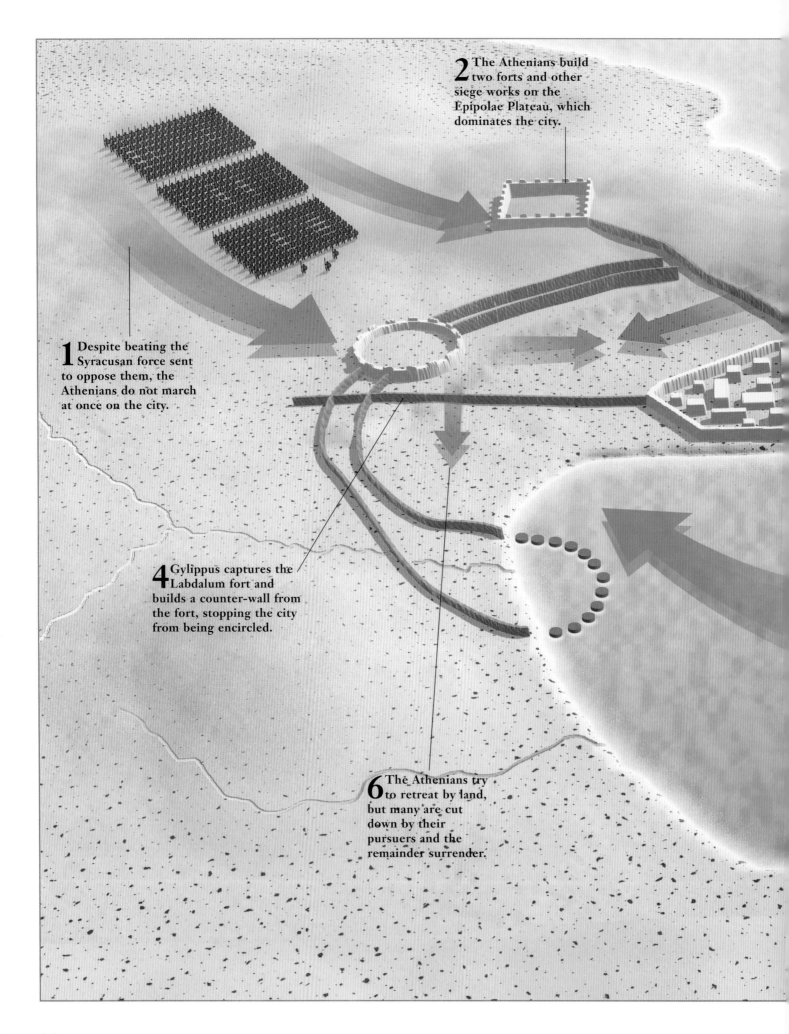

2 The Athenians build two forts and other siege works on the Epipolae Plateau, which dominates the city.

1 Despite beating the Syracusan force sent to oppose them, the Athenians do not march at once on the city.

4 Gylippus captures the Labdalum fort and builds a counter-wall from the fort, stopping the city from being encircled.

6 The Athenians try to retreat by land, but many are cut down by their pursuers and the remainder surrender.

SYRACUSE
415 BC

3 The Athenians neglect to finish their siege works, which allows the Spartan general Gylippus to reinforce the city.

5 The city traps the Athenian fleet by stretching a chain across the harbour mouth. The fleet is then abandoned.

the Syracusan cavalry and the best Athenian general, Lamachus, was killed in the fighting. While this was going on the Syracusans also mounted an assault on the Circle fort which they briefly captured before the Athenian general Nikias ordered it to be burnt to prevent it being held by the enemy. Nothing now prevented the Athenian construction work which proceeded apace. They also received further reinforcements of three 50-oared ships from Etruria.

GYLIPPUS ARRIVES

Dissension started to show in Syracuse and the Syracusan generals were replaced, with Heraclides, Eucles and Tellias taking over. At the same time the Spartan general Gylippus was on his way with two Spartan and two Corinthian ships and a further 14 following. This small force landed at Himera where they beached the ships and, with assistance from the Himerians,

marched to reinforce the city. Gylippus' force comprised 1000 hoplites, 700 sailors/marines, over 100 cavalry, some skirmishing infantry and about 1000 Sikels. Although they advanced boldly and offered to accept the Athenians' surrender, Gylippus could not get the poorly drilled Syracusan hoplites into a proper battle line and so stood off rather than attack.

The next day he captured the fort at Labdalum, which was not visible from the Athenian position, executing all he captured there. The Syracusans also captured an Athenian ship moored off the harbour. They also commenced another 'spoke' to prevent the Athenians completing their wall and fortified the entrance to the Great Harbour with three forts at Plemmyrium. The Syracusan cavalry was also making life hard for the Athenians, attacking small foraging parties wherever they could. A further battle took place, initiated by the Syracusans, between the walls. Here there

A Renaissance depiction of the Athenian landing. In fact, ancient crews lowered their masts before a battle, manoeuvring their vessels by oar alone. The elaborate stems and sterns of the ships are too exaggerated. On ancient galleys these (smaller) features helped to prevent a complete inversion if the ship capsized. The buildings in the background presumably indicate the three forts on the southern spur of the harbour. Syracuse would be behind the artist's left shoulder.

The Athenian general Alkibiades. This Renaissance painting reflects the artistic conventions and dress styles of the sixteenth century.

was insufficient room for their cavalry to operate successfully and they were again defeated and retired to the city. However, Gylippus rallied them and led them out again when the opportunity presented itself and deployed on more open ground where their superiority in cavalry showed. While the hoplites clashed head-on the Syracusan cavalry attacked the Athenian left and routed it, forcing the rest of the army to withdraw. The following night the Syracusans succeeded in crossing the Athenian building line with their own wall, depriving the Athenians of any chance of investing the city. To further tip the scales in favour of the Syracusans the Corinthian main fleet of 12 ships arrived, a much needed morale boost. Their crews helped complete the latest 'spoke' as well as bringing the Syracusan fleet up to fighting condition to challenge the Athenians at sea. As the summer ended Gylippus left the city to recruit more aid from the rest of the island and messengers were also sent to seek more aid from Sparta and Corinth. Of course the Athenians were doing the same, appealing for more troops and ships from home.

THE TIDE TURNS

Both sides readied reinforcing expeditions. The allies of Syracuse sent 600 Spartan hoplites, 300 Boeotians, 500 Corinthians and 200 Siconians in merchant ships. Meanwhile Athens despatched 65 ships with 1200 hoplites plus supports, together with the generals Demosthenes and Eurymedon, to share the command with Nikias. The Spartans also launched an invasion of Athenian territory in Greece, forcing her to fight on two fronts. Back in Syracuse Gylippus had succeeded in recruiting a substantial number of allies from around the island and laid plans to take the war to sea. The attack was mounted on three fronts. Gylippus led the infantry out in a dawn

attack on the forts at Plemmyrium, while 35 ships from the Great Harbour and another 45 from the smaller harbour executed a pincer movement against the Athenians. Manning this number of triremes takes time and must have been spotted, for the Athenians put 60 of their ships into action, 25 against the 35 and 35 against the Syracusan 45. The land attack was successful and all three forts were captured, their garrisons fleeing by small boats across to their main camp. At sea the Syracusans were initially successful, forcing the Athenian 35-ship squadron back into the

harbour, where they became disorganized. The Athenians rallied and sank 11 ships for the loss of just three.

However, at a strategic level, the Syracusans now held the upper hand. They now dominated, if not controlled, the entrance to the harbour, and the Athenians, not the Syracusans, now had supply problems. The besiegers had become the besieged. Athenian depots in Italy were raided and destroyed. Supply convoys were intercepted and vital material intended for the Athenian force now benefited the Syracusans. The Athenians knew they had to regain control of the harbour and launched an attack against the protective stakes the Syracusans had earlier planted to protect their ships beached within it. Some of these were visible above water, some were hidden beneath the surface to rip holes in the hulls of the enemy's ships. The Athenians equipped a huge ship with wooden towers and protective screens and pulled up or, using divers, cut off most of the stakes. This is all reminiscent of the pre-landing activity on D-Day, 2360 years later. However, the Syracusans replaced them within a few days with more stakes driven into the harbour bed.

Things were not going well for the Athenians at home either. Peloponnesian League forces had occupied a position near the city, which effectively dominated the Athenian hinterland and thus its ability to feed itself. The war effort was also draining the treasury and extra taxes had to be levied. This did not appear to sap the Athenian determination. A force of Sikels ambushed a reinforcing column, killing about 800, but the surviving 1500 made it through the lines

to reinforce the garrison of Syracuse. A further 500 hoplites, 300 skirmishing javelinmen and 300 archers from the Sicilian city of Camarina also managed to reach the city, plus 400 javelinmen and 200 cavalry from Gela.

FIRST NAVAL DEFEAT

By now the Athenian reinforcements from Greece were at Rhegium on the toe of Italy and the Syracusans had been busy. Following a Corinthian example, they heavily reinforced the bows of their ships and prepared for a head-on naval clash in the Great Harbour. Again Gylippus first led the army out from the city against a portion of the Athenian wall while skirmishers, backed by cavalry and 500 hoplites from their outpost at Olympieium, moved up from the other side.

This feint caused the Athenians to reinforce those parts of the wall and then the Syracusan fleet sallied forth with 80 ships to attack the Athenians' fleet. They quickly managed to man and launch 75 ships. This action was indecisive. But it did

In this re-creation by Hermann Vogel, columns of Athenian hoplites are destroyed by missile throwers and cavalry attacks as they retreat in panic. The near complete loss of the 40,000 Athenian allied army who sailed to conquer Sicily fatally weakened the Athenians' ability to wage war.

A portrait bust of Thucydides (471–411 BC). An Athenian aristocrat, Thucydides is famous as the chief chronicler of the conflict between Athens and Sparta, in his History of the Peloponnesian War. Thucydides' account of the siege of Syracuse remains a literary masterpiece and the chief source for historians studying the Sicilian campaign today.

prompt the Athenian commander to form a protective screen of merchant ships, anchoring them 61m (200ft) apart along the front of his fleet. The next day the Syracusans repaired their damaged ships and on the third day sallied out again, but earlier than before. They also had a plan. Before noon and the heat of the day their fleet backed water and headed back to the harbour side, apparently to feed their crews. The Athenians did the same. However, some of the Syracusans doubled back and attacked the unprepared ships. Annoyed, the Athenian ships came to ram speed bow-to-bow with the reinforced prows of the Syracusan ships. The Athenians lost seven ships and many more damaged while the Syracusans lost only two.

This defeat had a disproportionate affect on Athenian morale. They had always been the seafaring Greek city. To lose even a small naval battle was very disheartening. Not a moment too soon the long-awaited reinforcements arrived from Greece, comprising 73 ships carrying 5000 hoplites plus numerous javelin-, bow- and sling-armed skirmishing troops and the balance of power once more swung in Athens' favour. The new general from Athens, Demosthenes, determined to make a vigorous attempt to capture the city while he had the advantage of fresh troops. First he laid waste to a fertile region near the city to reduce the supplies available to the garrison. Then he brought up 'engines', probably scaling ladders on wheels, to the walls. However, these were set on fire by the Syracusans and the assaults driven back.

Undeterred he now launched a night attack on the last 'spoke' of the Syracusan wall built to prevent the Athenian wall being completed. He had the army provisioned for a five-day expedition and led them on an overnight march to Epipolae via Euryelus and captured the Syracusan fort. A rash counter-attack was defeated and the Athenians set about tearing down the Syracusan spoke wall. A major counter-attack was also pushed back. But the advancing Athenians became disordered and were charged by the Boeotian allied hoplites and routed. In the dark all was confusion on the Athenian side. Their troops were dispersed with new troops arriving from the night march and all asking for the password at the same time. The Syracusans were, by contrast, all together in one body, but cheering wildly at the Athenian rout.

Athenian troops fought each other in the confusion and the army retreated in considerable disorder. Many of the new arrivals got lost and were rounded up and killed by the Syracusan cavalry when daylight came. Gylippus set out again to recruit even more soldiers to the cause. He hoped to raise enough to really take the fight to the Athenians.

THE FINAL BATTLE

The Athenian generals held a full council to decide what to do as their army was disheartened and suffering a lot from sickness. Returning to Athens or finding a new base in Sicily from which to harry their enemies were both considered. In the end they decided to stay put and continue the struggle.

Gylippus had been successful at raising a new force and returned after some adventures, landing at Selinus. Seeing this new force the Athenians decided they had had enough and gave orders to sail at night. But an eclipse of the moon was taken as a bad omen from the gods and they had to wait for 27 days for the omen to be propitiated. News of this came to the

SYRACUSE

attention of the Syracusan commanders and they turned the pressure up on the vacillating Athenians. The Syracusan fleet went back into training and a two-pronged attack to be executed over several days was planned. On the first day they attacked the Athenian walls and a small force of cavalry and hoplites came out to meet them. This was routed and driven back. The second day 76 Syracusan ships sailed out and met 86 Athenian vessels. The Syracusans broke through the centre and cut off one of the Athenian generals, Eurymedon, who was killed and the ships of his squadron were sunk. While the naval battle raged, Gylippus led the army along the shore to attack the naval base. His vanguard was routed by Etruscan allies of the Athenians. They were forced back by the main force, which was, in turn, forced back by the Athenians' main force. The 18 ships briefly captured by Gylippus' men were recovered. To further discomfort their enemy the Syracusans deployed a fire ship, perhaps the first use of this weapon. But it was countered and did no damage. Despite the fact that they contained the land attack this was another blow to Athenian morale.

The Syracusans' next step was to reduce the navigable passage through the harbour entrance by mooring a line of ships across the entrance, effectively blocking the exit route for the Athenian force. Immediate escape was their only chance. They fortified a small area only large enough for the stores and the sick. Every able-bodied man was loaded onto the ships with the intention of

fighting a huge boarding action and 110 ships were so equipped. But all this action was clearly evident to the Syracusans, who stretched hides over the prows of their ships to negate the grappling irons of the Athenians. The Syracusans, using the same 76 ships as before, deployed part of their force at the harbour mouth. The rest were at various stations around the harbour, intent on attacking the Athenians from all directions, while their infantry stood ready on parts of the shore where the Athenians might land. The fighting was intense. Few naval battles have ever involved so many ships in such a small space.

At the end it was the Syracusans who carried the day. The Athenians lost around 50 ships and the Syracusans nearly 30. So the Athenians still had more ships. Those surviving beached themselves as and when opportunity presented and their crews made for their camp. Nikias put off an immediate retreat inland for a day or two. The Syracusans were after all celebrating both their victory and a religious rite. However, the Syracusans were not all idle. Gylippus had organized roadblocks and scouts to monitor the Athenian route and deployed the army to best counter the retreat. Finally, two days after the naval battle the Athenians set out, abandoning their sick and unburied dead. The force still numbered over 40,000. Marching in a hollow square formation, they had to carry everything they needed except food for there was none to be had in the camp they left.

The Syracusan cavalry and light infantry harassed their flanks all the way. The first defended ford was taken and the army camped just 7.2km (4.5 miles) from their original base. The next day they reached a

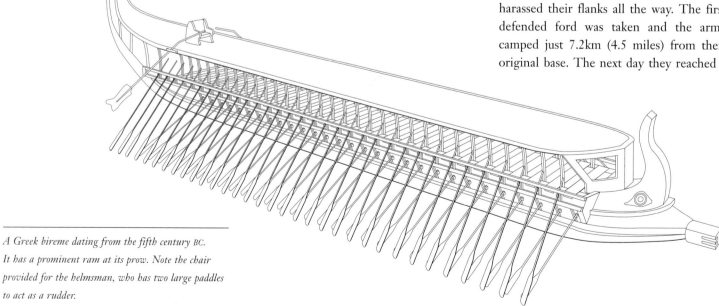

A Greek bireme dating from the fifth century BC. It has a prominent ram at its prow. Note the chair provided for the helmsman, who has two large paddles to act as a rudder.

small village and camped again to get what food and water they could. On the third day they set out but were forced back by the skirmishers. On the fourth day they came to Gylippus' blocking force. He had occupied a steep, narrow pass with a rocky gully on either side and fortified his position with a wall. The Athenians had no choice but to carry out a frontal assault on this formidable place with skirmishers and cavalry awaiting them below.

They tried, against almost impossible odds, moving up the pass and attempting to storm the temporary barrier Gylippus' men had erected. Beset by storms of missiles it was never going to succeed and they retired and rested. As they did so, part of Gylippus' force was building another wall in their rear, but its completion was prevented by the Athenian rearguard. Night fell, with the poor Athenians camped out on the plain. Nikias had them light numerous fires then tried to slip away towards the sea under cover of darkness. As they marched in the dark the three parts of the army became separated. The advance guard under Nikias reached the coast and turned to march along it. The first river they came to was being barricaded by light Syracusan forces

but they were brushed aside and the army continued. The rearguard was attacked while it lagged some 8.8km (5.5 miles) behind the others. They were surrounded in a walled olive grove. After a day under constant missile fire, terms were agreed and all 6000 Athenians surrendered.

AFTERMATH

The next day the Syracusan army caught up with Nikias and the remnants deployed on a hill; they declined to surrender. Three hundred of them escaped that night and the following morning the desperate Athenians marched on to the next river, harried all the way by Syracusan skirmishers. Syracusan infantry again held the steep opposite bank. But the Athenians had lost the will to fight and only wanted to drink. Thousands were slaughtered as they did so. Nikias surrendered to Gylippus to spare their lives and the rest were taken prisoner. The Athenian generals Nikias and Demosthenes were put to death, and 7000 prisoners were incarcerated in the stone quarries where many died before they were repatriated. The disastrous Syracusan campaign crippled the city of Athens and destroyed her ability to dominate Greece.

The amphitheatre was the centre of Greek culture in Syracuse. In its original form, the amphitheatre was built in the reign of Hiero I, around 470 BC. It was here that the tragedy The Persians by Aeschylus (c. 525–456 BC) was first performed in Sicily. Syracuse remained an important centre of Greek culture well into the third century BC, before the Roman conquest.

LEUCTRA
371 BC

THE BATTLE OF LEUCTRA WAS NOTABLE FOR TWO THINGS – THE DEFEAT OF THE SUPPOSEDLY INVINCIBLE SPARTANS AND THE METHOD OF THAT DEFEAT. THE THEBAN ARMY USED INNOVATIVE TACTICS INCLUDING A REFUSED FLANK TO BREAK THE CONVENTIONALLY DEPLOYED SPARTAN FORCE.

WHY DID IT HAPPEN?

WHO Theban forces numbering about 7000–9000 under Epaminondas (d. 362 BC) versus around 12,000 Spartans under King Cleombrotus (d. 371 BC).

WHAT A Spartan cavalry attack was repulsed, then Epaminondas used unusual tactics to break the Spartan right flank, killing their king and forcing a retreat.

WHERE 16km (10 miles) west of Thebes, in Greece.

WHEN July 371 BC.

WHY The Spartans invaded Theban territory in response to a request from several Boeotian cities for assistance in overthrowing their Theban overlords.

OUTCOME Up until this point, the Spartans were thought to be invincible. Their defeat at the hands of an inferior force caused irreparable damage to Spartan prestige.

It is a truism of warfare that military practices are shaped by the enemy they face, and that this can create dangerously one-dimensional forces. These always suffer when they meet an enemy who fights 'outside the box' of conventional military thinking. So it was at Leuctra in 371 BC.

War between the city-states of Greece was not uncommon as each jockeyed for political and economic advantage. Various states enjoyed a period of ascendancy and would then fall into decline or be pulled down by aggressive neighbours. Often the alliances that knocked an enemy off his pedestal did not even last long enough to celebrate the joint victory.

THE PHALANX

The supreme arbiter of these disputes was the phalanx, a great mass of spear-armed citizen-soldiers (hoplites) called out to fight for the honour, the interests or sometimes the survival of their home city. The phalanx was a product of its environment and the kind of warfare engaged in by the city-states. A quick decision was needed in any conflict, since even a victorious campaign would cause great damage to the economy of the polis (city-state) that had several thousand of its citizens away fighting for weeks or months on end.

Thus wars between city-states tended to be rather short and were decided in a few

Epaminondas was an innovator who defied the convention of the times to win his great victory at Leuctra. How much of this was genius and how much simple necessity is a matter for conjecture.

hours by the clash of phalanxes. To a certain extent, battles were a matter of mutual consent. Both sides wanted a decisive clash to avoid economic damage, so were not inclined to engage in long periods of skirmishing or manoeuvring. A suitable battlefield would be chosen and the armies would meet to force a decision as quickly as possible.

Greek armies of the period did contain troops other than the hoplites of the phalanx, but these were of secondary importance. Membership of the phalanx was prestigious, while service with the light troops was mainly left to those who could not afford proper hoplite equipment or were of lowly station in life. 'Peltasts' were light troops who guarded the flanks of the hoplites. They were variously armed. Javelinmen equipped with shields and swords were not uncommon but the light troops might also include slingers and archers. There was little honour to be found as a peltast, and so there were few volunteers for these forces. Those there were tended to be of poor quality and were regarded with either suspicion or disdain. Light cavalry were also employed, but mainly as scouts. Good horses were hard to come by and cavalry service was not popular for social reasons. There was, in the eyes of the Greek citizen-soldier of the fourth century BC, something just not quite right about a man who could afford to accoutre himself as a hoplite and take his place in the phalanx as a real man should, yet chose to buy a horse and go to war sitting down.

Thus it was that phalanx warfare was a part of the social order and thus was carried out even when other means might have been more efficient. The phalanx was the final arbiter of disputes. It carried with it the hopes and aspirations of its polis. To be part of that was the aspiration of all true citizens; who would choose to be elsewhere when matters were being decided in the manly clash of phalanx against phalanx?

Given the factors at work in inter-state warfare in Greece at that time, the concept of phalanx warfare was self-perpetuating. It gave the polis what it needed, a quick decision. It fitted with the social order as it existed, and it was suited to the terrain to be fought over – so long as the enemy also followed the same rules. When fighting other city-states who played the same game, this was entirely acceptable. As later events would show, when an enemy arrived from outside the Greek order of things and fought differently, the phalanx proved to be less than all-powerful.

Naturally, a standard way of doing things was evolved. Within the phalanx were several sub-units. Some of these might be professional, others citizen-soldiers. One advantage of the phalanx was that relatively little training was needed. The phalanx moved as a mass and did not undertake complex manoeuvres, so high standards of training were not necessary.

Nevertheless, some units were considered to be better than others, and by convention the most elite units took the position of honour on the right of the line. It was a compliment to a unit to be given the far-right position. Weaker or shaky formations were placed to the left. Against a conventional foe, this meant that the right almost always prevailed against the enemy's left, but in turn the enemy would win the fight on his right. In battle, hoplite forces would thus tend to wheel anti-clockwise around one another unless one side was markedly stronger all along the line.

THE CAMPAIGN

Sparta was at that time in the ascendant, a position gained mainly because of her impressive military prowess. So powerful was the Spartan army that to this day the city-state's name is a byword for austere military efficiency. By rigorous training and a social orientation towards warfare, Sparta had created a phalanx that was better than everyone else's. Even the Spartan left was a match for the right-flank units of most foes, and Sparta had risen to dominance on the back of this spear-bristling asset.

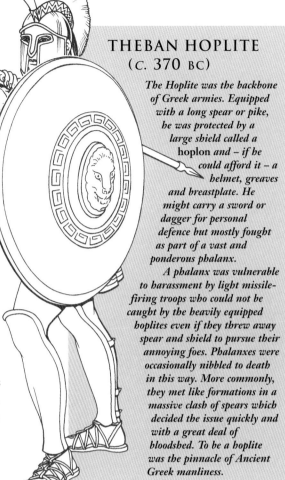

THEBAN HOPLITE (C. 370 BC)

The Hoplite was the backbone of Greek armies. Equipped with a long spear or pike, he was protected by a large shield called a hoplon and – if he could afford it – a helmet, greaves and breastplate. He might carry a sword or dagger for personal defence but mostly fought as part of a vast and ponderous phalanx.

A phalanx was vulnerable to harassment by light missile-firing troops who could not be caught by the heavily equipped hoplites even if they threw away spear and shield to pursue their annoying foes. Phalanxes were occasionally nibbled to death in this way. More commonly, they met like formations in a massive clash of spears which decided the issue quickly and with a great deal of bloodshed. To be a hoplite was the pinnacle of Ancient Greek manliness.

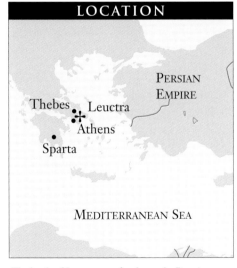

LOCATION

The battle of Leuctra was fought on the Boeotian plains just south of Thebes. It was ideal country for hoplite tactics, and the battle proved the previously invincible Spartans could be beaten.

Theban general Pelopidas, wounded seven times in a battle near Mantinea, is saved by Epaminondas, who wards off the enemy, preventing them from stealing his armour as spoils. Deeds of this kind were expected of Greek generals. Heroic leadership and personal bravery were necessities to reach high station.

THE OPPOSED FORCES

THEBANS (estimated)

Hoplites:	6500
Peltasts:	1000
Cavalry:	1500
Total:	***c.* 7000–9000**

SPARTANS (estimated)

Hoplites:	10,000
Peltasts:	1000
Cavalry:	1000
Total:	**12,000**

Thebes was also expanding, which brought her into conflict with Sparta. Indeed, in 382 BC the Spartans had captured and garrisoned the citadel in Thebes, though this was retaken in 379–378 BC. The Thebans were wary of Sparta as more than a rival – they had defeated a Spartan force and might face savage vengeance.

From the Spartan perspective, Thebes was a growing threat. Sparta had dominated Greek affairs since the defeat of Athens in 404 BC, although the victory had cost Sparta

dear and Athens was beginning to regain her prestige. But now Thebes was beginning to challenge Spartan ascendancy. Having fended off Spartan attacks over the past few years, Thebes had even managed to capture Spartan-controlled cities in Boeotia. She had recently concluded an alliance with the city-state of Pherae, which was also gaining in power.

Against the backdrop of this crisis, a group of Boeotian city-states decided that they did not want to be ruled by Thebes any

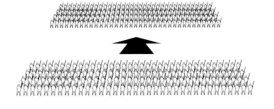

Greek battle tactics: The phalanx – as seen at Marathon – some four or more ranks deep.

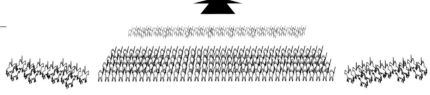

Later cavalry were introduced to protect the vulnerable flanks, while light troops (peltasts) harassed the enemy with javelins.

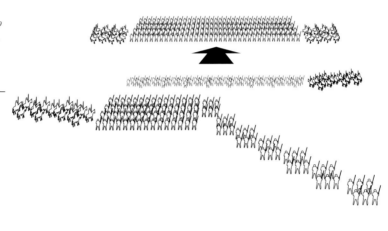

The Thebans used their peltasts and cavalry to pin one of the enemy's flanks while advancing in an oblique formation, with the lead unit heavily reinforced, to attack the other flank.

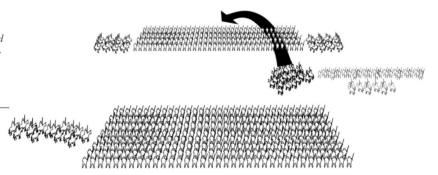

The Macedonian approach was for a deepened phalanx to advance to contact, with a unit of heavy cavalry breaking through a flank and hitting the enemy in the rear.

Key:
- Hoplites
- Light troops
- Cavalry
- Light cavalry

longer. They requested aid from Sparta, and the Spartan king demanded that Thebes remove her forces from Boeotia. Thebes declined to give up her hard-won territory, and so the stage was set for conflict.

SPARTAN INVASION

A Spartan army under King Cleombrotus marched on Thebes, taking an unexpected route and in the process capturing a Theban fortress. Epaminondas of Thebes had no choice but to confront the invaders, so he

placed himself at the head of his army and advanced to meet the Spartans.

The Theban force has been reported at somewhere between 7000 and 9000 men. At its heart was the Sacred Band, an elite force some 300 strong and recruited from young noblemen. The members of the Sacred Band were trained and fought as pairs, and were encouraged to become lovers as it was thought this would improve their willingness to stand and fight – and if necessary, die – together. The Sacred Band

was a potent fighting force and its members were both tough and skilled fighters. The Theban force also contained something in the region of 1000 peltasts, about 1500 cavalry and perhaps as many as 6500 hoplites equipped in the conventional way. Many of the troops were levies raised in Boeotia, whose reliability was suspect, but Epaminondas made the most of things by exuding confidence and hoping that this and the example set by the Sacred Band would inspire the rest of the army.

LEUCTRA
371 BC

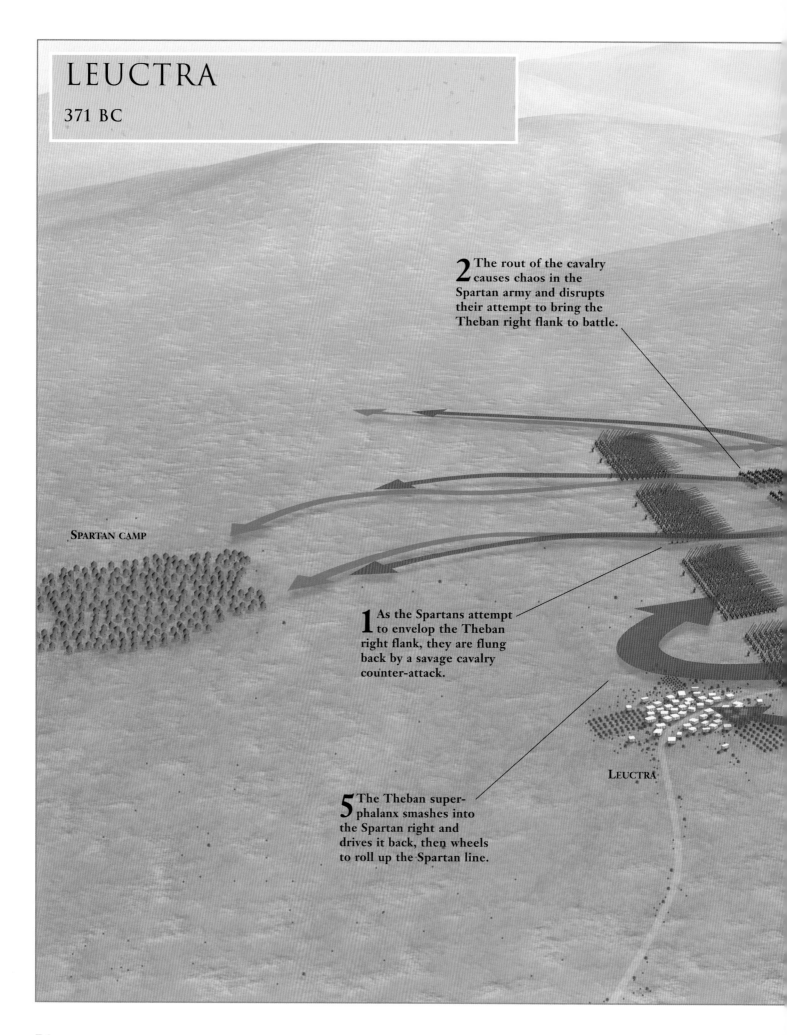

2 The rout of the cavalry causes chaos in the Spartan army and disrupts their attempt to bring the Theban right flank to battle.

SPARTAN CAMP

1 As the Spartans attempt to envelop the Theban right flank, they are flung back by a savage cavalry counter-attack.

LEUCTRA

5 The Theban super-phalanx smashes into the Spartan right and drives it back, then wheels to roll up the Spartan line.

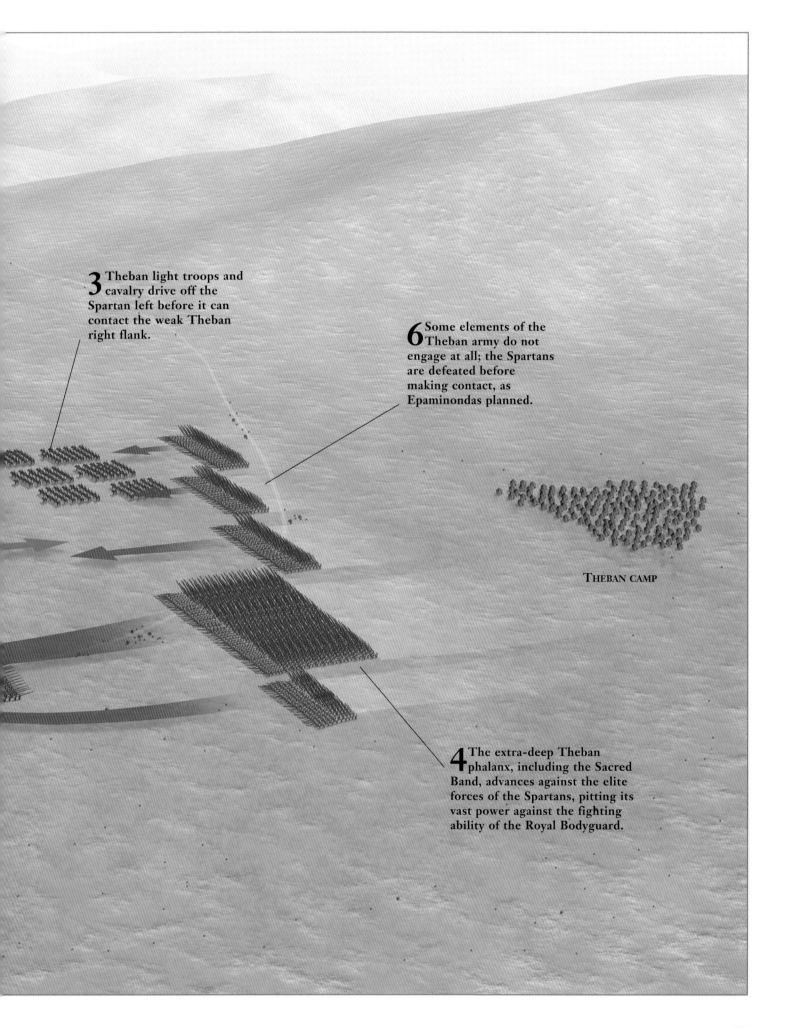

3 Theban light troops and cavalry drive off the Spartan left before it can contact the weak Theban right flank.

6 Some elements of the Theban army do not engage at all; the Spartans are defeated before making contact, as Epaminondas planned.

THEBAN CAMP

4 The extra-deep Theban phalanx, including the Sacred Band, advances against the elite forces of the Spartans, pitting its vast power against the fighting ability of the Royal Bodyguard.

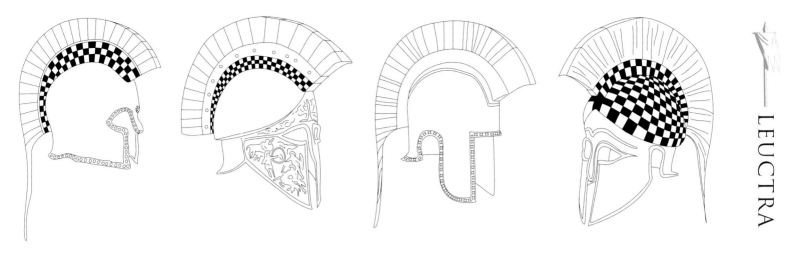

Epaminondas cannot have had any great confidence of success. He was outnumbered by about 50 per cent, and by Spartans, no less! Either of those factors would be frightening, but both together added up to a sure recipe for defeat. And then there was the fact that many of his troops were Boeotians – the very people who had requested Spartan aid to get rid of their Theban overlords. There was every chance that his army might just melt away or show a marked reluctance to fight for their continued oppression. Still, Epaminondas had no choice but to fight, so he offered battle near Leuctra.

The Spartan host numbered about 12,000, of whom around 10,000 were hoplites from Sparta itself, armed with the long pike and body armour and trained to fight in close order. The Spartans also brought around 1000 lightly armed peltasts to cover their flanks and about 1000 cavalry.

UNUSUAL DEPLOYMENT

Contrary to the conventions of the time, Epaminondas deployed his army with his strongest troops on the left of his line, and created a massive hammer in the form of a 50-deep phalanx there. In order to find the troops for this formation from an already inferior force, he had to thin the rest of his

line to a dangerous extent. Instead of deploying using the usual 12-man-deep formation, Epaminondas placed most of his troops in very thin lines facing the Spartans' more conventional formation. There was no chance that these weak units could withstand the impact of a deeper phalanx, but Epaminondas had planned for this. He drew up his army in echelon from left to right, with each unit positioned slightly further back than the one to its left. This created a 'refused' flank which was well back from the enemies facing it, with cavalry and peltasts to further confound an attempt to come into contact.

There has been much discussion about whether Epaminondas was deliberately inventing the oblique order of battle, which would be used to tremendous effect by Alexander of Macedon and Frederick II of Prussia (both perhaps not coincidentally known to history as 'The Great'), or was simply making the best of a bad situation,

Classic hoplite helmets. From left to right: a simple Corinthian helmet; the classic Corinthian design with long cheek pieces; a later Illyrian helmet; and a late Corinthian design with a space cut out for the wearer's ears to make hearing easier.

Peltasts versus a phalanx. The peltasts throw their javelins into the phalanx, but their lack of armour means that they can evade any attempt by the hoplites to bring them to battle. They can continue to wear down the phalanx with impunity.

Opposite: The Theban general Pelopidas (in green) sets off to free Thebes from the Spartan occupation. At the battle of Leuctra he contributed greatly to the success of Epaminondas' new tactics by the rapidity with which he led the elite Sacred Band of Theban crack hoplites to close with the Spartans.

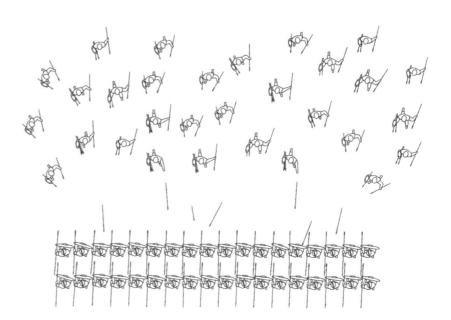

LEUCTRA

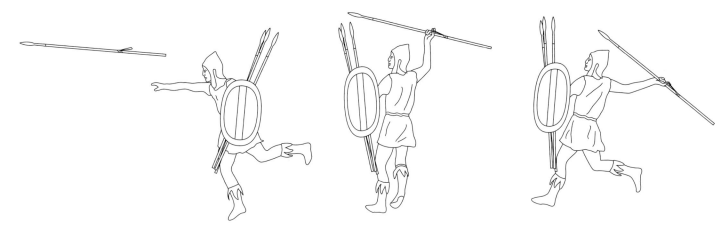

A Theban peltast throws his javelin. A leather loop on the javelin gave him much greater accuracy and power.

but whatever the case he did what was necessary to win the battle and demonstrated a new style of infantry warfare. By concentrating so much of his force on the left flank, Epaminondas was hoping to achieve a local superiority and use it to decisive advantage before his refused flank and centre could be broken. Now all that remained was to commit to battle and hope the tactic worked.

THE BATTLE

The Spartan force, realizing how inferior in numbers the Thebans were, tried to perform an encirclement. This is always a risky manoeuvre, and this time it failed utterly. The Theban cavalry launched a vigorous attack on the Spartan horse and routed it, sending a shattered mob of horsemen reeling into the Spartan lines. This was an unexpected event for the Spartans. They were used to winning, and to seeing their enemies waver simply because they were facing Spartans. An enemy who was undaunted by their fearsome reputation and who attacked so violently was a new experience, and an upsetting one. The Spartans had seen their cavalry driven from the field and they were dismayed. And the situation was about to get worse.

Under cover of the chaos caused by the cavalry fight, Epaminondas unleashed his hammer, sending the Sacred Band and the powerful left-flank phalanx at the Spartan lines. The enormous phalanx crashed home, smashing into the Spartan lines and driving powerfully forward. After the initial clash a phalanx battle was determined to a great

extent by the 'pushing power' of the phalanx. The Spartan force was deployed traditionally, 12 men deep, which meant that for every man in the Spartan phalanx there were four on the Theban side. Faced with such enormous pushing power, the Spartans were shoved bodily back and suffered many casualties in the press.

Whether Epaminondas knew it or not, he had deployed his Sacred Band opposite the bodyguard of King Cleombrotus, which was also 300 strong. This was the elite of the Spartan force, occupying the position of honour on the right of the line. The Sacred Band led the Theban super-phalanx right into the royal bodyguard and shattered it, overrunning it and driving onward. Fallen men were trampled to death or despatched with spear butts which were weighted to counterbalance the length of haft projecting forward and could batter through even a thick bronze breastplate if brought vigorously down on a foe. Among the dead was the Spartan king Cleombrotus. Never before had a Spartan king fallen in battle against fellow Greeks. The shock rippled though the Spartan force, which began to fall apart.

The Royal Bodyguard was virtually destroyed and the right wing, traditionally the strongest part of the army, was in disarray. Although the Thebans suffered considerable losses in the process, they were clearly winning. Elsewhere on the line, most of the superior Spartan forces had not managed to come into contact with the enemy. Some units had managed to enter combat but were badly shaken and did not perform well. The Spartan left, composed of the weaker units (though everything is relative; these were still Spartans) broke and began to retire before it had even struck a blow. Realizing that they were losing, and disheartened by the fact that their invincible right had been shattered, the Spartans began a general retreat. Epaminondas sent his cavalry in pursuit.

TRUCE

The retreating Spartans encountered a force of their fellows under Archidamos and rallied at his camp. They still did not believe they could defeat the Thebans, perhaps because of rumours that Jason of Pherae was coming to the Thebans' aid. Archidamos asked Epaminondas for a truce to bury the dead. The truce was granted, and the Spartans used it to send to their home city

for more troops as well as burying their dead, which numbered around 400 Spartan citizens and 600 allied troops. They were reluctant to resume hostilities with the Thebans, whose ferocity and unusual tactics had dismayed them. The Thebans were also strangely hesitant to continue the fighting considering their successes so far. They sent to their allies in Pherae, whose king, Jason, marched immediately to their assistance. Whether or not he was on his way to their assistance, as the Spartans had thought, now he came, and swiftly.

Spartan reinforcements had not arrived when Jason's army reached the field. The Spartans were now in a bad position and decided to withdraw. A second truce was requested, this time to allow the Spartan army to retreat. Whether or not

Epaminondas wanted to fight, Jason suggested that the Spartans should be given permission to retire. Since they obviously felt they could not defeat the Spartans without their allies, the Thebans were forced to agree to Jason's suggestion and permitted the Spartan army to return home unmolested.

While not a particularly dramatic ending to the campaign, this suited the Thebans' purposes. They had marched to war to repulse a Spartan army, and now it was going home. The job was done and Boeotia remained under Theban control.

AFTERMATH

The defeat of Sparta had important consequences. As conquerors throughout history have found, defeat tends to inspire rebellions. Sparta was forced to deal with troubles among its subject states, and a Theban force took advantage of the disruption to launch an invasion.

The Theban campaign in Spartan lands ran from 370 to 369 BC and was not particularly decisive. No great battles were fought, though the Thebans were able to advance to the outskirts of Sparta itself. The main outcome of this campaign was the creation of a state hostile to Sparta in the Messenian district.

This state acted as a counterbalance to Sparta and forced her leaders to keep their attention close to home instead of launching expeditions against more distant rivals. Sparta remained a powerful military force after Leuctra, but her failure to defeat the Thebans dispelled the myth of Spartan invincibility, after which her influence was greatly diminished.

Leuctra was important in other ways too. A young man named Philip, later to be King Philip II of Macedon and father of Alexander the Great, observed the Theban tactics at Leuctra and ultimately developed them to a fine art. His son used them to conquer the known world.

Epaminondas' kindly expression and soulful eyes are at odds with his warlike armour and skull-faced helmet. A leader of his times had to be gentle in peace and fierce in war; a good friend and a terrible foe.

GAUGAMELA
331 BC

ELITE FORCES FACED RESURRECTED AND EXOTIC TACTICS AND WEAPONRY IN THE BATTLE THAT DECIDED THE FATE OF THE KNOWN WORLD IN THE NEAR EAST. COULD THE MILITARY GENIUS OF ALEXANDER THE GREAT OVERCOME THE COLLECTED RESOURCES OF THE WORLD'S LARGEST EMPIRE?

WHY DID IT HAPPEN?

WHO Alexander the Great (356–323 BC) and his battered Macedonian army faced the final stand of the Persian Great King Darius (reigned 336–330 BC), who was well-prepared and on ground of his own choosing.

WHAT War elephants from India stood ready to smash the legendary Macedonian phalanx – while scythed chariots and picked bodies of special troops awaited their own part in the final struggle for control of the Persian Empire.

WHERE Gaugamela near the city of Arbela, in what is now northern Iraq.

WHEN 1 October 331 BC

WHY To Alexander and the Greeks before him, the Persian Empire stood as the very definition of world power. That taken, Alexander and his army would neither face nor fear a rival.

OUTCOME In a staggering display of tactical adaptability and superb military training, Alexander's army resisted and destroyed every Persian weapon and tactic. One subordinate's error resulted in a crisis, however, of Macedonian command.

Gaugamela, as the greatest victory of the Ancient World's undisputedly greatest military genius, deserves study from all angles as the tactical masterpiece it was. Under careful review, the battle takes on the appearance of having such intricate and careful construction that the very difficulties Alexander faced in controlling and preserving his own army in the face of the Persians ended up augmenting Alexander's plan, instead of hindering it.

Arrian's excellent *Anabasis* of Alexander's battles is the preferred source here.

DARIUS' ARMY

Alexander had been blessed in his principal opponent, Darius III, during his campaigns from 336 to 331 BC. For five years the boy-king of Macedon had laboured brilliantly to complete his father's dream of conquering the Persian Empire and territories in the East. The Persian Great King Darius was a

In this nineteenth-century magazine illustration, Alexander is shown as a young man listening to his tutor, the philosopher Aristotle (384–322 BC), while they sit in a palace in ancient Pella, Greece, c. 342 BC.

good leader but a below-par general, whose ability to bring huge numbers of Persia's military assets into the field did not live up to his skill in using them. Moreover, as it had been since Kadesh, the king was still the cause – if Darius could be captured, Persian organized resistance to the invasion could, and in the end did, collapse.

As a result, in every battle with Alexander, the circumstances of his position prompted Darius to make ever greater demands upon his empire's reserves of manpower as they became available. Alexander would not find many Persians of military age able or willing to resist him away from the battlefields where Darius' poor skills got many of them slaughtered or put to humiliating flight. As the centre of Persian command, Darius necessarily fled the battlefield as soon as Alexander's own advance posed a credible threat to his person. Such pusillanimity had not been the case when the Persians themselves had tried a 'decapitation strike' on Alexander at the battle of the Granicus in 334 BC. Alexander's bodyguard had prevented the Persian cavalry's effort to despatch him, while Alexander kept control of his anxieties and his army and won battle after battle.

At the core of Darius' forces were the celebrated, and dreaded, Immortals, the elite division of the Persian army. The unit's name came from the Persian practice of replacing each casualty in that 10,000-man unit with another picked soldier, whose spear would bear the golden pomegranate of the elite. The goal had been to raise the lighter Persian infantry to a level where they could face heavier Greek hoplites and prevail. At times they had come close, such as during the Persian Wars in Greece at Thermopylae and Plataea. Darius' ranks also included the assembled nobility of the Persian Empire, sons of all the empire's powerful families serving in the cavalry divisions under Bessus and Mazaeus.

In addition to these elite forces, Darius employed a sizeable force of Greek mercenary hoplites, hardened professionals who continued in Persian service despite the gruesome example Alexander had made of the Greeks in Persian service who had penetrated the Macedonian Phalanx at Issus, two years before. Many of the Greeks came from lands already subjugated by the Macedonians, eager to strike a blow – even for the hated Persians – against Alexander and the Macedonian conquerors. Darius' assurance in facing Alexander received additional support from the Persian king's confidence in two secret weapons he had procured in the time for preparation granted him by Alexander's two-year campaign south to Egypt.

From his Indian subjects, Darius had secured a number of war elephants, transported at great expense in time and fodder from the easternmost frontiers of Persian suzerainty. Untrained horses could endure neither the sight nor appearance of the strange monsters, who bore archers and javelin throwers upon their backs, and whose strength, Darius thought, might crack the Macedonian phalanx.

Alexander's entire army was aimed directly at him. Darius intended to be more than ready. Besides the elephants, Darius also had in his arsenal 200 of the most terrifying weapons from the traditions of

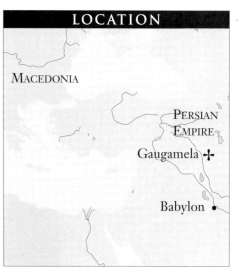

MACEDONIA

PERSIAN
EMPIRE

Gaugamela

Babylon

Gaugamela was the last stand of the Persian Empire. Darius escaped the staggering defeat Alexander inflicted upon his army, only to be executed by a subordinate disgusted by his cowardice and failures.

COMPANION CAVALRY

Companion Cavalry were literally that, the sons of the Macedonian nobility, raised along with Alexander under Philip's supervision and trained in the tactics Philip had learned from the Theban Epaminondas. Many of them were personal friends to whom he owed his life.

Companion Cavalry carried the shorter cavalry sarissa *and lighter armour, and always fought under Alexander's personal command. To the cavalry was given the decisive role in Alexander's battles. When the lumbering phalanx created a gap in the enemy's line, the cavalry would charge through and disrupt and destroy the enemy ranks by carrying out flanking attacks.*

GAUGAMELA

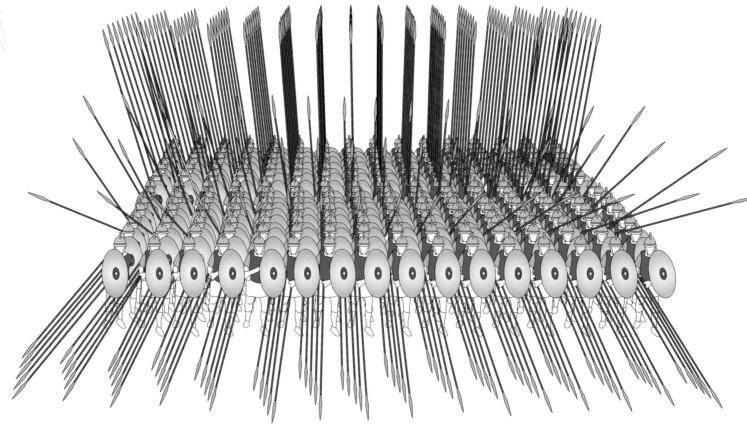

A forest of spears. A frontal view of a Macedonian speira, the unit making up the larger infantry phalanx. The ranks behind the front five would hold their counter-weighted pikes aloft until required to fill a gap, and in the hope of deflecting incoming missiles.

THE OPPOSED FORCES

MACEDONIANS (estimated)
Cavalry:	7000
Infantry:	40,000
Total:	**47,000**

PERSIANS (estimated)
Cavalry:	30,000
Infantry:	56,000
Chariots:	200
War elephants:	15
Total:	**86,000**

Eastern warfare: chariots equipped with scythe blades upon their wheels and traces, weapons designed to inflict dire casualties upon Alexander's infantry.

DISPOSITIONS

Darius took advantage of his ability to control Alexander's movements by being himself the objective of Alexander's campaign. He chose a wide and level battlefield near the city of Arbela, going so far as to have the terrain levelled to assist the operation of his chariots. For his own part, however, Alexander had taken the precaution of scouting the battlefield thoroughly. Darius' preparations provided his enemy with a very good idea about his plans. By giving Darius time enough to collect so great an agglomeration of resources and men, Alexander had either gambled heavily or allowed ample time for the final collection of resistance to be drawn together at a place where it could be found and destroyed. The outcome would determine which was the case.

Alexander, with the pragmatism of a genius, camped 6.4km (4 miles) from Darius' army, just far enough to prevent a surprise attack, and had one last interview with his sub-commanders. The leader's very confidence became a command asset in itself, for Alexander chose to leave his troops comfortably encamped, rather, than as their Persian counterparts, in arms and watchful throughout the course of a long and cold desert night. The commanding general himself managed such a good night's sleep that he had to be roused for action the following day.

With some justification, Alexander had come to feel that his subordinates were not quite worthy adjuncts to his genius. Alexander's father's adjutant and most competent general Parmenio approached him with his own plan for the battle, that being the very night attack the Persians were dreading. Contrary to Parmenio's usual reputation in the sources for prudence, such a suggestion was, in fact, bold and consequently risky. Controlling an army in broad daylight was hard enough, doing so in darkness legendarily difficult. Alexander's dismissive rejection, that he would not 'steal a victory', was the final word against such action, but Parmenio's very anxiety about the battle became yet another liability-turned-asset in Alexander's master plan.

It was a tendency of soldiers to move to the right in the course of an advance, as each sought to cover the exposed portion of his body with the shield of his comrade next in the line. The great Theban military genius Epaminondas had learned to exploit that tendency with an obliquely directed and focused attack on an advancing enemy line as it stretched and thinned in response. Philip himself had spent time in Thebes, and the tactic became an integral and vital part of Macedonian success in the decades following. Alexander's plan made full use of it when he formed his lines on the morning of the battle. Both Alexander's elite cavalry and the awe-inspiring Macedonian phalanx would move at the oblique angle into the much longer Persian line, impact, as usual, being set directly for Darius' visible position in the centre of his line. Layer after layer of the dreaded Macedonian pike, the *sarissa*, would menace the Persians and hold their attention. The Macedonian line would move at an angle as it advanced, and create a gap in the ranks of the apprehensive enemy.

While his attack was being launched, Alexander knew that Darius' cavalry, chariots and elephants would attempt to flank him and get behind his forces. His counter were his own selected special forces. These consisted of a unit new in Western warfare, crack light infantry, called 'hypaspists'. Experienced veterans, these men could move rapidly to oppose an attack with support from Alexander's allied Thessalian cavalry positioned at either end of his line. Both the hypaspists and the Thessalians fought in small units capable of dispersing in the face of a threat, then re-forming at need. In the course of the battle, these sub-formations would move aside in the face of elephants and chariots, showering javelins on those and the cavalry as they would inevitably be driven back by the Persian thrusts at Alexander's flanks.

Such was the genius of the Macedonian commander that the retreat of these smaller units became an asset to Alexander's grand plan. Behind his front line, under the worried Parmenio, Alexander placed a reserve phalanx, another rectangle of bristling pikes as difficult to attack as the

In this illustration, Alexander leads his Companion Cavalry across the Granicus, seizing the initiative from the Persians. Like most successful military commanders, Alexander was no stranger to luck.

GAUGAMELA

331 BC

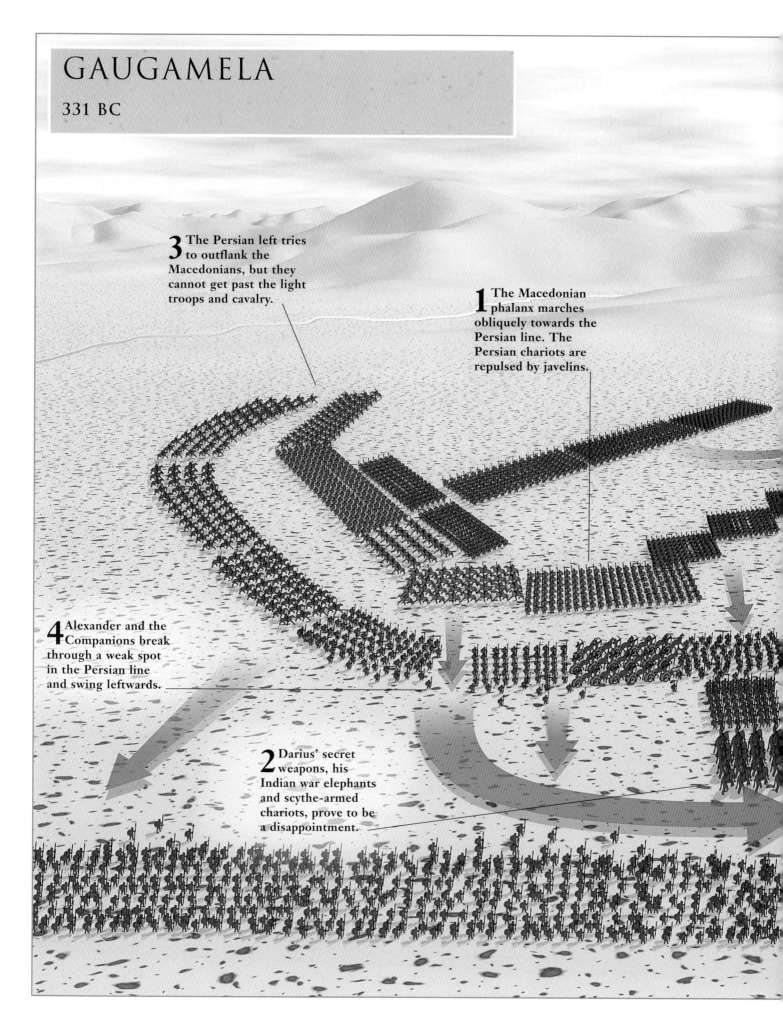

3 The Persian left tries to outflank the Macedonians, but they cannot get past the light troops and cavalry.

1 The Macedonian phalanx marches obliquely towards the Persian line. The Persian chariots are repulsed by javelins.

4 Alexander and the Companions break through a weak spot in the Persian line and swing leftwards.

2 Darius' secret weapons, his Indian war elephants and scythe-armed chariots, prove to be a disappointment.

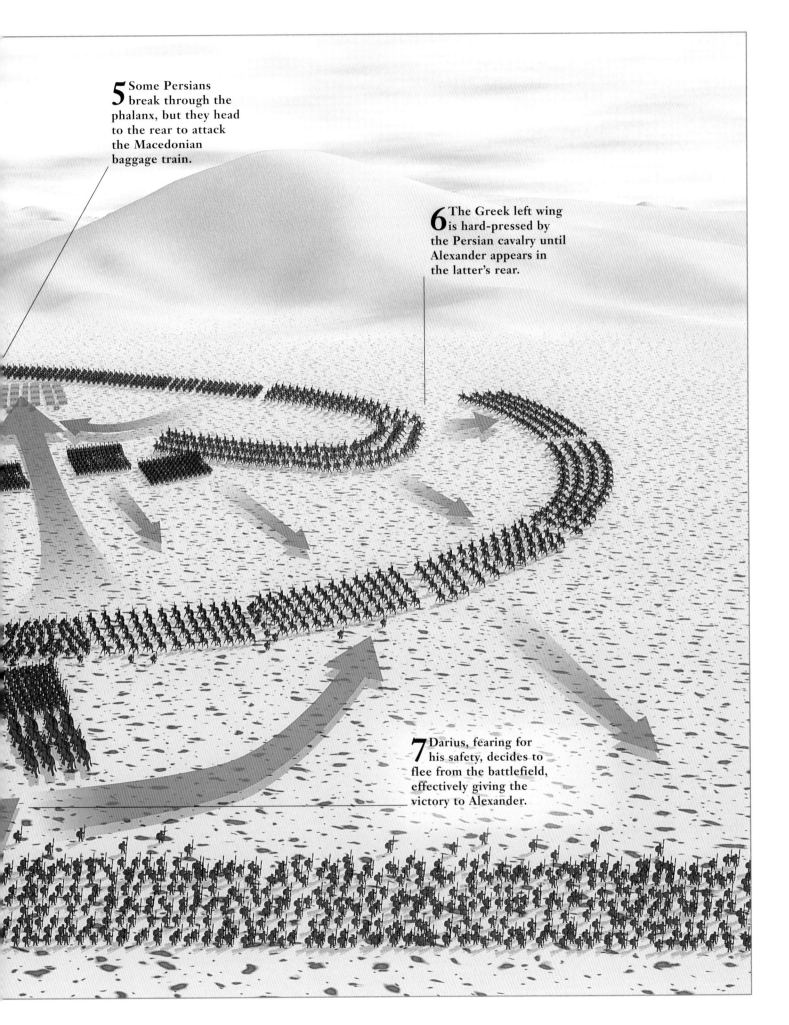

5 Some Persians break through the phalanx, but they head to the rear to attack the Macedonian baggage train.

6 The Greek left wing is hard-pressed by the Persian cavalry until Alexander appears in the latter's rear.

7 Darius, fearing for his safety, decides to flee from the battlefield, effectively giving the victory to Alexander.

GAUGAMELA

Darius breathes his last in this nineteenth-century depiction of the Persian ruler's death. Alexander's propagandists claimed that Darius had survived long enough to will his empire to Alexander with his dying gasp. Alexander found it more expedient after the battle to pose as Darius' successor, rather than rule as a foreign conqueror.

front line. The Thessalians and hypaspists would fall back into contact with the second line. In effect, as his smaller army waded into the massed Persian forces, Alexander's formation would become a forerunner of the British 'square' of the nineteenth century, a formation that became the stronger as it was driven into itself.

THE BATTLE

For the most part, the plan worked. Alexander's archers and javelin throwers killed the charioteers of the scythed chariots. In employing these, Darius had made another of his disastrous errors. The legendary ferocity of the chariots had come from their use by earlier empires to increase the slaughter of a disorganized and retreating enemy as the scythes took a fearful toll on frightened and defenceless men. In the face of Alexander's disciplined veterans, they failed miserably. Darius' second secret weapon proved no more successful. As often happened with elephants in warfare, the great beasts felt no

stake in the battle sufficient to wade into the bristling spears and arrows of the enemy, and proved useless and uncontrollable. Meanwhile Alexander's pike-equipped cavalry and infantry bore inexorably down, at the oblique angle, upon Darius' standard.

Meanwhile, Darius had nothing to stop the slow advance of the Macedonian infantry and cavalry toward a point near where he and his entourage clustered in mounting anxiety. Alexander was making an enduring demonstration of the utility of sending the strength of an army's forces against a single chosen spot in the enemy's front. Two British officers, Colonels Basil Liddell-Hart and J.F.C. Fuller, would cite Gaugamela as their inspiration when after the battle of Cambrai in 1917 they developed a new plan of battle. What those two officers outlined featured the concentration of force at a weak spot in an enemy line, penetration by an army's most mobile units to attack from the rear and spread havoc in the enemy's rear areas, culminating in the remaining frontal resistance of the enemy being crushed by infantry. The plan's adoption and successful use by the German army would give it its name: *Blitzkrieg*.

The moment of danger for Alexander and his army came when the onrushing Persian cavalry got past the Thessalians and hypaspists on the flank and drove for the Macedonian rear. Parmenio had not been able to keep the reserve in good order, the result of that failure coming as the Persians drove through his reserve line and moved miles to the rear to plunder the Macedonian camp. Only those Persians would have any taste of victory. Distance and Alexander's pressure upon him cost Darius the control of the most dangerous part of his army at that moment. Darius had no way of either summoning his victorious cavalry to his rescue or ordering it to take Alexander's line in the rear as a desire to win, as opposed to a desire to loot, should have prompted.

The Macedonian advance ground onwards, and as previously Darius' nerve failed. This final retreat was his most ignominious, as the Persian king abandoned his army and camp in wild flight. For a while longer at Gaugamela, however, the armies fought on. Alexander's plan had not survived contact with the enemy. Parmenio himself, under pressure and out of contact with Alexander's line, had abandoned the original idea of a box and sent frantically to the front to Alexander for assistance. Alexander returned to find that his Thessalian cavalry had counter-attacked, Parmenio had reversed the direction of the reserve advance and destroyed the Persians to the rear, and that Darius had, yet again, escaped him.

There would be a reckoning with Parmenio for his premature panic and disagreement with Alexander's plans and tactics, but, although it was not clear at the time, Alexander was for the rest of his life the virtual master of the entire Greek and Persian worlds.

AFTERMATH

Darius only bought a few more weeks of life by his flight. His disgusted subordinate Bessus executed his own monarch and attempted in vain to lead further resistance himself. Alexander wanted it all, and had the genius and the means to get it. He asked no more of his army than he himself was willing to give, but his army eventually lost its own willingness to march ever onward for more conquests, and Alexander's empire left him when a body wracked by wounds and disease could no longer support the powerful mind that had prevailed so brilliantly at Gaugamela. He died in the legendary city of Babylon in 323 BC.

Winning hearts and minds was Alexander's purpose behind his kindly treatment of Darius' surrendered family, depicted here in a 1566 painting by Paolo Veronese. Alexander went so far as to marry one of Darius' daughters, but his plan for a fusion of Persians and Macedonians under his rule did not long survive him.

HYDASPES
326 BC

ALEXANDER THE GREAT'S LAST MAJOR VICTORY SAW HIS MASTERY OF BATTLEFIELD TACTICS ONCE MORE OUTMANOEUVRE AND OUTFIGHT A SUPERIOR ENEMY ARMY, THIS TIME AGAINST MASSED WAR ELEPHANTS THAT COULD HAVE PANICKED HIS CAVALRY, THE MAIN ELEMENT OF ALEXANDER'S STRIKING FORCE.

WHY DID IT HAPPEN?

WHO The army of Alexander the Great (356–323 BC) against the army of the Indian king Porus.

WHAT Porus' army stood blocking Alexander's crossing of the River Hydaspes, but was outmanoeuvred and outfought by the tactically brilliant Alexander.

WHERE The banks of the Hydaspes river, now the Jhelum river on the northwest frontier of what is now Pakistan.

WHEN 326 BC.

WHY Alexander sought to carry his conquests on into India, to subjugate the known world to his rule.

OUTCOME Alexander accepted Porus' submission and appointed him a client king, but his plans for further conquest were later thwarted when his men finally refused to go any further.

It is difficult to know how large Alexander the Great believed the world really was. No maps from the fourth century BC exist, although there was an interest in geography, a subject which certainly would have been included in Alexander's tutoring by Aristotle and others. However large it was, Alexander believed that it was small enough for him to conquer it all, and he spent his entire reign trying to do so, ultimately adding Asia Minor, the Middle East, Egypt, Persia, Afghanistan, Pakistan and much of India to Macedonia, Thrace and Greece, lands left him by his father. His victory at the battle on the banks of the Hydaspes river was the culmination of these conquests.

For all of the ten years following his ascension to the Macedonian throne after the assassination of his father, Philip, in 336 BC, Alexander the Great fought wars. Rarely was his army more numerous than his opponents'; nor were his soldiers' arms and armour notably superior. But they were

certainly more disciplined, better trained, and much better led than anyone they faced. And the result was remarkable: to that time Alexander's were the most successful wars, achieving the most land gains in the shortest amount of time.

Facing an Indian army – led by a king known by the Greek name Porus – across the Hydaspes river in 326 BC, Alexander's forces differed little from those that had left the Greek mainland a decade before. At the core of his army were his Macedonian veterans. Alexander personally led his cavalry, elite horsemen, many of whom had learned their riding and fighting skills on the plains of Thrace. Alexander's own ability on horseback was legendary, even in his own lifetime. His taming of the seemingly untamable horse Bucephalas was known to all, and the fact that he still rode that steed into battle, despite having an obviously large number of younger and perhaps fitter horses to choose from – by the battle of the Hydaspes, Bucephalas must have been in his twenties if not older – showed his devotion to this fine animal on whom he had ridden to so many victories.

ALEXANDER'S ARMY

It has often been thought that without stirrups cavalry had little impact on the battlefield. Alexander's cavalry proves how wrong this is. His horsemen were rarely used as missile troops, but almost always in close combat. His cavalry fought not with javelins or bows, but used their lances and swords to thrust into opposing cavalry or down onto infantry. No doubt stirrups would have helped, but of course millions learned to ride without them before their

Alexander the Great is frequently depicted in contemporary sculptures. This coin, a Greek tetradrachm from Alexander's reign, is thought to depict his facial features accurately. He also wears his customary lion's head headdress, symbolic of his power.

invention, and, at least in Alexander's army, the best troops were heavy cavalry.

However, the Macedonian cavalry were never as numerous as the infantry, and Alexander the Great could not have won any battles without them. Naturally, after ten years of fighting, the numbers of original Greek infantry had declined, with few reinforcements coming to replace battle or campaign losses. Thus there was a need for recruitment of infantry, missile troops, and some cavalry among conquered peoples, a practice well known in ancient armies. They, too, were trained in the manner of the other Macedonian and Greek infantry soldiers, and, in fact, it is doubtful whether at the battle of the Hydaspes one would have been able to tell the different national origins of Alexander's soldiers.

The main body of Macedonian infantry which fought against the Indians at the Hydaspes river were phalangites clad in bronze and leather armour that covered the torso, hips, groin and back, a bronze helmet, and carrying a small shield. They were armed with a very long pike, known as a *sarissa*, which illustrations show reached as much as 5.5m (18ft) in length. The term 'phalangite' comes from 'phalanx', a dense formation of infantry that allowed for the *sarissas* of several ranks to thrust at the enemy whether the unit was on the offensive – moving at a slow pace as a solid mass of troops – or on the defensive. A group of 3000 infantrymen were called 'hypaspists'.

The literal definition of hypaspist is 'shield-bearer', although these troops, who always fought on the right of the Macedonian army, in the most honoured position, were clearly elite infantry, who may have been equipped more like the traditional Greek hoplite with a shorter spear than the *sarissa* and a larger shield. Lighter infantry, armed with javelins, bows and slings and wearing little, if any, armour were also used, as skirmishers and missile troops.

The veteran troops who had marched with Alexander the Great across the Bosphorus into Asia and had seen all of his conquests, either cavalry or infantry, were known as Companions. Alexander counted on these veterans to perform valiantly in all of his military adventures, and up to now they had never let him down.

PORUS' ARMY

The principle forces of the Indian army faced by Alexander at the Hydaspes also consisted of cavalry, heavy infantry and missile troops. Unfortunately, the sources do not describe these with much detail, leading some modern historians to belittle Indian arms and armour as

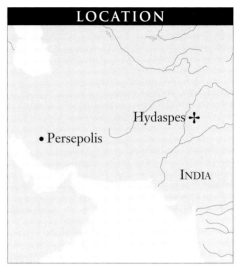

LOCATION

The battle of the Hydaspes was fought at the eastern extreme of Alexander's great empire. After the battle, he turned homewards, planning to sail around Arabia, but died in Babylon after a brief illness.

WAR ELEPHANTS

Although war elephants were exotic, dangerous and unpredictable, general after general in the Ancient World would use them as a means to gain a decisive edge in battle. By the very strangeness of their appearance and scent, elephants could and on more than one occasion did throw an enemy's cavalry into chaos as their horses panicked. The height and mobility of the howdah on the back of these animals gave these mobile strongpoints great allure; but the animals were difficult enough to control even without wounds from enemy missiles – and the mahout was dangerously exposed in his position astride the elephant's neck. Elephants could and did turn against their own side in the face of wounds or confusion, and the fail-safe – a mallet and chisel through the animal's spine – could only be employed if the animal's trusted driver was alive and willing to use it.

HYDASPES

While Alexander the Great's cavalry is justifiably celebrated for its battlefield skill, the core of his forces was the infantry. The discipline, training, unity and technology of these soldiers brought them victory over much larger armies.

being inferior to those of Alexander's army. There is little evidence to support this, though. There were, however, three units of the Indian army that were different enough from Alexander's earlier opponents to earn some detailed mention. First, Indian foot archers were outfitted with a very long bow, the string of which illustrations show was pulled to the archers' faces, in a manner not unlike English longbowmen of the later Middle Ages – although their arrows were

much less lethal, perhaps due to the bamboo used for both bows and arrows, or their weaker metal arrowheads. Second, Porus also used heavy chariots which carried six men – two shield-bearers, two archers, and two armed charioteers – numbered at 300 at the battle of the Hydaspes by Arrian and Quintus Curtius Rufus.

Finally, there were the Indian elephants. At least 200 war elephants were with Porus at the Hydaspes. He even rode one himself.

Alexander had faced elephants before, African elephants, but they were fewer in number and less well trained for combat. African elephants were also larger than Porus' animals, although scholars claim that the Indian elephants had larger brains, giving them a greater aptitude for training and discipline. As the action in this battle would show, this is not a bad assumption.

Porus' elephants were probably large, heavy bulls, although possibly gelded, up to

3.5m (11.5ft) tall at the shoulder and weighing up to 5 tonnes (tons). Each wore barding of ox or buffalo hide, with bells adorning this and its harness to make the animal more noisy when it moved. The elephant's crew consisted of a mahout who drove it and up to four warriors who carried bows or javelins and rode on its back. But undoubtedly it was the elephant itself that was the main weapon. It was certainly capable of trampling its enemy, clubbing him with its trunk, and goring him with its tusks, which illustrations seem to show may have been covered with iron sheaths. But even more important than the physical damage it caused, the elephant caused a psychological terror that affected not only the men who faced it, but also their horses. Horses had to be trained to fight against, or even alongside, elephants, and even then some were so terrified by the larger and louder beasts that they bolted at the very sight of them. By 326 BC Alexander was very much aware of the role elephants could play on a battlefield and he knew how to fight them, but if the sources are correct he had never faced as many as at the Hydaspes.

SOURCES FOR THE BATTLE

Unfortunately, 'if the sources are correct' is a phrase that often must be used in discussing the history of Alexander the Great. Although the great conqueror himself knew the importance of his historical legacy and employed at least two secretaries who recorded the details of his military expeditions, neither record has survived. Thus the modern historian must use narratives written long after the events they recount. All three are biographical in nature, with two – written by Arrian and Quintus Curtius Rufus – quite long and one a chapter by Plutarch in his lives of great ancients (which nevertheless contains some interesting details that the two longer biographies do not).

Still, all three of these authors do claim authority from the accounts written by Alexander's secretaries, and modern scholars have given them great credibility, especially as there appear to be very few contradictions or overt biases among them. On the other hand, without more contemporary sources available, and

War elephants were undoubtedly the most feared part of any ancient army, especially by horses untrained to fight next to them. Alexander's soldiers had never faced as many elephants as at the battle of the Hydaspes.

THE OPPOSED FORCES

MACEDONIANS (estimated)

Cavalry:	4000
Infantry:	40,000
Total:	**44,000**

INDIANS (estimated)

Cavalry:	4000
Infantry:	30,000
War elephants:	200
Total:	**34,000**

HYDASPES
326 BC

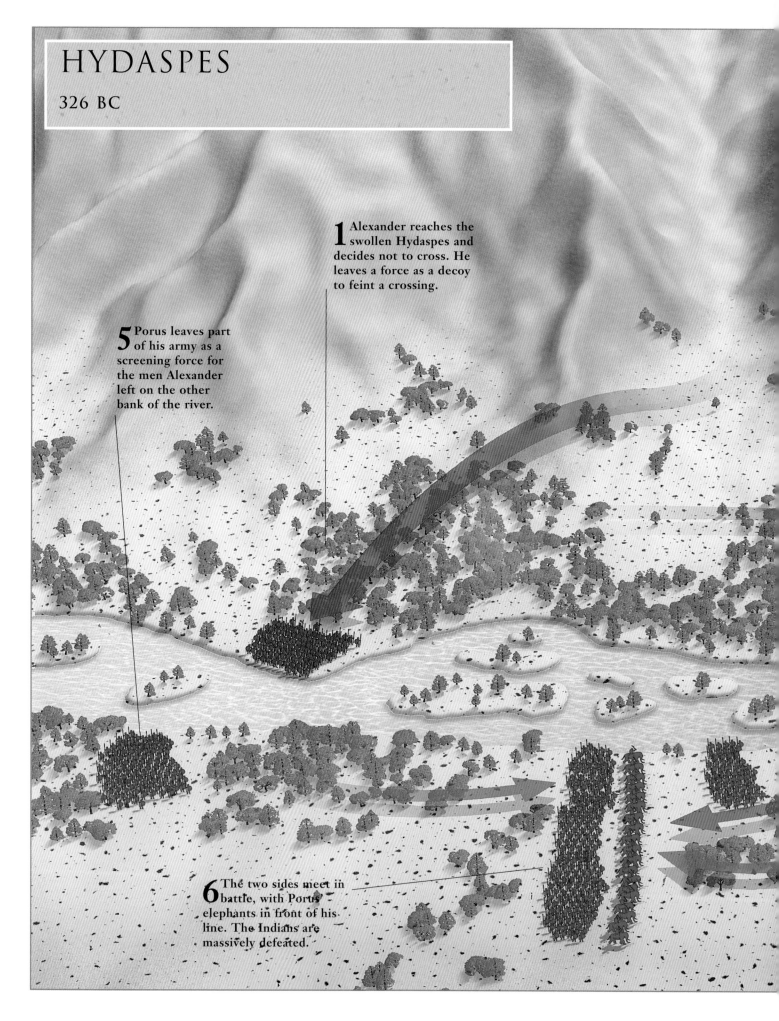

1 Alexander reaches the swollen Hydaspes and decides not to cross. He leaves a force as a decoy to feint a crossing.

5 Porus leaves part of his army as a screening force for the men Alexander left on the other bank of the river.

6 The two sides meet in battle, with Porus' elephants in front of his line. The Indians are massively defeated.

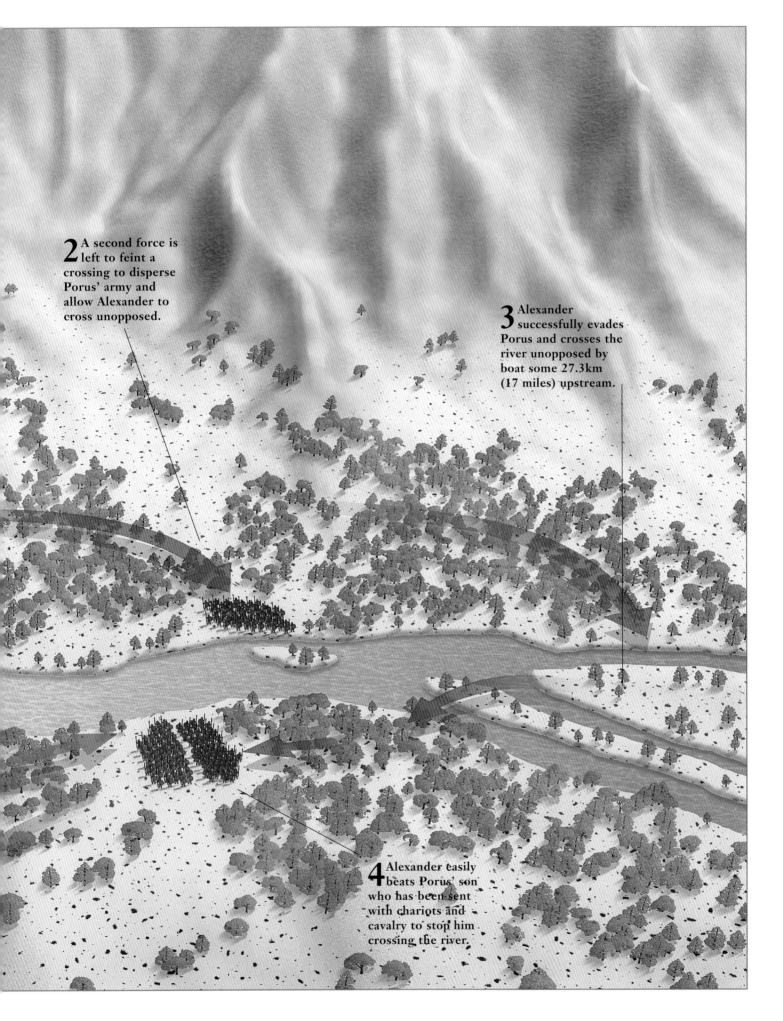

2 A second force is left to feint a crossing to disperse Porus' army and allow Alexander to cross unopposed.

3 Alexander successfully evades Porus and crosses the river unopposed by boat some 27.3km (17 miles) upstream.

4 Alexander easily beats Porus' son who has been sent with chariots and cavalry to stop him crossing the river.

HYDASPES

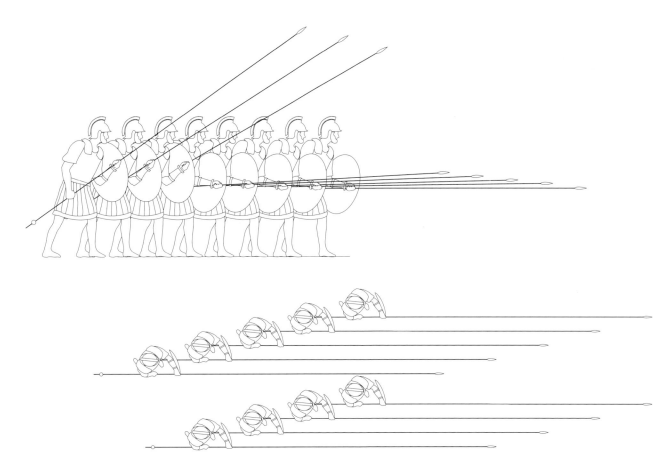

The Macedonian phalanx formation cannot be determined from ancient sources. These drawings depict three possibilities, all showing the hoplon attached to the soldier's left arm with the long sarissa held in both hands.

This battle scene is from one of Alexander the Great's 'elephant medallions'. It displays a Macedonian cavalry soldier pursuing an Indian elephant ridden by two spearmen. What these medallions represented is in dispute but must have celebrated Alexander's victory at the Hydaspes.

without anything written by any of his opponents, the accuracy of the following account of the battle of the Hydaspes, or any other of Alexander the Great's military adventures, must always be questioned.

CROSSING THE RIVER

Following Alexander the Great's recent successes in Persia and Bactria, several newly encountered smaller principalities surrendered to him without opposition. Their rulers felt that it was better to face their apparently inevitable loss without suffering the destruction of their towns and the ravishment of their populations. For months Alexander's army faced little resistance. But when it arrived at the Hydaspes river, Porus' army stood on the opposite bank. The sources suggest the two forces were almost equal in number, but Porus had the better ground, as he did not have to move, while Alexander – if he wished to continue his conquest – had to cross the river. This was to be far from easy. The Hydaspes was a deep river, swollen by the winter run-off. It would have been quite easy for Porus' soldiers to prevent such a crossing, if they could see it.

Alexander the Great was not planning to let them see his crossing, though. For several days and nights he kept Porus guessing while his troops executed feints up and down the river. So confused were the Indians, it seems, that when Alexander made his move to cross the Hydaspes River 27.3km (17 miles) upstream, Porus was almost completely unprepared.

Alexander led this force himself, after ordering one of his most trustworthy generals, Craterus, to remain with the remainder of his army in full view of Porus. He even dressed a look-alike in his own armour to confuse the Indians. All of this allowed Alexander a successful crossing, despite his mistaking an island in the middle of the river for a peninsula of land. By the time Porus knew what was happening and had reacted by sending an unnamed son to oppose him with 120 chariots and around 4000 cavalry, it was too late. The Macedonians had crossed the Hydaspes and set their formation on the same side of the river as the Indians. Before those sent to counter him could form their own lines, Alexander struck with his cavalry and swept them from the field.

THE BATTLE

However, Porus' main force still stood, and it still outnumbered the Macedonians. Arrian describes his formidable deployment:

In the van he stationed his elephants at intervals of about 100 feet [30m], on a broad front, to form a screen for the whole body of the infantry and to spread terror among the cavalry of Alexander. He did not expect that any enemy unit would venture to force a way through the gaps in the line of elephants … terror would make the horses uncontrollable, and infantry units would be even less likely to make the attempt, as they would be met and checked by his own heavy infantry and then destroyed by the elephants turning upon them and trampling them down (V.16).

Although not specifically mentioned in the sources, Alexander the Great must have had a plan to face the elephants. He knew that a large number would likely be in Porus' army, and he also knew that his horses would have difficulty fighting against elephants – only horses that had been raised with elephants, as in Porus' army, could endure their presence. Yet, Alexander's cavalry was his principal force, and his tactics were formed around it.

So, he charged his cavalry, not directly into the Indian elephants but around them. Alexander had used this manoeuvre before, at the battles of Granicus and Gaugamela, the speed of his cavalry easily able to outflank his Persian opponents in both of those conflicts. The same occurred at the Hydaspes, with one unit of the Macedonian Companion Cavalry quickly outflanking the Indians and, with the assistance of their allied Dahae horse archers, who shot their arrows in front of them, crashing into the cavalry of the Indian left flank. Having not yet completely deployed, Porus' cavalry was disorganized and vulnerable. A second cavalry unit, also of Companions, moving across the rear of the Indian army, reached the Indian cavalry on Porus' right flank and attacked them with great speed and force.

At the same time, Alexander's infantry had been crossing the river and moving into position. Their target was to be the elephants. Quintus Curtius Rufus reports

The Macedonian hoplite is often recognized as the best ancient infantry soldier. He differed from his Greek ancestor principally in the length of his spear, which could be as long as 5.5m (18ft), and the size of his round shield, which was smaller.

HYDASPES

The military activities of Alexander the Great have greatly interested painters of every generation. Here the seventeenth-century artist Nicolaes Berchem (1620–1683) depicts the battle of the Hydaspes with the romanticism for which his age was renowned.

the speech that Alexander had delivered to these troops before the battle:

Our spears are long and sturdy; they can never serve us better than against these elephants and their drivers. Dislodge the riders and stab the beasts. They are a military force of dubious value, and their ferocity is greater towards their own side; for they are driven by command against the enemy, but by fear against their own men (VIII.14.16).

Some historians have seen this speech as being dismissive of the Indian elephants. However, as his tactics at the battle of the Hydaspes showed, Alexander was far from dismissive of these beasts, so this speech was meant rather to inspire his infantry for the obviously daunting task ahead.

Porus commanded his elephants (and supporting infantry) to march towards the Macedonian infantry, and Alexander moved

his infantry forward to meet them. Initially, Alexander's missile troops – javelinmen and archers – drawn up on the flanks and perhaps in front of the phalanxes, had little effect, although unloading 'a thick barrage of missiles on both elephants and drivers'. The elephants quickly strode among the Macedonian infantry, pushing them back and causing havoc. Curtius continues:

A particularly terrifying sight was when the elephants would snatch up men in armour in their trunks and pass them over their heads to the drivers (VIII.14.27).

But the well-disciplined Macedonian soldiers did not break from their phalanxes, and eventually the tide of battle began to turn in favour of Alexander's army.

Soon the Indian elephants started to be worn down, fatigued, wounded and confused. Unlike the phalanxes, Porus' elephants panicked and could not be controlled by their drivers. Curtius claims:

They charged into their own men, mowing them down; their riders were flung to the ground and trampled to death. More terrified than menacing, the beasts were being driven like cattle from the battlefield (VIII.14.30).

Arrian is more detailed in his description, reporting that Alexander used his cavalry and infantry to 'box up' the elephants, leaving them no room to manoeuvre, so that in an effort to get away they trampled many of their own troops, *whereas the unfortunate Indians, jammed up close among them as they attempted to get away, found them a more dangerous enemy even than the Macedonians* (V.18).

AFTERMATH

Alexander the Great had won the battle of the Hydaspes. His phalanxes locked shields and marched forward. The Indians who could not flee surrendered. One of these was Porus himself. According to Curtius, Porus had ridden into battle on the back of an elephant that *towered above the other beasts* (VIII.13.7). While others had fled, he had stayed on the field, fighting until his elephant was killed under him and he had been wounded. Only then did he surrender.

This bravery impressed Alexander, who had seen the Persian king Darius flee from him at the battle of Gaugamela five years before. He rode up to Porus and addressed him: 'What do you wish that I should do with you?' 'Treat me as a king ought,' was Porus' reply. Alexander continued to be impressed: 'For my part, your request shall be granted. But is there not something you would wish for yourself? Ask it.' 'Everything is contained in this one request,' answered Porus. In response, Alexander preserved Porus' life and even returned him to power, as a client king.

Arrian reports that nearly 20,000 Indians lay dead on the banks of the Hydaspes river after the battle, while the Macedonians had lost fewer than 200 – Curtius and Plutarch give no death tallies. Both numbers may be exaggerated. However, one of Alexander's losses was more significant than any other. His horse, Bucephalas, his constant companion since his legendary taming when Alexander was only ten or twelve, and on whose back the Macedonian king had ridden into every conflict, was slain. At the advanced age of 28 or older, Bucephalas' death was as legendary as his life had been. It was said that although he had been mortally wounded, the horse was so faithful to his master that he did not stumble or fall until Alexander could safely dismount from him.

While one might expect that Alexander the Great would have slain Porus for fighting against him, not only did he preserve the Indian king's life, for his bravery in the battle he rewarded him by retaining him on his throne, as a client king to the Macedonians.

TREBIA
218 BC

WHY DID IT HAPPEN?

WHO Four Roman legions and their allies under Publius Scipio and Tiberius Sempronius Longus faced a collected band of barbarians, mercenaries, elephants, and an elite officer corps under the direct command of Rome's bitterest foe, the Carthaginian general Hannibal Barca (247–183 or 182 BC).

WHAT The Roman legion was the single most feared – and successful – military formation of the Ancient World. It would take overwhelming brilliance and guile to overcome the morale and experience of the Roman army fighting upon its native soil.

WHERE The banks of the river Trebia, near what is now Piacenza in northern Italy.

WHEN December 218 BC.

WHY The first Punic War had set the hatred of Carthage for Rome in stone. The struggle would only end with one power crippled – or in ruins. Hannibal had to be stopped from entering Italy, if he was to be stopped at all.

OUTCOME Rome's greatest military disaster in the field would soon be followed by others even worse.

AT THE THRESHOLD OF WORLD EMPIRE, THE ROMAN MILITARY MACHINE GLORIED IN AN UNBROKEN RECORD OF SUCCESS, PROVEN TACTICS AND THE FINEST SOLDIERS IN THE WORLD. IN RESPONSE, THE HATED CITY OF CARTHAGE THRUST FORTH MERCENARIES, ELEPHANTS – AND AN AVENGER IN THE PERSON OF HANNIBAL.

Westwards in the Mediterranean, two differing products of a differing international situation were engaged, like eaglets in the nest, in a struggle to see which of the two would survive. In the wake of Alexander's comparatively well-documented successes, commanders in succeeding ages acquired an appreciation of what a skilled general could accomplish by the careful use of his military assets.

Nationalism was becoming a force to be reckoned with in the military picture. Philip II of Macedon's creation of a national army, paid by the king and loyal to the king, had allowed his son and heir Alexander to defeat the subject armies of the Persian Empire and the smaller, divided armies with which the Greek city-states had sought to prevent his hegemony. Professional armies were a parallel development.

PROFESSIONAL ARMIES

The very idea of a professional army revolutionized warfare in the Ancient World – although the older formula of the citizen-soldier had its adherents. While the crops grew in the summer and early autumn, farmers could fight – but could they fight as well as men who stayed in the field or the barracks all year round? Even the Roman armies used mercenaries at times to supplement their levies, and the wealthy merchants of Carthage had their choice of veterans of wars and armies from all over the civilized world.

The general-kings who fought over Alexander's empire used the captured treasuries they inherited to finance their campaigns with armies composed of professional soldiers who had literally spent decades in the field. One of the most

A terror to horses. Hannibal hoped to use elephants from his native Africa to frighten off Rome's cavalry as Pyrrhus had employed them previously. Skilled mahouts and military engineers managed to get the animals into Italy, but the chill of the northern Italian winter soon proved more fatal than Roman weaponry.

successful of these had been Pyrrhus, king of Epirus, a smaller nation next to Macedonia, who had briefly conquered that country and sought conquests in the West. Pyrrhus' celebrated encounters with the national army of the Roman Republic between 280 and 275 BC contrast that general's skill in battle with the Romans' grim determination to win, which, in the end, prevailed. Roman infantry had eventually learned to cope with the huge, grey 'Lucanian Cows' (elephants) Pyrrhus had brought with him from the East to frighten them. That general left a written memoir of his achievements against the Romans (a major source for Plutarch's biography of him), and one of his most avid readers, and so the beneficiary of that general's experience, was a descendant of the ancient Phoenician traders by the name of Hannibal Barca.

THE PUNIC WARS

Hannibal's hatred of Rome and Romans was hereditary and legendary, but it was never blind. Rome had defeated Punic Carthage with great difficulty in the first Punic War of 264–241 BC, but what made a second struggle as inevitable as the Versailles Treaty made World War II was the Romans' opportunistic seizure of Sardinia and Corsica while Carthage was in the throes of a revolt by its own army of mercenaries. A Roman declaration of war against Carthage in 238 secured not only the two islands, but required also an indemnity of 1700 talents of silver and the undying hatred of the Barcid family for Rome.

The 'Grandpa's Knee' school of military education was the Ancient World's sole source of education for commanders. The transmitted experiences of the last generation were never more manifest in Classical Antiquity than in the wars of Carthage and Rome. Hamilcar Barca was the general who suppressed the insurgent mercenaries, only to see the Romans ruthlessly exploit his nation's weakness and make additional demands upon Carthage in its travails. The cabal of merchants who ran Carthage sought new revenues and new opportunities in Spain, and sent to secure them was Hamilcar, who took his eldest son for an education in the field.

That was Hannibal, who succeeded his father in command after Hamilcar met his own death by drowning in a river crossing. Carthage's greatest general at once began a long military career with marked successes against the fierce inhabitants of Spain. Roman efforts to circumscribe his operations, obviously directed in the end against them, prompted Hannibal to move his mostly mercenary army from Spain to Italy through the Alpine passes in the dead of winter in a lightning stroke nearly as difficult to believe as it was to execute. Willpower and planning made possible a tremendously difficult and effective piece of military haste.

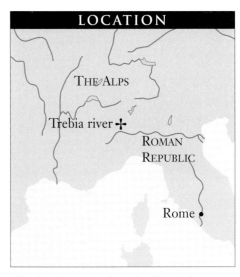

LOCATION

After his epic crossing of the Alps, Hannibal encountered Sempronius, the Roman consul, on the Trebia. The Roman defeat left the way open for Hannibal to march on Rome.

TREBIA

The movement of Hannibal's elephants through the difficult terrain of the Alps would have startled this Roman patrol more than the elephants themselves. The strange appearance and scent of the large grey beasts put many Roman cavalry horse into terrified flight.

THE CROSSING OF THE ALPS

To crush the younger child of a military family, the Romans sent as consul in 218 BC the patriarch of a famous military family, Publius Cornelius Scipio. With the coming of war, the elder Scipio had already decided to attack Hannibal's base of supply in Spain, but Hannibal's speed in arriving in Italy forced him to send an officer he trusted, his brother Gnaeus, ahead with limited forces to Spain while he himself returned and sought to bring Hannibal to battle near the crossing of the Po river valley.

Hannibal's deft handling of his army, on top of the incredible feat of transporting elephants over wide rivers and tall mountains in winter, made him by far the most terrible opponent Rome ever had or would encounter. Publius Scipio met Hannibal's superbly trained and skilfully

handled cavalry and light infantry at the crossings of the Ticinus river. For all his own expertise, Scipio could not halt the Carthaginians there and found himself severely wounded and forced to retreat backward into the fortified city of Placentia.

The Roman Senate quickly despatched reinforcements. A second consular army under Scipio's co-consul, Sempronius Longus, soon arrived at Placentia. The Senate had previously intended that Sempronius and his two legions should invade Punic Africa, taking the war directly to Carthage. Such a move would later win Rome's war with the Carthaginians, but Sempronius' march north was ample proof of how decisively and effectively Hannibal's rapid movement had wrested the initiative from the Romans. Carthage would instead take the conflict to Rome.

Some paired Roman executives were allies, others political rivals. A personal quest for glory soon played a devastating role in a vital tactical decision. A minor success in a skirmish with the Carthaginian advance guard convinced Sempronius that a decisive victory and political success were his for the taking from an enemy that could not have been anything but weakened by its winter crossing of the Alps. With Scipio still suffering from his wound, Sempronius took sole command and moved to the Trebia river with the combined consular armies of some 40,000 men. It was December 218 BC.

THE BATTLE

Hannibal enjoyed Napoleon's vital prerequisites for a successful commander, incredible good luck and a stupid enemy. Rome's traditional Gallic enemies had flocked to Hannibal as their liberator, but these undisciplined reinforcements would not linger long in the Carthaginian camp without the prospect of action. Hannibal had good and capable subordinates as long as he had younger brothers. Taking one such, Mago, with him, Hannibal scouted

THE OPPOSED FORCES

ROMANS (estimated)
Cavalry:	5000
Roman legionaries	16,000
Allied infantry:	14,000
Total:	**35,000**

CARTHAGINIANS (estimated)
Cavalry:	10,000
Heavy infantry:	20,000
Total:	**30,000**

Personal leadership was one of Hannibal's great strengths as a commander. By sheer force of personality and intelligent management the Carthaginian general welded a polyglot force of mercenaries, tributaries and a thin leavening of North African officers into an army that could execute tremendously complex – and deadly effective – manoeuvres.

the course of the Roman advance and found a declivity where Mago and 2000 infantry and cavalry could be concealed until an opportune moment.

Perhaps the bitterness of a Roman survivor influences Livy's enduring account of the suffering of the Roman army as it walked shivering into Hannibal's intricate trap. At dawn, Hannibal's Numidian cavalry appeared in front of Sempronius' fortified camp and invited the Romans to battle with a shower of javelins and other missiles. It was by no means the last time that Hannibal would turn Roman confidence from a historical advantage into a devastatingly exploitable weakness.

Sempronius at once sent his own cavalry and light infantry to exhaust their bodies and missile weapons in a vain response, despite a worsening winter storm and his men's lack of food or fire. The Trebia river itself was bitterly cold, and came up to the chests of the Roman infantry as they grimly forded it and advanced toward the cheerful fires of the Carthaginian camp, where Hannibal's well-fed and well-warmed troops awaited them. With any wind at all, even the hardy Romans would have had hypothermia added to their daunting list of enemies. Sempronius could and did choose to ignore the condition of his men in his

personal quest for glory, but their worsening physical and mental condition would soon exert tremendous influence upon the strength and nature of their fighting.

Hannibal's plan of battle took the shape of an intricately crafted meat grinder, with light infantry, the Baliares, set in front of his line with the heavier infantry. These skilled soldiers retreated in good order as the enemy advanced and showered the lumbering Romans with javelins at a safe distance. There had to be that distance for Hannibal's plans to work, but lightly equipped and warm men had no trouble maintaining the required space as the chilled and more heavily burdened Romans struggled forward.

Sempronius did have Rome's sterling military tradition to help him arrange his fight. Taken on its own terms, his line of battle was close and effective in the early

Legionary discipline required loud and proper signalling, left to experts such as this Roman field musician and his high-frequency horn, the cornu. *The legend of Romulus and Remus, raised by a She-Wolf, dictated the selection of the specialized soldier's cowl and insignia.*

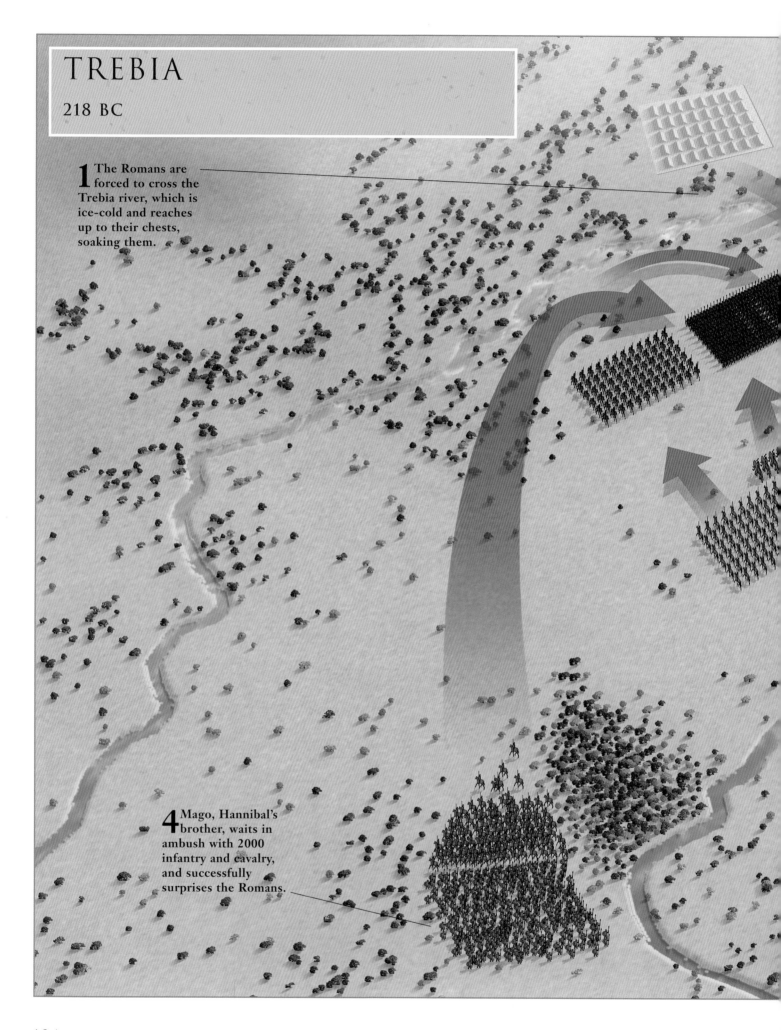

TREBIA

218 BC

1 The Romans are forced to cross the Trebia river, which is ice-cold and reaches up to their chests, soaking them.

4 Mago, Hannibal's brother, waits in ambush with 2000 infantry and cavalry, and successfully surprises the Romans.

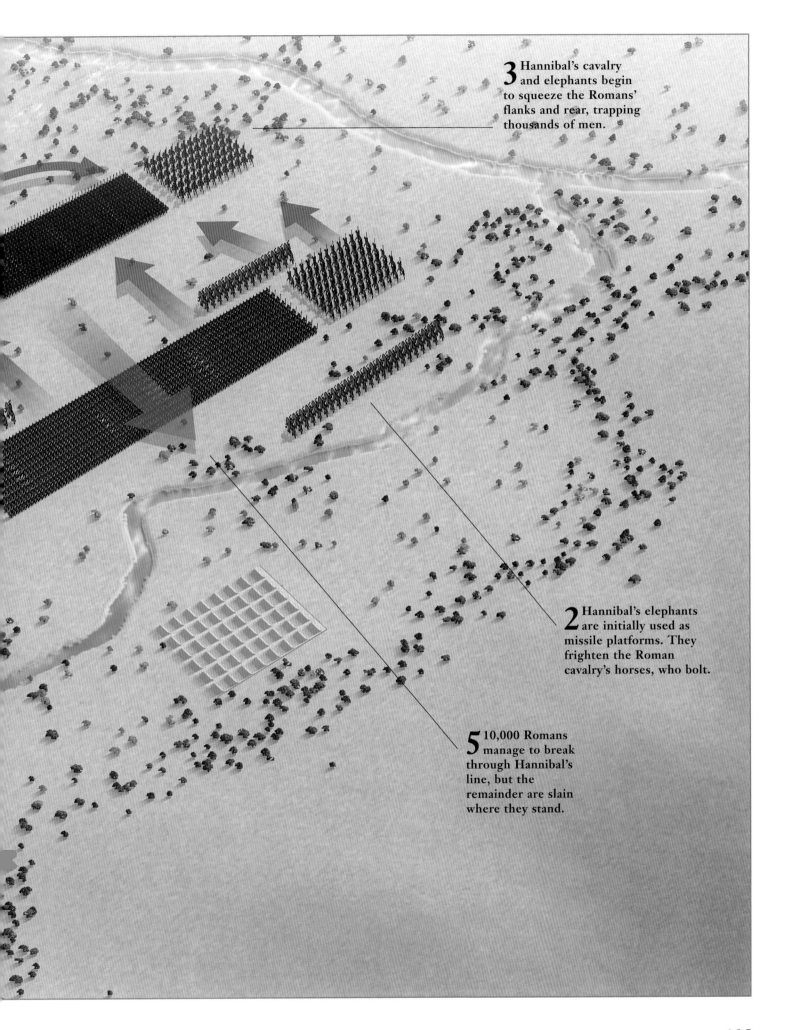

3 Hannibal's cavalry and elephants begin to squeeze the Romans' flanks and rear, trapping thousands of men.

2 Hannibal's elephants are initially used as missile platforms. They frighten the Roman cavalry's horses, who bolt.

5 10,000 Romans manage to break through Hannibal's line, but the remainder are slain where they stand.

TREBIA

The consternation inflicted by Hannibal's elephants weighed more heavily on frightened horses than the legionaries seen here in Raphael's romanticized depiction of the Trebia. Hannibal employed his elephants as missile platforms and as strongpoints around which his own forces could rally and coordinate their manoeuvres.

Republican heroes such as Publius Cornelius Scipio Africanus left accurate likenesses behind to inspire an admiring posterity. Hannibal's eventual destroyer had the interval between wars to study his opponent's tactics before taking the conflict to Carthage in a shattering assault.

stages of the combat. In all he had eight legions, four composed of Roman citizens in the centre, four levied from Rome's Italian subject allies on the wings. Having read his accounts of Alexander at Gaugamela and Pyrrhus' battles with armies as large or larger, Hannibal kept his elephants behind his line of battle, where they could serve as missile platforms in some safety, while his light infantry made a well-organized withdrawal behind the long line of Hannibal's 20,000 Spanish infantry and an unknown number of Gallic allies.

There is something to be said for following a military tradition when that is a good and sound military tradition, and Rome's legionary tactics, centuries in the

evolving, continued to serve the Roman army well. The legionaries' own throwing javelin, the *pilum*, made a strong response to Hannibal's bombardment as the legions drew near to the very centre of the Carthaginian line. The Roman cavalry, however, discovered the reason that Hannibal had gone to such great lengths to transport his elephants into Italy. The Italian horses could not abide the sight and smell of the huge, strange animals, and bolted, and the elephants and Hannibal's superior cavalry began to drive in the Roman flanks.

Sempronius' marked limitations as a commander could offer him no better solution for the worsening tactical situation than to continue his advance directly into Hannibal's centre, a tendency in Roman commanders Hannibal would exploit with horrific results in the subsequent battle of Cannae. Hannibal turned his elephants against the Roman light infantry (*velites*), who drove the animals off, and sprang Mago's ambush by some means or other that succeeded despite the continuing deterioration of the weather. In so doing, however, the guards of the Roman flanks had lost all contact with the centre.

Sempronius, out of touch with the whole of his army and the true and dire nature of the situation, thought he had the victory when a quarter of his army burst through the Carthaginian centre, but those 10,000 men proved to be the sole survivors of a truly disastrous defeat as the rest of Hannibal's forces methodically slaughtered the remaining two-thirds of the Roman army. The survivors escaped through the storm to Placentia in small groups.

AFTERMATH

Family connections would determine much of the rest of course of the fighting. Publius Cornelius Scipio would eventually join his brother in Spain and operate in Hannibal's rear, defeating and being defeated by Hannibal's younger brother Hamilcar until both men's defeat and death in 211 BC. Hasdrubal himself would die caught by a fresh Roman army while attempting to join his brother in Italy at the Metaurus river in 207 BC. Seeing his brother's head left in his line of advance by a Roman cavalryman, Hannibal is reported to have finally despaired of victory.

The son of Publius Scipio, meanwhile, had enjoyed great success with his father and uncle's remaining forces in Spain, and would meet and defeat Hannibal himself in Africa at Zama in 202 BC, winning the legendary name of 'Africanus' for the feat. Supposedly the two met off the battlefield in the Greek city of Ephesus, years later. Plutarch's account has Hannibal and Scipio Africanus walking along and discussing the great leaders of their own history. Hannibal ranked Alexander first, Pyrrhus second, and himself third. 'And if you had beaten me?' asked Scipio. 'I would have ranked myself first,' said Hannibal.

The last of Carthage's elephants make their final advance at the battle of Zama, fought in Africa 16 years after that at the Trebia. Hannibal had been correct in his own intention to win the war on enemy soil – yet another of his plans studied, copied, and put into effect by his Roman destroyers.

CANNAE
216 BC

WHY DID IT HAPPEN?

WHO A Roman army under the consul Varro moved to attack the Carthaginians under Hannibal Barca (247–183 or 182 BC).

WHAT The Roman cavalry were driven from the field by the Carthaginian cavalry. The Roman and allied infantry, in a very deep formation, pushed the enemy back until their own flanks were exposed to the longer Carthaginian line which squeezed their formation even more. The returning Carthaginian cavalry attacked the rear of the Roman infantry, severely restricting the ability of individuals to respond.

WHERE Apulia, Italy.

WHEN 216 BC.

WHY Hannibal was attempting to wrest Rome's recently acquired Italian allies from her and so weaken her ability to continue the war.

OUTCOME More than half the Roman force was cut down. But Rome raised another army and continued the war to ultimate victory.

AFTER THE BATTLES OF TREBIA (218 BC) AND TRASIMENE (217 BC), AT CANNAE HANNIBAL WON HIS THIRD AND GREATEST VICTORY OVER THE ARMIES OF ROME IN ITALY. A TACTICAL MASTERPIECE, THIS BATTLE HAS PROVIDED A MODEL FOR GENERALS FOR OVER 2000 YEARS. YET ROME SURVIVED THIS CATASTROPHE TO DEFEAT THE CARTHAGINIANS.

In its early manifestation Rome was a city-state, just like all the others in Greece and Italy. However, Rome first defeated and then formed alliances with the other city-states in Italy. Rome was also aware of the older city of Carthage, which had great influence amongst the numerous independent cities on the island of Sicily. This became the centre of the first Punic War (264–241 BC) and ended with the defeat of Carthage. Thirty years later another area of dispute arose in Spain. In this, the second war between Carthage and Rome, half of the latter's power base comprised fairly recently acquired Italian allies. By taking the war to Italy the Carthaginian general Hannibal Barca hoped to break at least some of those alliances and reduce Rome's power in the field, while other Carthaginian leaders continued the struggle in Spain, where much of the second Punic War (218–202 BC) was fought.

THE CAMPAIGN

Roman strategy had been, initially, to immediately confront the invader in the field. This proved disastrous as Hannibal out-thought his amateur opponents on every occasion and slaughtered Roman soldiers in their tens of thousands. There was then a change of tack, and a policy of attrition was introduced by the consul Fabius Maximus: Hannibal was to be denied a victory in the field and his army was to be allowed to wither in the open countryside. Unfortunately, a lot of the countryside belonged to powerful politicians who didn't

Hannibal entering a northern Italian town in triumph. Elephants had helped Hannibal in his crossing of the Alps, but once the Roman troops and cavalry became inured to these strange beasts, they were relatively ineffective on the battlefield.

appreciate their farms and incomes being destroyed in this way.

To avoid the possibility of a popular army commander taking over the state and declaring himself king, the army of the Roman Republic was commanded by a pair of annually elected politicians, called consuls, each in charge on alternate days. In the year 216 BC the consuls Paullus and Varro were elected to command. They could not have been more different. Paullus was cautious, thoughtful and valued the lives of the men he had been entrusted with, while Varro was brash and full of unfounded confidence. Neither had held high command before. The consuls, bringing reinforcements which increased the field force by half, joined the army near Samnium, close to Hannibal's base camp. The Roman force was billeted in two camps, one smaller than the other.

FORAGING

Hannibal had his own problems. The army had eaten out the surrounding countryside and had only ten days' food left. Also, the lack of battle and thus plunder was making his largely mercenary troops discontented almost to the point of desertion. Inevitably, with two hostile armies so close, there was a lot of skirmishing between scouting and foraging parties. Within days of the consuls arriving, the Romans had the best of a large skirmish which left 1700 enemy soldiers dead for the loss of about 100 Romans. Paullus, in charge that day, called off any pursuit, suspecting a trap.

This is exactly what Hannibal planned for the following night. His army stole out of camp fully armed and ready for battle but leaving behind some of their tents, food and treasure. The baggage train also set off in plain view along a rising valley making it look as though he was fleeing in some haste. But the army was hidden either side of this valley, infantry one side, cavalry the other. Would the Romans take the bait and follow the baggage?

It was Varro's turn to command and he was nearly taken in, being on the point of ordering a precipitate advance. Luckily, Paullus sent word that the omens from a sacrifice of chickens were bad, foretelling disaster (how right they were!) and two

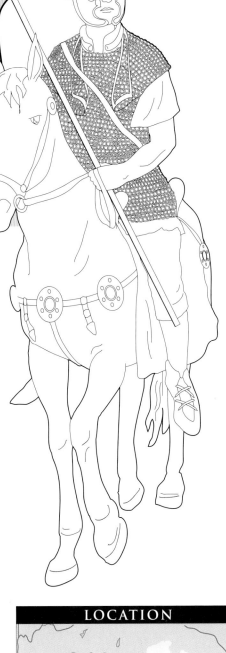

Roman captives who had escaped from the Carthaginian host returned just in time to expose the ruse. Both sides returned to their respective camps. To alleviate his supply problems, Hannibal decided to move on into Apulia. He set out leaving the camp as he had before at night and with all sorts of paraphernalia lying around. By the time the Romans had cautiously scouted the area he was well ahead of them. However, he was tracked and soon the Roman army caught up with him near the village of Cannae.

DISPOSITIONS

This was no whim or accident. Hannibal's position at Cannae provided him with several advantages. Firstly, his army deployed on hills giving them a height advantage. Secondly, they had their backs to the prevailing wind, which was prone to kick up dust squalls and impair the vision of anyone advancing into it. Thirdly, but perhaps most importantly of all, the frontage was restricted. He knew the Roman army outnumbered him almost two to one. The ground he chose forced them to deploy with a river on their right and steep hills to their left. This restricted their frontage, the gap being only 3.2km (2 miles) wide, and forced their infantry into a much denser formation than normal.

However many men they had, only the front rank could fight. The Athenians had used the same ploy in their first battle with the Syracusan army 200 years earlier and it

LOCATION

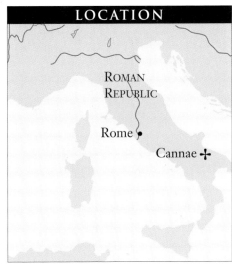

Cannae was perhaps Rome's greatest defeat, but typically the Republic soon recovered, and Hannibal, neglecting to march on the capital, was effectively isolated in the south of Italy.

CANNAE

THE OPPOSED FORCES

CARTHAGINIANS

Heavy infantry:	32,000
Light auxiliaries:	8000
Cavalry:	10,000
Total:	**50,000**

ROMANS

Legionaries:	58,000
Light auxiliaries:	16,000
Cavalry:	6000
Total:	**80,000**

would be used again by the English at Agincourt some 1600 years later. This negated the principal Roman advantage at a stroke. Hannibal's genius would turn that negated advantage into a crushing millstone around the neck of the Roman army.

When the Romans arrived they again fortified two separate camps on either side of the small river Aufidus. Again, skirmishing took place with the Numidian cavalry in the pay of the Carthaginians, causing havoc amongst the Romans as they went to fetch water from the river. Meanwhile, the consuls argued bitterly as to the right course of action. On Varro's day, without consulting his fellow commander, he led the army out and deployed for battle in the traditional style, with infantry in the

centre and cavalry on each wing. This time the Roman cavalry was on the right wing next to the river, next to them the Roman infantry, then the allied infantry and finally the allied cavalry. Along the front of the infantry were the skirmishers, armed with a throwing javelin, bows or slings. Many of these had been loaned by Syracuse, at that time allied with Rome.

Hannibal had a plan. Like the Romans, he placed unarmoured infantry skirmishers, including slingers from the Balearic Islands, along his front. On his left, facing the Roman cavalry, he deployed his own Gallic and Spanish cavalry. Gallic and Spanish mercenaries made up the main infantry centre. If they died he would not have to pay them. The line was deliberately bellied

out towards the Romans. This line, right and left, was tipped by his African infantry, now sporting the Roman armour captured in previous victories. On his right flank were his famous Numidian cavalry.

THE ROMAN ARMY

The Roman army was relatively homogeneous. It always included priests and purified beasts for sacrifice to try and placate the gods. It is likely the Carthaginians did the same. The infantry was organized in legions of about 5000 men. These deployed in a standard way. The front line consisted of light infantry skirmishers, *velites*, armed with javelins and carrying a round shield. The second and third lines were of *hastati* and *principes*

armed with the heavy throwing javelin, for which the Romans were famous, known as the *pilum*, and carrying a large, flat, oval shield. The richer members of this class would wear a mail shirt, otherwise a simple square of bronze worn on the chest had to suffice for protection. The last line was formed of *triarii*. They were equipped with a long thrusting spear and, being the older members of the community, were more able to afford mail armour. The second, third and fourth lines normally deployed in companies of around 80 men, maniples, arranged in a chequerboard formation. This allowed mutual support and maximum flexibility as well as breaking up the rigid battle lines of many of their opponents. The restricted frontage at Cannae must have

The site of the battle at Cannae today. Stand on the ridge above the river as Hannibal must have done and let your imagination conjure up the enthusiastic Romans rushing into your trap. Then go down by the river and dwell upon the despair and frustration of the men who were so hemmed in by their fellows they could not strike back as they were cut down.

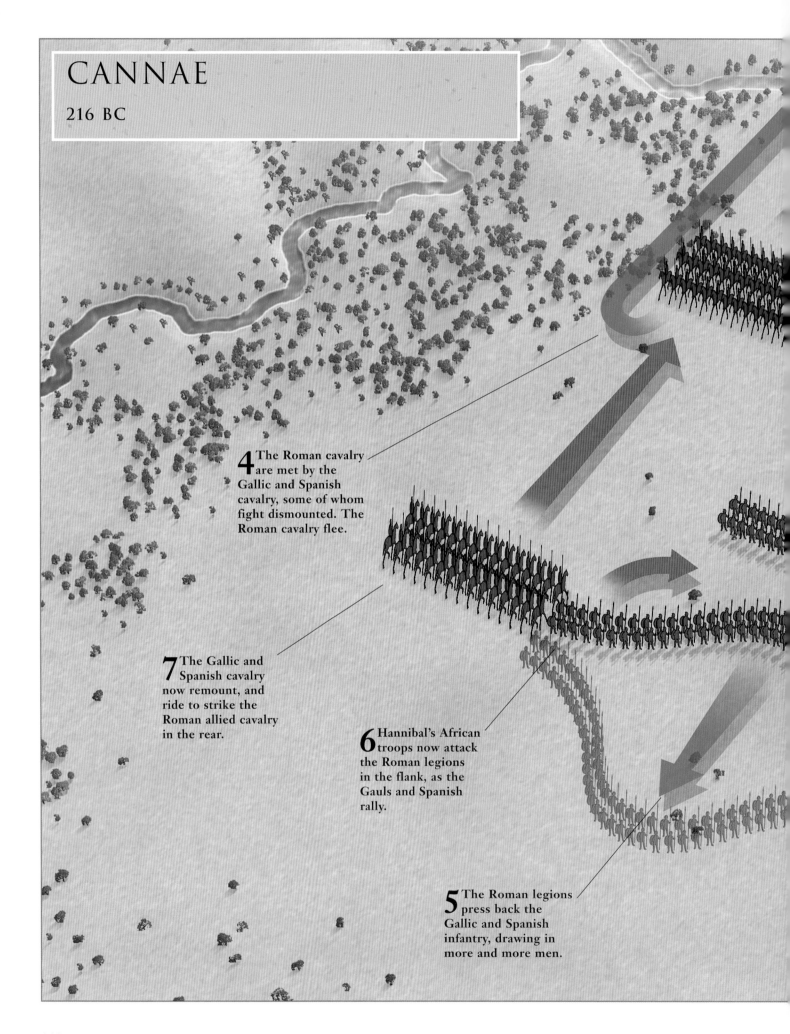

CANNAE

216 BC

4 The Roman cavalry are met by the Gallic and Spanish cavalry, some of whom fight dismounted. The Roman cavalry flee.

7 The Gallic and Spanish cavalry now remount, and ride to strike the Roman allied cavalry in the rear.

6 Hannibal's African troops now attack the Roman legions in the flank, as the Gauls and Spanish rally.

5 The Roman legions press back the Gallic and Spanish infantry, drawing in more and more men.

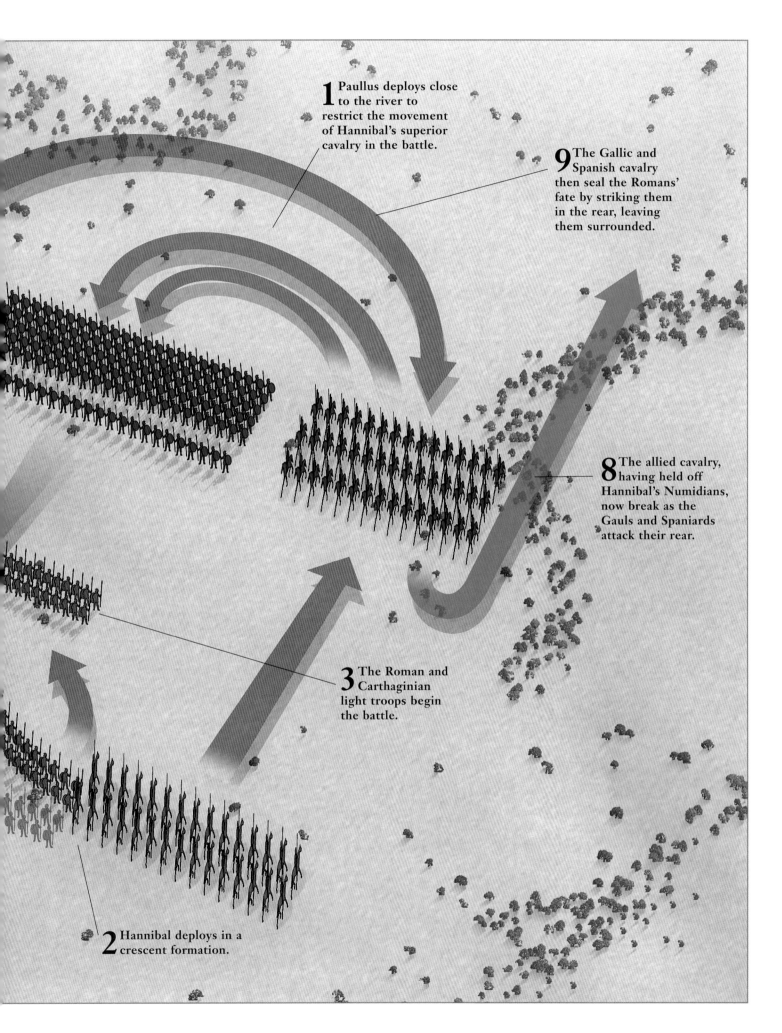

1 Paullus deploys close to the river to restrict the movement of Hannibal's superior cavalry in the battle.

9 The Gallic and Spanish cavalry then seal the Romans' fate by striking them in the rear, leaving them surrounded.

8 The allied cavalry, having held off Hannibal's Numidians, now break as the Gauls and Spaniards attack their rear.

3 The Roman and Carthaginian light troops begin the battle.

2 Hannibal deploys in a crescent formation.

Roman cavalry shields. From left to right: a round, spined design from 200 BC; a first century BC Celtic style; a typical first century AD oval design; an AD 300 design, with a rounder, more dished shape.

cancelled the chequerboard formation and the resulting departure from their training contributed to their defeat.

Have sympathy for the poor Roman cavalryman. His was a much under-developed branch of the army. There were no stirrups, so he had to maintain his own balance, grip with his knees and control his reins with his left hand which also held his shield. At the same time he had to wield his spear in his right hand, listen for orders and try to spear the man facing him before he was speared himself. Although he wore a muscled cuirass in thin bronze, his shield was made of buffalo hide which tended to go soft in damp conditions. His principal weapon, a light javelin, was not really up to the job either. It was too thin, making it wobble and difficult to aim at the vital moment. When it broke, there was no butt spike and he was left wielding a broken stick! Even though he carried a sword, vital

seconds would be lost in drawing it just when the opponent was upon him, and by then it might well be too late.

The principal weakness of the Roman army at this period was a collective belief in their own invincibility. This often led to rash command decisions, as we shall see, and to the soldiers clamouring to get at the enemy, not to mention unauthorized advances. A large part of the army would have been trained but inexperienced. Rome had already lost 30,000 men in the previous two years in battles against Hannibal. Yet tactics and equipment remained unchanged. Although about half the army was provided by Rome's allies, they were similarly armed and organized. In this battle Varro commanded the allies on the left wing while Paullus commanded the Roman right.

HANNIBAL'S ARMY

The Carthaginian army was a very different beast. Hannibal had brought some troops with him from Africa and collected many more mercenaries on his long march from Spain where they had already won many victories. The core of the army was African spearmen from both Carthage and Libya. They wore a tunic to below the knee, an iron helmet and carried a large oval shield. The principal weapon was a spear about 1.8m (6ft) long, quite short for the period. By the time of Cannae many of these spearmen were wearing armour looted from the Roman dead at previous battles.

Cavalry from the city carried a round shield and wore muscled bronze breastplates. These horsemen were supplemented by numerous Numidian cavalry from the pre-desertified hinterland. A simple sleeveless tunic to the thigh, a shield and a few javelins were their equipment. They were nevertheless fearsome in their charge and formidable horsemen. They had mastered the art of

controlling their horses with only their knees and body weight and did not encumber their shield arms with reins. This gave them a tremendous advantage in a melee. Although Hannibal had also brought elephants from Africa they had all died, mainly from the cold, two years before.

In Spain he recruited large numbers of native Celtiberians. These warriors sported black helmets made from sinew, a large oval shield and their typical dress was a white tunic with a purple border. They used a

Romans and Carthaginians contest the battle of Lake Trasimene (217 BC) during the second Punic War.

Opposite: The death of the Roman general Paullus at the battle of Cannae. This Eighteenth-century illustration shows legionaries wearing a form of armour introduced nearly 300 years after the battle and a breed of horse popular in the Eighteenth century. But it does confirm Cannae's place in world history as the defeat of overconfidence by intelligent planning.

CANNAE

A Numidian light cavalryman from around 200 BC. He is armed with a javelin and small shield. These horsemen were such good riders that they had no need of a bridle to control their mount.

completely iron javelin, the *angon*, not unlike the Roman pila in effect. They also provided a contingent of cavalry. The Spanish cavalry carried a small shield of boiled leather and a pair of robust javelins so they could be hurled in a close-quarters mounted scrum without disarming the rider. Hannibal's only significant missile force was a number of slingers from the Balearic Islands.

In Gaul he added more tribal infantry and cavalry, again with big oval shields, javelins and long, slashing swords. They were the only ones in either army to wear trousers! The Gallic mounted warriors carried the wooden shield like their infantry and a stout spear. These separate groups spoke different languages and fought in different styles. The Gauls preferred a huge, wild, headlong charge whereas the Celtiberians threw their javelins and charged like the Romans.

Hannibal also had greater control in the field. For this battle his right wing, opposite the allied cavalry, was commanded by Marhabal. The Gallic and Spanish cavalry

facing the Roman horse were under the command of his brother Hasdrubal. Hannibal personally led the centre with his brother Mago. He had four experienced battle commanders facing just two novices. It is an oft-omitted tribute to Hannibal's abilities that he managed to weld this disparate group into an army that regularly beat the Romans and kept it in the field in Italy for about 16 years.

THE BATTLE

The Roman cavalry were the first to give way. They were hemmed in by the river on one side and the massed infantry on the other. Frankly, the Romans should have placed all the cavalry in reserve ready to plug gaps or exploit success as required and held the riverside with infantry. Outclassed by the veteran Gallic and Spanish cavalry, the Romans first gave ground and then turned tail and fled.

The skirmishers exchanged missiles and withdrew through the ranks of the main infantry as they closed. When they met it was with a tremendous clamour. Buoyed up by the war horns and shouts of their own side they would have appeared to hesitate about 30m (32 yards) apart, while the *hastati* and *principes* on the Roman side and the Gauls and Spanish on the other hurled their javelins at each other.

To the war cries and clash of weapons would be added the screams of the injured. Then the lines would quickly collide in melee, raising the noise to painful levels as shield clashed against shield and swords began their deadly work, seeking out unguarded limbs and bodies. More screams and a bass undertone of grunting, shoving men in a mortal scrum added to the din. Slowly but surely the Roman and allied infantry pushed back the centre of the Gallic/Spanish line.

But this was Hannibal's trap. As the Romans pushed forward the line flattened then went concave. As it did so the already

Opposite: Despondency in Rome after defeat at Cannae. Hannibal still did not feel strong enough to besiege the city. So a stalemate ensued in Italy and the seat of the war moved to Spain. It ended with the Roman invasion of Africa and the battle of Zama in 202 BC.

CANNAE

This nineteenth-century illustration shows Hannibal and his army stripping the defeated Romans of arms and armour after their victory at Cannae.

cramped Roman and allied infantry became increasingly crowded, restricting the space they needed to wield their weapons. The Gauls and Spaniards started to run in feigned rout. This also left the two tips of African troops on the wings of the infantry. These fresh troops now launched themselves at the flanks of the tiring Roman infantry. The Romans had observed that a man can fight with maximum vigour for

about eight minutes. To fight and beat one enemy takes a lot of energy. To be then faced by a new, fresh foe is a blow to the spirit as well as a physical challenge. Added to that, the encircling movement they could perceive to their rear would have further sapped the Romans' will. However, they were not yet ready to throw in the towel. They desperately turned to face the new foe but they were already bloodied and

reported to have said: 'They might as well be delivered up to me in chains.'

On the Roman left about 500 of the Numidian cavalry had pretended to desert and were escorted through the allied cavalry lines. When the cavalry battle on this flank became general they showed their true colours and attacked the allied cavalry in the rear with weapons they had hidden earlier. Outnumbered and attacked front and rear, it was just a question of time before the allied cavalry too fled the field.

As casualties mounted and men started to leave the field Hasdrubal, Hannibal's brother, who commanded a reserve of Numidian cavalry, launched them in a bloody slaughter of the fugitives, for it is when an army breaks and is pursued that most casualties are inflicted.

In the early stages of this pursuit they cut down the consul Paullus who was still trying to make a fight of it. The Gauls and Spaniards were now recalled to the fight for the Africans were tiring of the butchery. The instinct to fight or flee is a strong one. When fighting becomes suicide, flight takes over and so it was at Cannae that day. The Roman army lost cohesion under this onslaught and fugitives ran in all directions: 10,000 made it to the larger camp, 7000 to the smaller and 2000 to the unfortified village of Cannae. Varro escaped with 70 cavalry to Venusia. The dead numbered 48,000. The Carthaginians captured 4500.

AFTERMATH

Although it was another great victory and he had now killed nearly 80,000 Roman soldiers in three years, Hannibal still did not feel strong enough to attempt to storm Rome. Meanwhile, Roman general Publius Scipio was subjugating Spain. A decade later, he went on to invade Africa and beat Hannibal at the battle of Zama, so ending the second Punic War in 202 BC.

Hannibal escaped and went to serve the Seleucid king Antiochus, who in turn became one of Rome's bitterest opponents. In the final war between these great powers the Romans besieged and captured the city of Carthage in 146 BC, slaughtering all the inhabitants and salting the surrounding countryside in the hope that Carthage would never rise again.

Dating from the third century BC, this Roman cavalry helmet – without its cheek guards – was recovered from excavations in Italy.

disorganized. They didn't stand a chance.

As the African steamroller hit, the confused Romans were thrown closer and closer together, unable to fight back. The sources speak of butchery rather than fighting. A slingshot had injured Paullus, commanding the right wing of the army. Unable to stay mounted he ordered his bodyguard to dismount to continue the fight. When he learned this Hannibal is

PYDNA
168 BC

THE BATTLE OF PYDNA WAS THE PIVOTAL MOMENT OF THE THIRD MACEDONIAN WAR. IT WAS A CLASSIC PHALANX VERSUS LEGION CLASH, WITH THE LEGIONS EMERGING VICTORIOUS. THE BATTLE ALSO MARKED A SIGNIFICANT SHIFT IN POWER, WITH ROMAN MILITARY MIGHT FIRMLY ESTABLISHING THE NEW ORDER IN THE MEDITERRANEAN.

WHY DID IT HAPPEN?

WHO Roman legions and supporting forces under Lucius Aemilius Paullus (*c.* 229–160 BC) versus Macedonian forces under Perseus, king of Macedon (*c.* 212–165 BC).

WHAT A clash between troops gathering water developed into a full-blown battle which was won by the Roman legions after initial reverses. The Macedonian left was shattered by elephants and the central phalanx massacred.

WHERE Near the city of Pydna, Macedon.

WHEN 22 June 168 BC.

WHY Roman dissatisfaction with the indecisive third Macedonian War, which had begun in 172 BC, resulted in a new campaign to subdue the increasingly anti-Roman Macedonians.

OUTCOME The Macedonians were decisively defeated in battle and Macedon became a Roman province.

The great civilization of Ancient Greece influenced many others, including that of the Romans. The early armies of Rome were influenced by Greek hoplite forces, but over time they evolved into the more commonly recognized form. Early in the history of the Roman Republic, Greece was in decline but remained a power in the Mediterranean region. Conflicts between Roman and Greek forces were not uncommon, and the Greeks threatened the very survival of Rome at times.

THE PHALANX

By the second century BC, the classical Greek hoplite armies of citizen-soldiers had given way to the pike-armed Macedonian phalanx developed by Alexander the Great's father Philip II (382–336 BC), made up of veteran professional soldiers, with which Alexander had gone on to conquer the known world.

Delivering the crushing blow of a phalanx charge was the main factor in Greek tactics. Light forces might scout and skirmish, but the issue would be decided by the phalangites. Each man was armed with a *sarissa*, a very long pike which required surprising skill to handle since the shaft bent under its own weight, causing the head to jump around as the phalangite wielding it advanced. Macedonian-style phalangites were less heavily armoured than their predecessors. Instead of the large shield that gave the hoplites their name, they had a smaller shield strapped to their left arm, leaving both hands free to wield the *sarissa*. This left them at a disadvantage in close combat if they were forced to drop their pikes and draw their sidearms.

The Greek phalanx was a powerful force on the battlefield but its day was passing. Against the more flexible Roman legions, the phalanx was too unwieldy to prevail unless the opposing commander made the mistake of trying to face it head-on, in which case the phalanx crushed its foes in the traditional manner.

The main advantage of these hugely long pikes was the depth of formation that could fight. For every man in the front rank there were several pike points projecting forward; those of the front ranks made a deadly hedge while those more to the rear were left pointing straight up and allegedly gave some protection against missiles. The latter was mostly psychological. The depth of the phalanx, 16 ranks, was important also for psychological reasons – charging forward into the teeth of an oncoming wall of spear points was a daunting prospect – but it had real advantages too. The shock of impact was absorbed by the press of men behind the spears, and once the two phalanxes were jammed together a sort of gigantic rugby scrum then ensued, with the side with more 'pushing power' gradually driving the other back until it broke.

The phalanx was a potent formation but it required certain criteria to be effective. First, it needed level and clear terrain to get a run at the enemy. It could be broken up by difficult ground and once cohesion was lost it was largely ineffective. Second, the phalanx was very vulnerable to flank attack. It was not possible to wheel quickly to face a new opponent, especially with 6.4m (21ft) long pikes to handle. The phalanx was also vulnerable to infiltration. In the noise and dust of a clash, men jammed close together could not see what was going on around them. It was not unknown for light troops armed with daggers or swords to get inside a phalanx (usually from the side) and move among the phalangites stabbing as many as they could. Even if he realized he was about to be attacked, in the press it was difficult for a man to defend himself and of course by doing so he contributed to the disruption of the phalanx.

For this reason the phalanx was normally protected by lighter troops who kept the enemy's light forces from harassing it while it went about the business of winning the battle. Faced on its own terms, the only answer to a phalanx was another phalanx, and even then the clash would be bloody, if swift to a decision. It was a foolish enemy that allowed the massed pikes to come at him head-on.

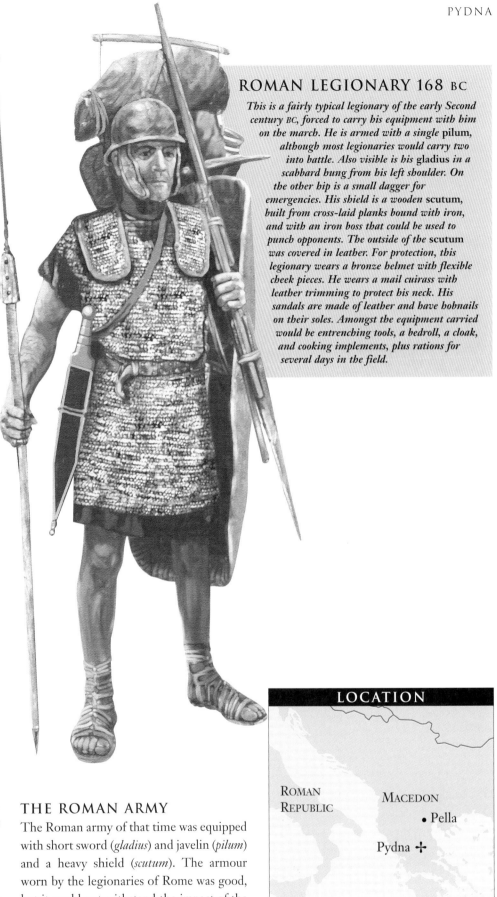

ROMAN LEGIONARY 168 BC

This is a fairly typical legionary of the early Second century BC, forced to carry his equipment with him on the march. He is armed with a single pilum, although most legionaries would carry two into battle. Also visible is his gladius in a scabbard hung from his left shoulder. On the other hip is a small dagger for emergencies. His shield is a wooden scutum, built from cross-laid planks bound with iron, and with an iron boss that could be used to punch opponents. The outside of the scutum was covered in leather. For protection, this legionary wears a bronze helmet with flexible cheek pieces. He wears a mail cuirass with leather trimming to protect his neck. His sandals are made of leather and have hobnails on their soles. Amongst the equipment carried would be entrenching tools, a bedroll, a cloak, and cooking implements, plus rations for several days in the field.

THE ROMAN ARMY

The Roman army of that time was equipped with short sword (*gladius*) and javelin (*pilum*) and a heavy shield (*scutum*). The armour worn by the legionaries of Rome was good, but it could not withstand the impact of the Macedonian *sarissa*. Long spears are extremely effective at penetrating armour, since they magnify the effort of the wielder by flexing, storing up energy in the wooden shaft. This is then delivered as the shaft tries to straighten, driving the point through whatever is in its path. A Roman soldier's

LOCATION

ROMAN REPUBLIC

MACEDON
• Pella

Pydna ✝

Pydna marked the end of Macedonian power in the Eastern Mediterranean, and the beginning of Roman hegemony. Macedon was divided into four republics under Roman protection.

PYDNA

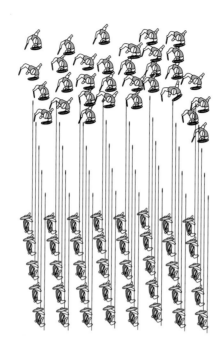

A Roman legion versus a phalanx: the legionaries throw their pila *in an attempt to disrupt the phalanx. They then close with the formation, trying to get into hand-to-hand combat range, where the superior sword-fighting skills of the Romans will tell.*

to defeat such a force? The answer lay in tactical manoeuvre, something that the Roman legions did very well and the phalanx hardly at all. The battle of Pydna in 168 BC is a textbook example of how the phalanx could be destroyed by an apparently inferior force.

THE MACEDONIAN WAR

The days of Macedonian greatness under Philip and Alexander were over, though the state remained powerful in Greek affairs. It was also supposedly a Roman ally. King Philip V of Macedon had supported Roman campaigns against the Aetolians and Seleucids. This was in his own interests to some extent, since he did not want powerful rival states to prosper. However, in time his interests began to diverge from those of Rome, and he began his own campaign of expansion into Thracian lands. Philip V was succeeded in 179 BC by his son Perseus, who continued his father's work. Perseus disposed of his brother, who was thought to be pro-Roman, and allied himself with Germanic tribes that were distinctly unfriendly to Rome.

armour and even his shield was scant protection against such force. True, the legionary had a heavy javelin he could hurl into the phalanx from beyond the range of its pikes, and this would undoubtedly cause casualties. But the phalanx was large and deep, and for each man in the Roman line there were several spear points. He now faced them with only his short sword.

Accounts of Roman troops engaging Greek forces tell of soldiers trying to beat aside the pikes with shield or sword, or grasping them and pulling them down. There were too many of them, though, and this tactic was wholly ineffective. The legionary force, facing an oncoming phalanx, was entirely outmatched in terms of equipment and fighting power. How then

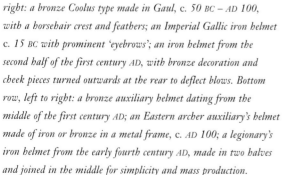

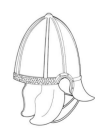

Roman legionary helmets and auxiliary helmets. Top row, left to right: a bronze Coolus type made in Gaul, c. 50 BC – AD 100, with a horsehair crest and feathers; an Imperial Gallic iron helmet c. 15 BC with prominent 'eyebrows'; an iron helmet from the second half of the first century AD, with bronze decoration and cheek pieces turned outwards at the rear to deflect blows. Bottom row, left to right: a bronze auxiliary helmet dating from the middle of the first century AD; an Eastern archer auxiliary's helmet made of iron or bronze in a metal frame, c. AD 100; a legionary's iron helmet from the early fourth century AD, made in two halves and joined in the middle for simplicity and mass production.

This was unacceptable in Rome, and so in 172 BC the legions marched on Macedon to instil a more appropriate attitude. An experienced army was put together – perhaps a little too experienced, as many of the veterans recruited to the legions were getting quite long in the tooth – and sent eastwards. Thus began the third Macedonian War. The Romans had encountered Greek forces many times since 280 BC when King Pyrrhus defeated the legions with a combination of phalanx and elephants. The campaign ultimately failed in the face of Roman tenacity rather than the fighting power of hastily raised citizen-legions, and Pyrrhus' main contribution to history was a phrase ('pyrrhic victory') referring to a battle won at high cost.

This time, however, things were different. Unlike Pyrrhus, Perseus had no elephants while the Romans did. The Roman force was highly experienced and well disciplined and, above all, confident. It numbered around 37,000 infantry and 2000 cavalry in the form of a consular army. In all, two legions of around 6000 infantry and 300 cavalry, plus supporting troops, advanced into Macedonia. Perseus met the consular army with some 39,000 infantry and 4000 cavalry.

Over half the Macedonian infantry was concentrated in the great phalanx, with supporting troops and mercenaries covering its flanks. It was a powerful but unwieldy force that Perseus took into battle with Rome. After some initial successes, Perseus went onto the defensive, hoping to defeat the Romans by use of good terrain in the mountains that formed the borders of Macedon. A Roman breakthrough forced the surrender of several cities but there was no decisive victory.

PAULLUS TAKES COMMAND

Rome was not satisfied with the results of the Third Macedonian War, and amid much arm-waving and wrangling in the Senate, Lucius Aemilius Paullus was appointed consul. He was 60 years old at the time, a seasoned campaigner in Spain and Liguria. His father had fallen at Cannae in 216 BC and he was brother-in-law to Scipio Africanus, who had defeated Hannibal at Zama in 202 BC.

Paullus was given command of the army that had fought against Perseus in the third Macedonian War, with a draft of fresh troops to bring it back up to establishment. He worked hard to train up his army and build morale among his veterans and new recruits alike, meanwhile carrying out reconnaissance of the enemy positions. One of Paullus' innovations was in the field of manoeuvre. Instead of simply ordering a formation to undertake a manoeuvre, which might cause chaos in a unit strung out along the line of march, Paullus implemented a policy of issuing warning orders to the tribune in charge, who would then plan the manoeuvre in conjunction with his centurions. When the time came to undertake the evolution, the unit was ready to implement it smoothly.

A lictor (a Roman civil official) on horseback carries the fasces, symbol of his office. The fasces was a bundle of sticks and an axehead, representing the power and strength in unity of the Roman people.

THE OPPOSED FORCES

ROMANS (estimated)
Total: 38,000

MACEDONIANS (estimated)
Total: 44,000

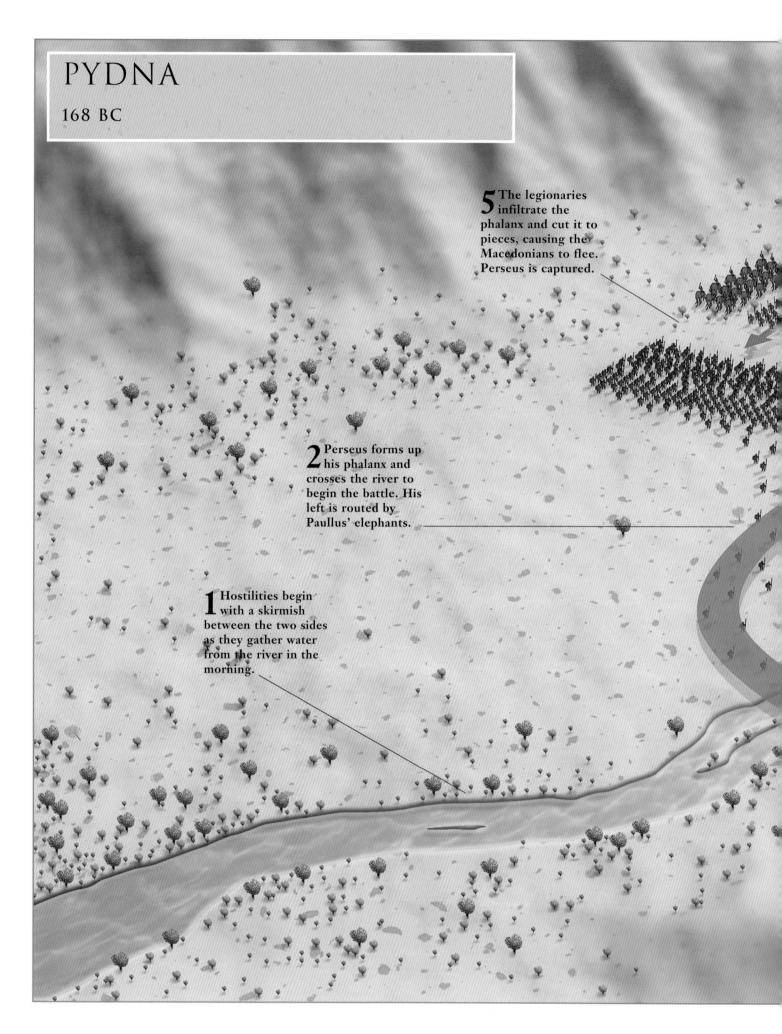

PYDNA
168 BC

5 The legionaries infiltrate the phalanx and cut it to pieces, causing the Macedonians to flee. Perseus is captured.

2 Perseus forms up his phalanx and crosses the river to begin the battle. His left is routed by Paullus' elephants.

1 Hostilities begin with a skirmish between the two sides as they gather water from the river in the morning.

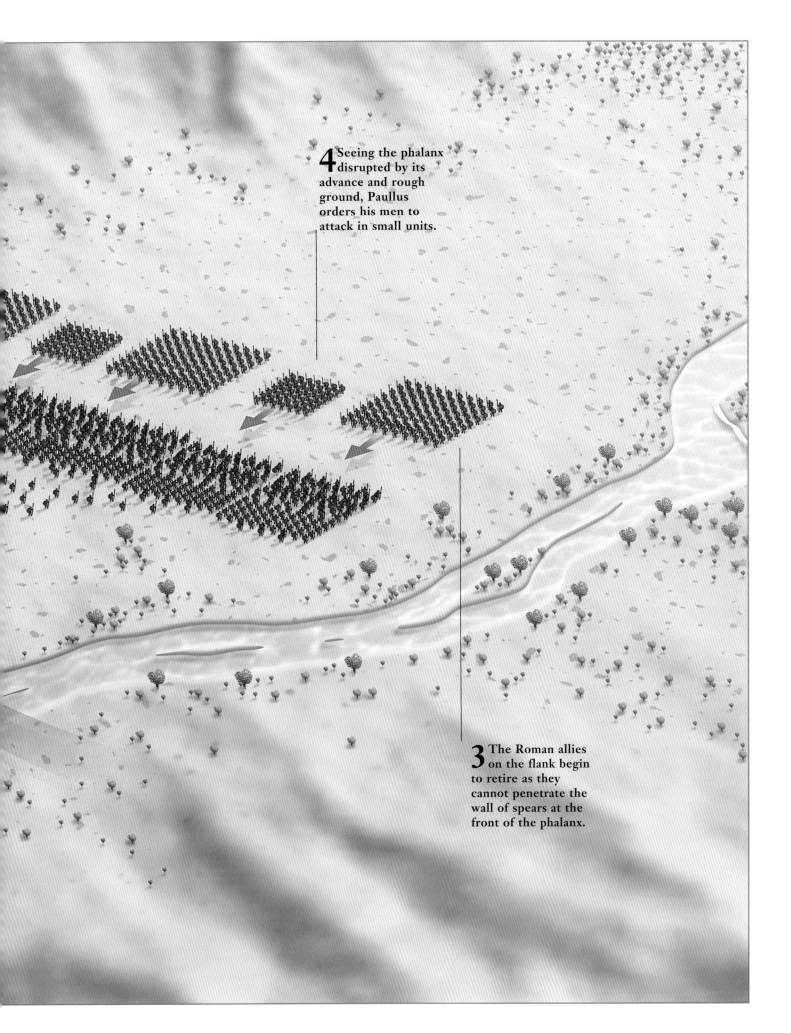

4 Seeing the phalanx disrupted by its advance and rough ground, Paullus orders his men to attack in small units.

3 The Roman allies on the flank begin to retire as they cannot penetrate the wall of spears at the front of the phalanx.

PYDNA

ENTERING MACEDON

Perseus had not been idle, and had created a line of fortifications in case the Romans renewed hostilities. Breaking through these fortifications was going to be a difficult task, and afterwards the real campaign would begin. Some centurions favoured a head-on assault on the forts, and this might well have worked but the cost might have jeopardized the subsequent campaign. Paullus had other ideas.

When the Romans got news that the Macedonians' most important allies had suffered a heavy defeat in Illyria, Paullus decided to take advantage of the moral effect on the Macedonians and began his advance. However, he opted to employ a stratagem rather than for a straightforward assault. Sending off a detachment, ostensibly to meet his fleet in Heracleum as if to conduct seaborne raids up the coast, Paullus began to make a series of demonstration attacks against Macedonian outposts in the mountains. These made no real impression, and Paullus kept the enemy's attention focused by being seen searching for an alternative route.

On the third day, Paullus' detachment made its strike. After moving to Heracleum, the force had secretly night-marched into position to force a pass. Attacking by surprise, the detachment broke through and advanced on Dium. With Romans in his rear, Perseus decided to retreat from his forward defence line and Paullus was able to advance unopposed.

THE MACEDONIANS STAND

As Perseus drew back from his forward positions and tried to concentrate his army, the Romans also reunited their forces. Perseus made his stand near the city of Pydna. Seeing the obvious determination of the Macedonians, Paullus did not launch an immediate assault, although he drew up his force in battle formation.

The Macedonians were less tired than their Roman pursuers, and had ample time to make ready for battle whereas the Romans were deploying from the line of march and while they were very good at this kind of evolution, the 'friction' inherent in all manoeuvre would have disrupted their dispositions somewhat. Paullus wisely

decided not to risk all on a headlong assault but waited and, when the Macedonians did not come at him, began to set up camp for the night. It was obvious to Paullus that Perseus wanted a fight here, on this ground, and Paullus was quite willing to give him one. However, he had no intention of doing so on Perseus' terms.

To tackle the phalanx head-on from a hasty deployment with tired troops would be sheerest folly, and Paullus had not marched all this way to throw away his army. That night there was a lunar eclipse, but some of Paullus' officers knew about it in advance and were able to reduce the effects the strange phenomenon had on their men. Paullus himself made a sacrifice of oxen and heifers, and the omens suggested that the Romans were best to remain on the defensive.

THE BATTLE BEGINS

Paullus had under his hand two Roman legions plus two allied Italian legions and supporting troops which included Numidian cavalry and 34 war elephants. It was the foreign troops who were camped nearest the enemy. A stream ran between the two forces and was used as a source of water by both sides. For some hours a wary and unspoken truce seemed to be in place as water was gathered before an incident over an escaped mule provoked fighting between troops watching the river on both sides, and as the conflict spread, both generals formed up their armies for battle.

The Macedonian force numbered some 38,000 infantry, of whom 21,000 formed the phalanx. There were also 4000 cavalry. Rather than challenge the phalanx immediately, Paullus launched his war elephants at the Macedonian left wing. This was ironic, since in previous wars the Greeks had fielded elephants against the Romans. Now the situation was reversed and the Macedonian left crumbled under the onslaught.

A reconstruction of the battle of Pydna demonstrating how the broken ground disrupted the Macedonian phalanx, allowing the Romans to close with the phalangites and use their superior swordsmanship to good effect.

PYDNA

This Victorian depiction of Paullus in triumph, complete with cherubic children and adoring common soldiers, is a typical example of nineteenth-century illustration of classical themes and scenes.

forward in the traditional manner, crushing its foes like a giant spiked steamroller. However, the phalanx inevitably lost some of its cohesion as it advanced uphill over the bodies of the fallen and in the face of stubborn resistance. Gradually its onslaught slowed to a crawl and was finally halted by the arrival of more Roman troops.

STALEMATE IN THE CENTRE

The central area of the battlefield was now the scene of a desperate infantry struggle. On one side the 16-deep Macedonian phalanx strove to resume its advance and regain its cohesion, and on the other the tough legionary maniples began to force their way into the gaps between the pike units. This was the great weakness of the phalanx; its strength was as a mass, and that mass had to all point in the same direction. Attacked from the flank, it was vulnerable. Infiltrated by enemy troops with more handy weapons it was what some day would be termed a 'target-rich environment'.

The clash had become a 'soldier's battle' where individual initiative and the actions of small units were decisive. This was where the Romans had the advantage, for their training and organization emphasized initiative, aggression and flexibility. Led by their centurions and enterprising soldiers, maniples and smaller bodies of Roman soldiers began forcing their way into the gaps in the pike hedge and attacking the phalangites from the flanks. Here, the deadly *gladius* was far more useful than the enormous *sarissa*.

THE BALANCE SHIFTS

Now the Macedonians were in deep trouble. Their left flank was shattered and the phalanx was under assault from within. There were no reserves to back it up – Greek armies rarely maintained a significant reserve – and the only way to meet this new challenge was for the phalangites to throw down their pikes and resort to their sidearms.

They were equipped with small shields and swords or daggers for self-defence, but their training with these was minimal and their morale was already dented by the aggressive Roman assault. The dropping of pikes was also an irrevocable act – there was

However, in the centre the legions had to face the mighty phalanx, and this proved to be a problem. Faced with a huge wall of long spears the Roman infantry were struggling to make any impression, and Paullus was doubtful of success. The legionaries fought hard to penetrate the hedge of spears, but those that were not killed outright were shoved back. Roman officers despaired. One 'rent his garments' in impotent fury. Another seized his unit's standard and flung it in among the enemy, and his men made a desperate charge to recapture it. They were beaten back despite inflicting some casualties.

Other Roman units were reluctant to close with the phalanx, and it pressed simply no way the phalanx could reform, regain its pikes and begin trying to win the battle again once the troops had resorted to their hand weapons. The balance had shifted and now the phalanx was fighting not for victory but for survival.

Against these inadequate weapons and training the *gladius*-armed Roman legionary was unstoppable. The *gladius* was primarily a thrusting weapon, and would kill or disable foes instantly with most blows. Even when used to cut, a less effective mode of operation, it was still deadly.

Roman troops could slam their heavy shields into a foe, driving him back against his fellows to pin him, despatch him quickly, and move on to the next target. Their blood was up and they wanted revenge against the phalanx that had recently been driving them back to defeat. Now, in the midst of the enemy formation, they took that revenge.

THE END COMES SWIFTLY

The great phalanx was shattered and the pursuit began. In ancient warfare casualties were usually fairly slight until one side broke, and then a massacre ensued. Pydna was no exception. Something like 25,000 Macedonians were reported killed or taken prisoner. Allowing for inflation on the part of the victors this is still a tremendous number, especially when Roman casualties are listed as being around 100 men.

Among the Romans there were several heroes. Paullus' son, Scipio Aemilianus, was thought lost for a while, but it turned out that he and a handful of friends had been pursuing the broken Macedonians. The son of another prominent Roman, Cato the Elder, lost his sword in the fighting and was determined to regain it. Gathering some followers he attacked every Greek in sight (history does not record with what) and finally recovered his precious weapon from under a heap of dead Macedonians.

There were also heroes on the Macedonian side. One elite unit of the phalanx, around 3000 men, put itself on high ground (or was cornered there) and fought to the bitter end, with the loss of almost every man. Other units were less heroic. At the collapse of the phalanx, most of the Macedonian cavalry fled the field. Perseus was among them. He retreated to his capital at Pella.

The Roman victory at Pydna was the result of flexibility and initiative rather than outright fighting power. The phalanx was more powerful than the units that opposed it, but more vulnerable to 'friction', which quickly eroded its effectiveness. With every moment of combat, every step forward over uneven ground and the bodies of the fallen, it lost cohesion. The phalanx had to win quickly, where the legion formation could battle on for hours without significant reduction in its capabilities. At Pydna, the legions did not have to do this; the battle was won in around an hour.

AFTERMATH

Perseus surrendered and was taken to Rome to be paraded through the city in celebration of Paullus' triumph. He pleaded not to be so humiliated, and Paullus replied by saying that he could always avoid it by committing suicide. Many towns were plundered by the Romans and vast numbers of Greeks were enslaved. The kingdom of Macedon was divided up into republics governed from Rome, and in time these were also dissolved. Macedon then became the first Greek province owned by Rome.

Perseus of Macedon surrenders to the Roman commander, Paullus. The victory at Pydna was considered worthy of a triumphal procession through Rome and although Perseus begged to be spared the humiliation, Paullus was not inclined to be merciful.

AQUAE SEXTAE
102 BC

THIS CAMPAIGN ESTABLISHED THE ROMAN PREFERENCE FOR LONG-SERVICE PROFESSIONAL TROOPS, WHO EARNED THEMSELVES THE NICKNAME OF 'MARIUS' MULES'. IT ALSO RESULTED IN SOME POLITICAL CHANGES IN ROME AND THE ETERNAL GLORY OF MARIUS HIMSELF, NAMED AS THE THIRD FOUNDER OF ROME.

WHY DID IT HAPPEN?

WHO A Roman consular army under Gaius Marius (157–86 BC), consisting of two legions and two *alae* of cavalry, plus supporting units for a total of around 30,000–35,000 Roman troops, versus a large number of warriors of the Germanic Teutones tribe.

WHAT Migration by the Germanic tribes threatened the security of Rome. Marius led his forces to deal with the problem and brought the enemy to decisive battle.

WHERE Aquae Sextae (now Aix-en-Provence) in southern France.

WHEN 102 BC.

WHY Friction between Rome and the Germanic tribes was constant, and the migratory nature of some tribes inevitably brought them into conflict with Rome.

OUTCOME The Germanic barbarians tried to charge uphill against formed and waiting legionary troops, and were crushingly defeated.

Conflict with the Germanic barbarians to the north was a constant threat for Rome around 100 BC. In 390 BC Rome itself had been sacked by a Gallic army under Brennus of the Senoncs, and invasions of Italy had occurred from time to time. Some of the Gauls and Germans were allies of Carthage, so deliberate attacks could be expected as well as more or less random conflicts caused by internal Germanic politics or tribal migrations.

MANPOWER PROBLEMS

True, much had changed for the Romans since Brennus smashed their hoplite army three centuries before. No longer using Greek-style tactics, the Romans now had a citizen-army built around a core of veterans and backed up by auxiliary and allied troops. Their equipment was very different, too, being suited to individual combat (though as part of a larger unit). Troops were armed with the *gladius*, a short sword ideally suited to close-quarters combat, plus a shield and a heavy javelin, or *pilum*.

At this time service in the Roman army was required of all citizens who owned more than a certain amount of property. However, service could be a problem. The maximum term of conscription was 16 years, but for the yeoman farmers who provided the bulk of the recruits, being away for even a year or two could be severely detrimental. Each campaign reduced the pool of available manpower a little further. Not all these people were killed, of course. Most were lost due to devaluation of their untended property whilst serving in garrisons in Gaul, Spain and Macedonia for years on end. The richest of Rome's citizens became ever richer as a result of overseas gains, and many used their money to buy up small estates that had fallen on hard times, working them with slaves who naturally were not available to serve in the army.

Thus not only was service in the army resented by those required to present themselves at need, but there were real concerns about the availability of sufficient manpower to maintain an effective military. By 107 BC, it had become normal to recruit troops from among the *proletarii*, even though these lowly citizens were not officially eligible for service under the existing laws.

A Celtic shield from the first century BC. Such shields were similar in size to the Roman scutum, *but were made of wooden planks covered with a stretched piece of hide, which was usually decorated.*

MARIUS' REFORMS

Gaius Marius was sent on campaign in Numidia in 107 BC in command of an army that was partly raised in the traditional manner, following the directives of the *dilectus* (the levying of soldiers for military service), and partly made up of professional soldiers recruited from the poorest of Rome's citizens.

Normally citizens of the classes eligible to be called for military service were expected to have appropriate weapons and equipment (exactly what was determined by their social class) and to have been taught to handle them during their adolescence. However, Marius' force was raised from scratch and had to be issued with weapons and equipment, for the new troops had none of their own. They also had to be trained in the use of their equipment and, perhaps most seriously, had no military traditions nor expectations to inspire them.

Marius was a skilled strategist and a good handler of troops. He trained his mixed force until it was an integrated military machine, and he blooded it in easy victories to improve its confidence. Marius was not a brutal disciplinarian – at least, not by Roman standards – but led by example and by appealing to the soldiers' pride. Marius prized mobility, and dispensed with

as much of his cumbersome baggage train as possible. This meant that each soldier had to carry his own equipment and food, and he was not permitted pack animals or slaves to help him. It became standard practice to carry the pack on a pole over the shoulder, so that it could be dropped quickly if action threatened.

As a leader of men, Marius had much in common with Napoleon Bonaparte. He would live among his soldiers in the same conditions and would eat the same rations. When the army camped, Marius would personally tour the defences and inspect the sentries. He was seen by his men to be a 'soldier's soldier' rather than a soft general who fell asleep in his tent as soon as the army halted. He spoke to the men under his command in the same rough soldiers' language, praised them when they deserved it and censured them when appropriate.

After his successful campaign in Numidia, Marius took over command of an army raised by Rutilius Rufus. This force was also largely recruited from among the *proletarii*. Rufus had implemented some training practices that became standard in the Roman army, partly because Marius

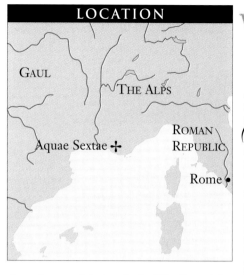

Aquae Sextae and the later battle of Vercellae sealed Marius' military reputation, and put an end to the danger to the Roman Republic from the migrant German horde.

LEGIONARIES

The primary weapon of the legionary was his deadly sword, used from behind the protection of his shield. Enemies were softened up before a charge, or their charges were broken up, by massed volleys of pila, or javelins. The pilum was a 'fire' weapon used to weaken the enemy so that the 'shock' effect of the legionary assault could more easily shatter his formations and drive him from the field. The combination of fire and shock has been a fundamental concept in successful tactics for centuries, and the Romans had it down to an art.

AQUAE SEXTAE

The might of Rome. The greatest advantage enjoyed by Roman forces lay in organization. Each man knew his job and with an effective command and control mechanism in place, sub-units or entire legions could be wielded like a surgical blade rather than the blunt instrument that so many barbarian armies represented.

THE OPPOSED FORCES

ROMANS (estimated)
Six legions, with cavalry
and auxiliaries: 35,000
German auxiliaries: 5000
Total: **40,000**

GERMANIC TRIBES (estimated)
Total: **110,000**

continued them. Soldiers were first given a wooden post to practise on, then they would fight other soldiers. The wooden training equipment was heavier than the standard-issue weapons and shields the legionaries would fight with in battle. It is telling that Rufus' army was specifically trained to fight Germanic barbarians. Marius continued Rufus' work, imposing his own leadership style and concentrating on physical fitness. He was hard on his troops, but played fair by them.

Exactly how fair Marius was is illustrated by an incident in camp involving his nephew, Gaius Lusius. Lusius was an officer, and had tried repeatedly to seduce a soldier named Trebonius despite a law that forbade homosexual activity in the army – it was punishable by death. The main reason for this law was that relationships between soldiers might weaken the command structure of the army. Lusius eventually

attacked Trebonius for refusing his advances, and Trebonius killed him. Trebonius was of course charged with the murder of a superior officer, but upon receiving testimony from the defendant and his comrades, Marius ruled that not only was Trebonius not guilty, but he should be awarded a *corona civica* for his actions, which had defended both his personal honour and the integrity of the legion. The fact that Marius would apply the law fairly even to a common soldier who had killed his nephew added to the general's reputation as a hard but fair man.

THE THREAT GROWS

However, while Marius was building his legend and training his army, the expected threat from the north was becoming a reality. Large numbers of Germanic tribesmen were on the march. A veritable flood of Ambrones and Teutones, plus lesser numbers of Cimbri and Scythians, were heading southwards in search of new land to settle. As they passed through Gallic lands, some Gauls also joined the march. Some accounts claim as many as 300,000 warriors plus their dependants, meaning that three quarters of a million or more people were on the move, though an exact figure is impossible to obtain. The migrants moved in groups of varying sizes along roughly parallel routes.

In Rome, the movement was observed with growing alarm. It was not clear exactly who these people were or where they had come from – nor why they had chosen to move – but the threat they posed to Rome was obvious. Already some areas had been plundered by raiding parties from the migrating tribes, and armies under Gnaeus Papirius Carbo and later Marcus Junius Silanus had been roughly handled by the Teutones.

In 107 BC, a consular army under Lucius Cassius Longinus was destroyed by the Tigurini tribe and the survivors enslaved. This triggered uprisings against Rome in Transalpine Gaul and although Quintus Servilius Caepio was able to suppress them, his joint expedition with Gnaeus Mallius Maximus in 105 BC ended in disaster. Jointly commanding a huge force, one of the largest ever fielded by Rome, Caepio and Maximus failed to work together effectively and were resoundingly defeated in a disaster that rivalled Cannae in its magnitude. Only the fact that the wandering tribes decided to enter Spain rather than Italy prevented another catastrophe.

MARIUS TO THE FORE

Things looked bad. It seemed that Rome could not field an effective army nor a competent commander, and that another sack of Rome was becoming inevitable. In desperation, Rome turned to Marius to provide a solution.

Marius was out of favour, mainly for his harsh criticism of Rome and her leaders, and in any case was forbidden by law from holding a consulship as he had already served a term within the last decade. Perhaps it was Marius' reputation for fairness that swayed the decision in the end, but for whatever reason Marius was elected consul for a second term and then, when the expected invasion of Italy was delayed, a third and a fourth.

Finally, in 102 BC, the threatened invasion materialized. The Ambrones and Teutones diverged from the rest of the migration and headed towards Italy. Marius had placed his force in a fortified blocking position, all the while maintaining a constant training regime and allowing his troops to become used to the sight of barbarians in order to reduce their fear of these unknown but reputedly invincible enemies. The Teutones attacked Marius' force in its fortified position, and were repulsed with heavy losses. The tribesmen broke off their attack and headed for Italy with Marius' army in pursuit.

The barbarians had given Marius what he wanted, however. Up to that point they had beaten every Roman force sent against them and had gained a reputation as

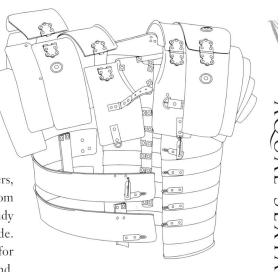

A reconstruction of the lorica segmentata *showing how the iron segments were held together with hooks and riveted leather straps to produce a flexible yet effective piece of armour.*

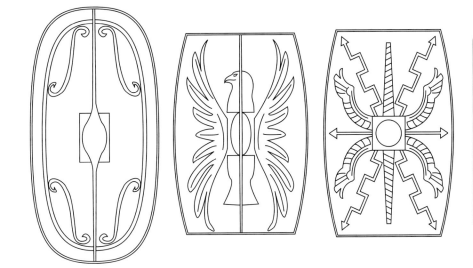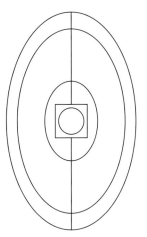

Roman legionary shields. From left to right: a scutum *used from the seventh century* BC *to around* AD *50; a 'squared-off'* scutum, *c. 10* BC, *used until c.* AD *175; a shield with a circular boss to save weight, c.* AD *20; a rectangular shield from c.* AD *40 used until after* AD *200; an oval shield used from c.* AD *150 to Rome's fall.*

AQUAE SEXTAE

102 BC

4 As Marius advances down the hill, Marcellus sends his men against the German rear, causing them to break and flee.

2 Marius takes up position on the hill at the end of the valley, waiting for the Germans to charge uphill.

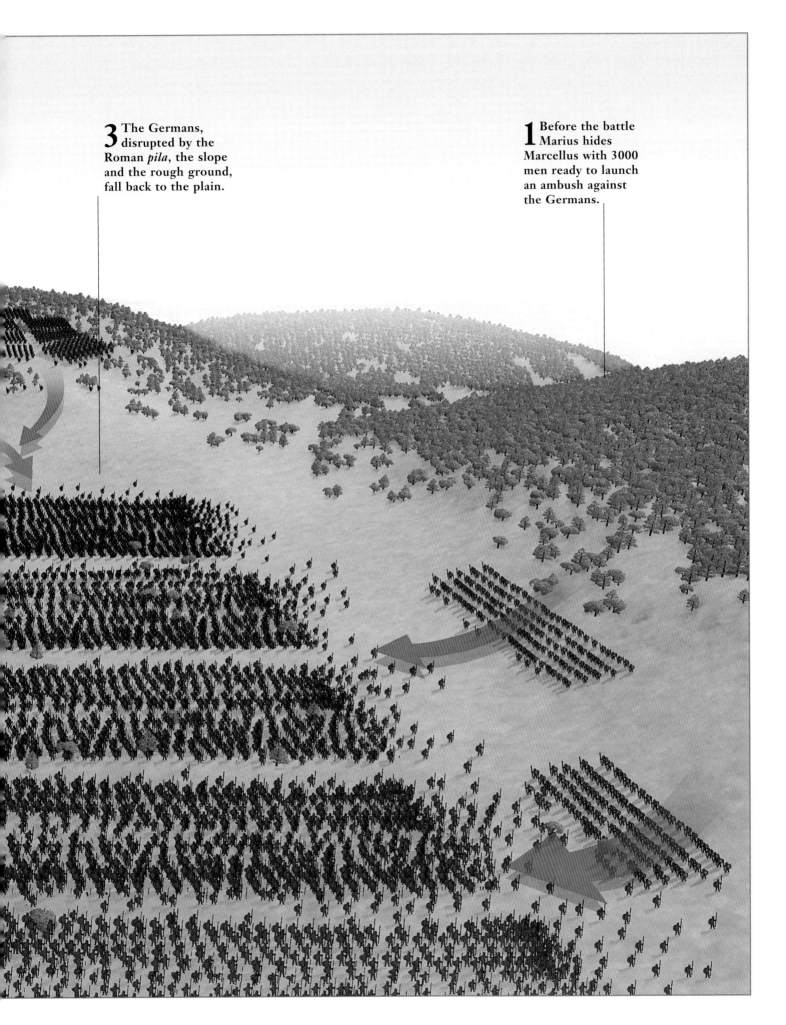

3 The Germans, disrupted by the Roman *pila*, the slope and the rough ground, fall back to the plain.

1 Before the battle Marius hides Marcellus with 3000 men ready to launch an ambush against the Germans.

AQUAE SEXTAE

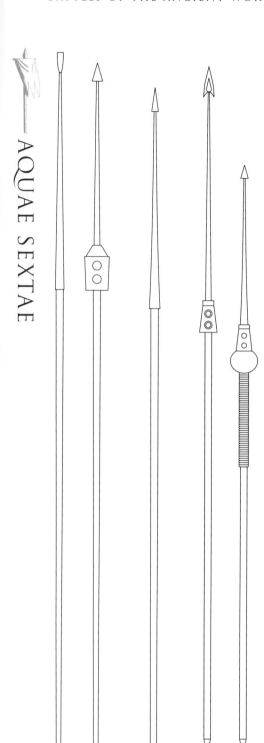

A selection of Roman pila. *From left to right: a fifth-century BC Etruscan version; a fourth-century BC* pilum *with riveted tang; a light* pilum *of the third century BC; a* pilum *of the first century AD; a* pilum *from AD 100 with an added bronze weight.*

tremendous fighters. Marius had shattered that myth, revealing to his men that they could beat this foe in a straight fight. And knowing that, it was time to have one.

Marius marched his army on a parallel course to the barbarians, and his long emphasis on fitness and marching training paid off when his force was able to intercept the enemy near Aquae Sextae, which today is called Aix-en-Provence.

As always the Roman army built itself a fortified camp while parties were sent out to collect water. The watering parties were attacked by Germanic warriors, and Roman forces went to their aid. These included Ligurian auxiliaries and some legionaries, who quickly established dominance over the barbarians. The tribal warriors, mainly Ambrones, were repulsed with heavy losses and the Roman force settled into its camp to rest, ready for the coming fight.

DISPOSITIONS

The barbarians were quite well organized. Their force was made up of experienced and even somewhat disciplined warriors who fought in a dense formation. However, their equipment left a lot to be desired. Most men were armed with a spear with a soft iron head, which was very poor against an armoured opponent. There was little armour among the tribes, so the dense formation made a wonderful target for missile weapons such as the massed *pila* of the legions. Some warriors were equipped with stolen or captured equipment, including Roman gear, but they were in the minority. Thus for all their physical prowess and organization, the barbarian warriors were at a disadvantage against the better equipped and organized Roman force.

Marius was confident of his legions' ability to manoeuvre and to obey orders, and had faith that his legionaries could outfight the Germanic warriors either man-for-man or in units. Taking advantage of the close terrain – the battle took place in a valley surrounded by steep sides, with heavy forestation – Marius sent off a force to make a flank march. Having detached six cohorts, around 3000 men, under the tribune Claudius Marcellus, Marius drew up the rest of his force for battle. He retained

personal control of the cavalry, using it to screen his deployment. Then he took his place in the front rank of the legion and awaited the barbarian attack.

Marius had so far done everything right. His soldiers knew they could beat this enemy, because they had already done so. They had faith in their leader, who shared their hardships and treated them well. Now he stood, sword in hand, in the front rank. At 56 years old and a Roman consul, some would say Marius had no place in the actual fighting, but his presence there was an inspiration to his men. If such an important man, at his age, who did not have to be there, would stand against the first charge, could they do any less? They could not, and Marius knew it.

Now, all Marius needed was for the enemy to oblige him and charge.

BROKEN CHARGE

The Germanic warriors were an aggressive and hot-blooded lot, in whose society personal courage counted for a great deal. The stolidly waiting legionaries presented a target they could not resist, and so they advanced uphill to the attack. As the Germans advanced into range, the legionaries hurled their *pila*, drew their swords and set to work. The charge was slowed and disrupted by the slope and the close terrain, and the shower of javelins exacted a heavy toll among the Germanic warriors, made worse by their lack of protection and dense formation.

The two forces came into contact, Romans stabbing confidently at their tired opponents, working together as a coherent unit while the barbarians were disrupted by the struggle uphill and the slaughter caused by the *pila*. The fight became a bitter close-quarters struggle in which the Romans' professionalism and training met Germanic aggression and courage. The decisive

Opposite: A bust of Gaius Marius. Not only did Marius reform the Roman army into its classic (and most effective) form, but his campaign saved Italy from invasion and may have prevented the sack of Rome. He restored the confidence of the army and was rightly praised as the saviour of his people.

MARIC

AQUAE SEXTAE

This early Twentieth-century book illustration shows Germanic warriors charging a Roman legion. Although effective in battles such as Teutoberger Wald (AD 9), the concentrated warrior charge relied on massed momentum to be successful. At Aquae Sextae, Roman tactics and weaponry proved superior.

weapon was the *gladius*, which was ideally suited to such combat while the barbarians' spears were not only clumsy but also hard-pressed to penetrate Roman armour.

THE BARBARIANS RALLY

Inevitably, the Teutones were pushed back down the hill with their foes in close contact. Still they would not break and on the level ground at the bottom of the valley they rallied and began to form a shield wall. This would have been tough to penetrate and might have held the Romans, but for the intervention of the flanking force.

The shield wall was a classically 'barbarian' tactic whereby each man overlapped his shield slightly with that of his neighbour, effectively creating a barricade from behind which to fight. Spears were an excellent weapon to fight with in a shield wall, since they could thrust out and did not require a great deal of movement, unlike swung weapons like axes or the slashing swords used by many barbarian tribes. Men in the rear ranks could add their weapons to the fight, creating a hedge of points facing each enemy trying to cut his way into the wall.

A shield wall was primarily a defensive tactic, which suggests that the Teutones' morale may have been severely dented. They were no longer fighting to win but were trying to survive the Roman

onslaught. Had they succeeded in repulsing the Roman attack in turn, they might have been sufficiently heartened to resume the offensive. However, the final blow was about to fall.

FLANKING FORCE ARRIVES

While Marius' force held the enemy's front and drew the complete attention of the barbarian warriors, Marcellus entered the fray with his six cohorts. Attacking from the rear with added momentum imparted by the slope, the Romans crashed into their enemies with an impact that was as shocking to morale as it was physically.

The Teutones were smashed. Those nearest the point of impact were cut down straight away. The formation broke up, allowing Marius' men to storm through the shield wall. The fast-striking *gladius* was deadly here too, slaying anyone who did not flee fast enough.

Within moments the Teutones' force had dissolved into a routing mass, with the Romans in vigorous pursuit. The barbarians' camp was stormed, sacked and burned, with many non-combatants killed in the process.

Some Roman sources claim as many as 100,000 were killed, including warriors and non-combatants. Enemy casualties are always inflated in Roman accounts of their victories, but it is plausible the figure is not very much exaggerated. What is certain is that the Teutones had ceased to be a threat to Rome. Several of their chieftains were captured and taken to Rome where they were publicly executed by strangulation.

AFTERMATH

The Cimbri were still advancing on Italy, and before Marius could celebrate his victory he was sent against them in turn. Bringing his army from Gaul he confronted the invaders on the plain of Vercellae. Although the Cimbri were better equipped than the Teutones, 'Marius' Mules' were tougher, better trained and physically fitter, and after a fierce battle fought amid huge clouds of dust thrown up by the cavalry of

both sides, finally overwhelmed their adversaries and ended the threat of the Cimbri to Rome.

Marius was hailed as a great hero and revered as a third founder of Rome. He eventually served as consul no less than seven times. Many of the practices of his victorious force became standard in the Roman army. Thus it was that future legionaries were recruited mainly from among the poor, carried their own kit and were subjected to a harsh training regime that kept them fit to march and fight. In many ways, Marius' successful defence of Italy ushered in a new era for the Roman army and established the pattern for its many successes in future years.

After smashing the Teutones, Marius went on to defeat the Cimbri in a hard-fought battle. The Roman army marched faster than news of the Teutones' defeat – at this parley before the battle, the Cimbri demand land and concessions for themselves and their Teutone allies, not knowing that they had already been defeated.

CARRHAE
53 BC

CRASSUS' PARTHIAN CAMPAIGN OF 53 BC WAS ONE OF THE GREAT MILITARY DISASTERS OF ROMAN HISTORY. A ROMAN INFANTRY FORCE OF 42,000 WAS HARRIED TO DEFEAT BY HORSE ARCHERS, WHOSE TACTIC OF THE 'PARTHIAN SHOT' HAS ENTERED THE LANGUAGE.

WHY DID IT HAPPEN?

WHO The Romans under Marcus Licinius Crassus (115–53 BC) made an unprovoked invasion of Parthian territory.

WHAT The Romans formed a hollow square, but 5500 were lured out in pursuit of the horse archers and massacred by the cataphracts. The rest were steadily shot down. An overnight halt at the unprovisioned town of Carrhae failed to halt the killing.

WHERE Carrhae, 48km (30 miles) south of Edessa in Syria.

WHEN 53 BC.

WHY Crassus needed a military success to further his political rivalry with the other Triumvirs, Pompey and Julius Caesar.

OUTCOME Only 5000 of the Roman army escaped, 10,000 surrendered, and the rest, including Crassus, were slaughtered.

Over the centuries there have been many excuses for starting a war. One of the most despicable is simply to further one's own career and yet this is what the enormously rich and jovial Marcus Licinius Crassus did. He had supported the winning side in the Roman civil war between Sulla and Marius and taken a large part in the destruction of the Slave Revolt under Spartacus in 73–71 BC, as had Gnaeus Pompey (106–48 BC). In the turbulent politics of the Roman Republic, Crassus, Pompey and new boy on the block Gaius Julius Caesar (100–44 BC) formed a stable, but unofficial, political clique which became known as the Triumvirate. Caesar won military laurels in his conquest of Gaul, and Pompey had achieved great success against the pirates in the Eastern Mediterranean, so

Crassus needed something similar to maintain his position in the gang of three. When he was made consul, for the second time, at the age of 60, he made his plans and chose his victim. Parthia, modern Iraq, Iran and more besides, was known to be fabulously wealthy. The Arsacid Parthian tribe had come from northeastern Iran and taken over the empire from the successors of Alexander the Great's conquest of Persia, a process completed around 174 BC. Other eastern states, Crassus reasoned, had proved to be fairly easily conquerable by Rome, so why not Parthia? This was a misjudgment for which he and his men would pay dearly.

THE CAMPAIGN BEGINS
The Romans had little experience of fighting against this new foe. In campaigns

Roman General Marcus Lucinius Crassus. A recurring failing throughout human history is the triumph of greed and ambition over knowledge and ability. His expedition against Parthia was simply his attempt to score one over his political rivals Pompey and Caesar. He hoped for glory and riches, he got tragedy and death.

in the north and west of modern Turkey they had encountered armies with a familiar Macedonian heritage: large numbers of infantry armed with pikes, spears and javelins, and lightly armoured cavalry like their own. There were also a few cataphracts. These were altogether a new troop type and the Romans were unable to emulate them for nearly 400 years. Now they would meet an army whose backbone was entirely composed of these new troops. They were supported by mounted archers and there was, in the field at least, a complete absence of any infantry at all. Furthermore, the Romans were accustomed to fighting in mixed terrain – rivers, hills, villages and so on. This made it easy to delineate the boundaries where they might expect to fight and to identify key objectives on the battlefield. Rome's legions were unused to the vast emptiness of the north Syrian Desert.

Crassus left Rome in November 55 BC, having summoned seven legions with their attendant light infantry and cavalry, hired 1000 Gallic cavalry from what is now France and engaged 6000 local Arabs to form his army. In his haste to sail from Brundisium in the heel of Italy he lost several ships with all their crews to winter storms.

He was faced with two principal alternative routes into the Parthian Empire. He could take the northerly route through the mountains and passes of Turkey then turn south down the Tigris. This was a longer route, but hilly and mountainous terrain favoured the infantry, while marching alongside a river secured at least one flank and ensured a water source for thirsty men and animals, and supplies carried on boats meant less fodder for draught animals. Or he could cross the desert along one of the trade routes. It would be more than 500 years before they were called the Silk Road. This was shorter but more appropriate to all cavalry armies like the Parthians and it was harder to keep an army supplied with water. An army the size of Crassus' would need more than 100,000 litres (22,000 gallons) of water every day for the fighting troops alone.

Crassus brought his army overland through modern Turkey. When he crossed the Euphrates and arrived in Parthian territory a number of cities capitulated without a fight. But, one, Zendotia, had to be assaulted with the loss of 100 men. The population was sold into slavery and all valuables added to the growing pile of booty. The cities were garrisoned, taking a further precious 7000 infantry and 1000 cavalry from his force and he retired into winter quarters in Syria to wait out the winter rains, which turned the desert into a

LOCATION

• Byzantium

ROMAN EMPIRE

Carrhae ✝

Carrhae was the result of the Romans' first campaign against the Parthians, who gave their name to the 'Parthian shot', an arrow delivered as the bowman fled on his horse.

The Roman Legionaries who marched into Parthia were ill equipped to meet their foe. Their feet were very vulnerable to arrows and their shields and mail armour were inadequate against the lances of the Parthian armoured horsemen, known as cataphracts. Their own spears, pila, were thrown at short range so had no chance of hitting the longer ranged mounted archers.

THE OPPOSED FORCES

PARTHIANS
Cataphracts:	1000
Horse archers:	10,000
Total:	**11,000**

ROMANS
Legionary infantry:	28,000
Light infantry:	4000
Gallic cavalry:	1000
Roman cavalry:	3000
Arab cavalry:	6000
Total:	**42,000**

muddy quagmire, and the arrival of the Gallic cavalry. At this juncture, the Parthians sent emissaries who politely enquired whether this was a raid at the personal instigation of Crassus or war declared by the Roman state. They were remarkably better informed about Roman affairs than the Romans were about Parthian matters! Crassus, as consul, was able to declare that this was official.

DISPOSITIONS
In May, he again crossed the Euphrates at Zeugma and, against the advice of the Armenian king but at the behest of a reputedly double-dealing guide, headed off on the desert road to the city of Seleucia, 30km (18.6 miles) south of modern Baghdad. The Parthian response was twofold. The king, Orodes II, who had recently beaten his rival in a two-year civil war, led an army into Armenia to preoccupy the Armenians and prevent them from joining forces with the Romans. Their armoured

cavalry, with horse and foot archers, would have been a good match for the Parthians and the advice of their experienced king would have been invaluable to Crassus. This also placed the Parthian king's army on the distant flank of the advancing Romans.

Meanwhile the Parthian regional governor, the Surena, gathered his forces to directly oppose Crassus' advance. When scouts reported the presence of this force, Crassus first formed his army into a long thin line. Then, having been advised of the impossibility of securing his flanks in such open terrain against a cavalry army, he re-formed his forces into a huge hollow square. Forming the line, even half-heartedly, then re-forming it into square would have taken a long time. This was not a rehearsed battlefield drill movement.

So issuing the orders, transmitting them and getting the right troops in the right place with all four corners touching and no gaps between units could easily have taken two and a half hours. The Parthian army must have been a long way distant but their scouts would certainly have witnessed this spectacle. Certainly tempers would have frayed dreadfully inside the square as the troops marched and counter-marched to get into position and got hotter and thirstier in the sun.

THE 'PARTHIAN SHOT'

By this period, the Roman army had been reorganized, the principal architect being the consul Marius, who had lost the civil war with Sulla. He had abandoned the four types of foot soldier (*velites*, *principes*, *hastati* and *triarii*) and instead adopted one type of soldier, the legionary, with all his equipment being provided by the state as well as regular pay and a pension. He was armed with the *pilum*, a heavy javelin, and the *gladius*, a short stabbing sword. A bronze helmet, the familiar semi-cylindrical shield and a short-sleeved mail tunic provided his protection. The tactical unit, known as a maniple, of 80 men was replaced with the cohort of 480 men, except the first cohort of each legion, which was 800 strong.

Each side of Crassus' square was composed of 12 cohorts, about 5700 infantry. Allowing for campaign losses this would make a square of about 1300m (1422 yards) on each side. In addition a body of cavalry providing a local, mobile counter-strike capability supported each cohort. In the centre of the square were all the baggage and camp-followers, plus the light infantry and a reserve of legionaries as well as the cavalry. It would have been very cramped and, in the absence of sanitary arrangements, very smelly!

In this formation they crossed a small stream but were not allowed to camp or rest. Instead they pressed on until the enemy came in sight, at which point the

The Parthian horse archer rode a small pony of 11–12 hands. He had a very rapid gait, which makes a fairly stable ride and therefore a good platform to shoot from. The horse archer could shoot through about 270 degrees. The only blind spot was to his rear right. His sophisticated bow was made from laminated wood and sinew, and had a range of 150 metres (500 ft).

6000 Arab horse rode off. Well, they had been paid and they knew how good the Parthians were at fighting in such conditions. The Surena immediately began to play on the morale of the Romans. He had ordered his armoured cavalry, the cataphracts, to conceal their armour until a given signal. When this was given, the Romans were dazzled by light glinting off the polished metal scales on heavily armoured cavalrymen riding heavily armoured horses. The Romans had nothing to match it. Their legionaries' only armour was a short-sleeved mail tunic reaching to the mid-thigh; and mail, whilst being good protection against a cutting blow, was very poor against a penetrating thrust from lance or arrow. These Parthian cataphracts were covered from head to toe in a coat of small metal plates sewn on to a cloth or leather backing. This gave good protection against ordinary bows, a

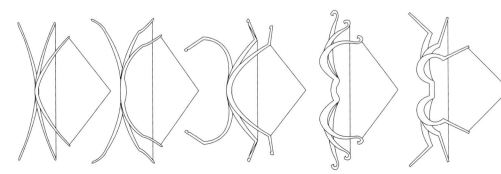

Different ancient bows, from the simplest on the left to the most advanced composite on the right. The diagram shows the bows in three positions: before stringing, at rest when strung, and when fully drawn, ready to release an arrow.

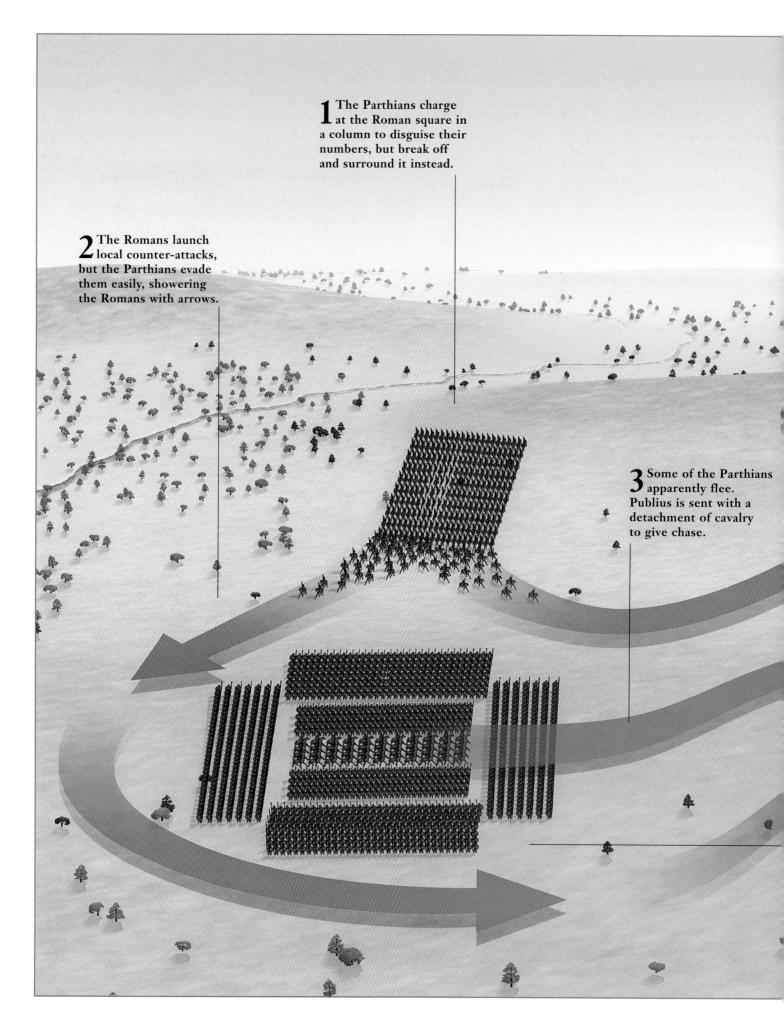

1 The Parthians charge at the Roman square in a column to disguise their numbers, but break off and surround it instead.

2 The Romans launch local counter-attacks, but the Parthians evade them easily, showering the Romans with arrows.

3 Some of the Parthians apparently flee. Publius is sent with a detachment of cavalry to give chase.

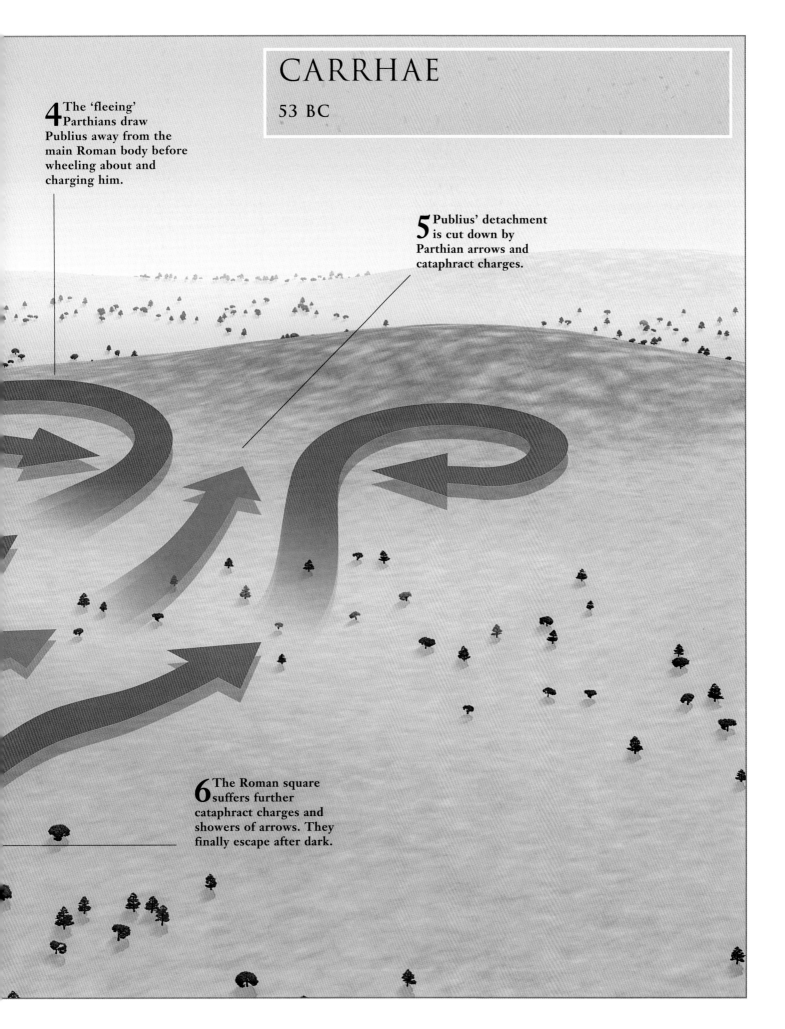

CARRHAE
53 BC

4 The 'fleeing' Parthians draw Publius away from the main Roman body before wheeling about and charging him.

5 Publius' detachment is cut down by Parthian arrows and cataphract charges.

6 The Roman square suffers further cataphract charges and showers of arrows. They finally escape after dark.

CARRHAE

cutting stroke or a thrust, unless it came from below. Modern reconstructions have also proved this armour to be remarkably flexible. Even their horses, considerably bigger than the average European horse, carried twice as much armour as a single legionary. However, the Surena only had 1000 such warriors. The rest were bow-armed, pony-mounted steppe tribesmen, but he had 10,000 of these. Whereas the cataphract cavalry were encumbered by armour, the horse archers relied on the nimbleness of their ponies to keep them out of trouble.

They had two principal tactics. A formation the Romans knew as 'scythian' whereby a small group would ride round in a rough circle within range of the enemy. Those nearest would loose their arrows and while they rode around would fetch, nock and draw the next arrow ready to loose again when they came to the front of the circle. This laid down a continuous high volume of fire on a fairly confined area. The 'Parthian shot' was their other tactic. Riding directly away from his enemy at speed the archer would skew anti-clockwise round in his saddle and shoot his bow directly over his horse's rump.

A right-handed man had a blind spot to his right rear quarter. This was a very difficult manoeuvre to counter. One either had to lay down a greater barrage of missiles, which the Romans did not possess, or catch the horse archers against terrain they could not cross, like a river. The best answer the Romans developed was mobile bolt-throwers which had a range of 400m (437 yards) and were very accurate. But they came 150 years too late to help Crassus and his men.

The Romans braced themselves to receive a charge, but it did not come. Instead, the horse archers spread around the square and closed in to do their work. At a range of perhaps 120m (131 yards) they would let fly with their arrows. Although Crassus' army included light troops, probably less than half of these would have had bows, just 1500, which were not enough to counter the massive missile superiority of the Parthians.

Fairly early on in the battle Crassus ordered a counter-attack by his other light troops but these were easily forced back by a hail of arrows. The Romans' problems were that they could not catch the light cavalry and they could not stop them shooting their arrows, and all the time they were taking casualties. There was no prospect of the Parthians running out of ammunition as they had brought up a whole camel train laden with arrows. Crassus ordered his son Publius, who was in command of the Gallic cavalry, to see what he could do. He led them plus 300 other horse, 500 foot archers and eight cohorts of legionaries out to attack the horse archers. They simply rode on before him firing backwards over their horses at the rapidly advancing Romans. Publius and his force followed on until they were a considerable distance from the main square. Then the horse archers turned. Others joined them from the flanks and the armoured cavalry blocked their front.

Expecting to be charged, the Romans halted. But this just made an easier target for the archers, who never stopped launching their deadly rain. The infantry were suffering dreadful wounds in their exposed legs and arms and were beginning to resemble bloody pincushions. They could not go on. The cavalry made a brave attempt but they were unarmoured, other than a shield, and only carried light spears about 1.8m (6ft) long. The Parthians carried lances twice that length.

Although they came to grips, the Gauls, who were also suffering from the unaccustomed heat, were soundly beaten. The force retreated to a hillock and formed a shield wall on foot in serried ranks on its slopes. This just gave the archers a better target. Of the 5500 who sallied forth just 500 were taken prisoner by the Parthians. The rest were shot by arrows or ridden down by the cataphracts. Crassus' son Publius was amongst the dead.

Right: Roman cavalry chase fleeing barbarian infantry. The Romans usually used their cavalry to either cover the flanks of their infantry or pursue a retreating enemy. At Carrhae, this limited role was exposed by superior Parthian cavalry tactics: Publius' cavalry detachment were isolated and destroyed by Parthian horse archers and cataphracts.

CARRHAE

This sculpture from the second century shows a Parthian horse archer. The horse archers would normally operated in a loose line in front of and within range of the enemy. Within that line small groups of archers rode round in a circle shooting and reloading in turn. This presented a constantly moving target to the enemy. If charged they turned and fled, shooting backwards, the famous Parthian shot, as they went.

THE END

The Parthians then returned to attack the shrinking square, bringing Publius' head mounted on a spear. As the horse archers continued their work, the cataphracts made a series of controlled charges, murderously effective in a small area, but quickly pulling back if they seemed threatened. There simply were not enough of these heavy cavalry to plough through the whole Roman army, where they risked being overwhelmed by the more numerous legionaries. Eventually dusk fell and the Parthians pulled back about 16km (10 miles) to avoid a night attack, and made camp.

There could be no rest for the Romans. 300 cavalry made it overnight to the town of Carrhae, modern Harran, but instead of stopping there they merely informed the garrison commander of the battle, but not the result, and rode on to re-cross the Euphrates at Zeugma. Back with the main army, 4000 wounded had to be abandoned on the field and the rest made a long, weary and frightening night march to Carrhae, to be finally escorted in by the garrison in the small hours of the following morning, except for four cohorts, which had got lost in the dark.

When the Parthians returned to the battlefield, they slaughtered the wounded and set off to locate Crassus and the remains of the army. They came across the lost cohorts and made short work of finishing them off. While the Romans huddled in Carrhae, the Parthians swept the plain for stragglers, so it was the next morning before the Surena and his host arrived at the walls

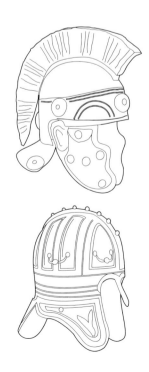

Right: Roman cavalry helmets. Clockwise from top left: an 'Attic' type, first century BC, made of iron with bronze decoration; an officer's crested helmet from c. AD 75, again with bronze decoration; next is an iron helmet from c. AD 350, made in two halves and joined in the centre; the last is an iron or bronze helmet from c. AD 250, with a hinged mask attached by a leather strap.

of the city. Here he demanded that Crassus and his second-in-command, Cassius, be handed over in chains.

Although this demand was rejected, the army seems to have lost all confidence in Crassus. There were insufficient supplies in the town for the survivors so another night march was necessary. Crassus placed his faith in the Arab guide who had already proved faithless and tried another night march to escape north to the hills and Armenia. This went round in circles in the dark and eventually Cassius led some back to Carrhae. About 5000 men, under a commander called Octavian, made it to a hilly district called Sinnaca. Crassus was still outside the city, lost in a marshy area with his 'guide', four cohorts, a handful of cavalry and the five lictors (they carried the axes and rods symbolizing Roman justice) appropriate to his office. After all the fighting this force numbered perhaps 1500. As they were attacked by the Parthians, Octavian's men managed to join them and drove off the first assaults. The Surena then offered terms but a brawl ensued between the Roman officers and the Persian servants during which Crassus, Octavian and the other officers were killed. Leaderless, the rest of the army surrendered.

AFTERMATH

The Romans admitted to 20,000 killed and 10,000 captured, 5000–6000 fighting their way out. A number of the prisoners were shipped out to the far east of the Parthian Empire where 200 found themselves garrisoning a city in Sogdiana under the command of a lunatic nomad leader called Chi-Chi who had managed to rouse the ire of the Chinese. The 40,000-strong Chinese army easily captured the city, killing Chi-Chi in the process. Amongst the captives were 145 survivors of Carrhae who were shipped further east to garrison the town of

Li-chien in Khansu province. With the Roman army eliminated, peace was agreed between the Parthian and Armenian kings. The Parthians went on to try and capture Antioch but could make no progress against the walls because they had brought no siege equipment. However, Cassius and 5000 survivors were able to ambush the retiring army and inflicted a significant defeat on them.

The Armenians successfully played Roman off against Parthian, or their successors, the Sassanians, for hundreds of years before finally becoming a Roman province. The Romans and their successors, the Byzantines, fought the Parthians and

A romantised version of the death of Spartacus, slave gladiator of the Romans. He led a revolt against his masters which they found difficult to put down. In the end Marcus Lucinius Crassus succeeded in quelling the revolt and 5,000 slaves were crucified along the Appian Way as a warning to the others.

their successors, the Sassanians, again on numerous occasions. Finally the newly Islamic Arabs swept north from the Arabian peninsula and took over the Persian world, culture and technology and eventually also took the Byzantine capital, Constantinople, which we now know as Istanbul.

ALESIA
52 BC

THE FALL OF ALESIA WAS THE DEATH KNELL FOR GALLIC INDEPENDENCE. DEFEATED BY THE ROMAN ARMIES UNDER GAIUS JULIUS CAESAR, THE GAULS FELL UNDER THE SWAY OF THE EXPANDING REPUBLICAN EMPIRE. OPERATIONS CONTINUED INTO THE FOLLOWING YEAR BUT IT WAS AT ALESIA THAT THE GAULS WERE BROKEN.

WHY DID IT HAPPEN?

WHO Roughly 70,000 Roman troops under Gaius Julius Caesar (100–44 BC), versus around 80,000 infantry and 15,000 cavalry under the Gallic chieftain Vercingetorix (d. 46 BC) besieged inside the fortress. Perhaps as many as 250,000 more Gauls formed the relief army.

WHAT The Roman forces built extensive field fortifications to pen the Gauls within their fortress and to prevent relief. Gallic reinforcements and relief efforts were beaten off and the siege was maintained.

WHERE Mount Auxois, near what is now Dijon in France.

WHEN 52 BC.

WHY Julius Caesar embarked on a campaign to pacify Gaul and bring the Gallic tribes within the empire. The Gauls resisted fiercely.

OUTCOME Break-out and relief attempts were contained, and finally the starving Gauls were forced to surrender.

It has been said many times that history is written by the victors. In the case of *The Gallic War*, this is literally true – Julius Caesar himself wrote the definitive account of the campaign and his role in it. He uses a third-person perspective throughout, giving the illusion of objectivity, but the fact is that Caesar wrote the history of his own campaign. How much of his account is self-publicity and how much is truthful journalism is open to conjecture. Additional books were written by others after the mopping-up operations in 51 BC and generally agree with Caesar's account of events during the campaign.

Gaius Julius Caesar rose to military prominence fairly late in life, in his forties. He did have a solid background as a solider

of Rome, however, having won a *corona civica* whilst on campaign in Asia in 80–78 BC. He was taken hostage by pirates on his voyage home, and after being ransomed took his revenge. On his own initiative, Caesar raised local forces and smashed the pirates. He probably served as a military tribune in 72 BC and may have fought in the campaign against Spartacus' revolt, which began the previous year.

Like all Roman field commanders he was a political figure as well as a military one. He had held office as praetor and *Pontifex Maximus*, and governorship of three provinces had been conferred on him. He was thus responsible for both military and political command (the two were inextricably entwined) within a large region

A reconstructed fort at modern-day Alesia. The double ditch and abatis (sharp poles projecting from the wall) were not intended to stop intruders so much as to slow them down so that missile fire from within the fort could kill more of them. After a struggle through the ditch under fire, the wall with its brushwood palisade and frequent towers was a formidable obstacle.

of the empire, which included Transalpine Gaul and Cisalpine Gaul.

Later Caesar would use 'his' army to make him master of Rome but at the outset of the campaign in 58 BC, Caesar was no more than an officer of the Republic tasked with the subjugation of Gaul and given the resources to tackle this difficult task. He was an important and powerful man when he led his army into Gaul, but it was during the Gallic campaigns that he went beyond being a servant of Rome and became potentially her master.

THE CAMPAIGN OPENS

Caesar's Gallic campaign was triggered by the migration of the Helvetii people in search of more fertile land to support their growing population. This move would take them into Transalpine Gaul, and Caesar was determined to prevent any incursions into Roman territory. He rushed to the frontier to take stock of the situation.

Although the Helvetii requested permission to move through Roman territory and gave guarantees of their good conduct whilst doing so, Caesar refused, though not immediately. After stalling the Helvetii for nearly three weeks, he gave notice that their request would be rejected. In the intervening time, Caesar's legions had built field fortifications. These were defended against all incursions and the Helvetii eventually chose to take a different route into Gaul.

Caesar, who was out to make a reputation for himself and seeking plunder, was determined to fight the Helvetii. At the head of a force consisting of five legions plus supporting troops, he advanced against the Helvetii, citing complaints from Roman-allied tribes that they had been raided. The Helvetii, hit hard, tried to negotiate a settlement whereby the Romans would give them a place to settle in return for peace, but Caesar wanted none of it. After a period of manoeuvre and skirmish, Caesar's force brought the Helvetii to battle and soundly defeated them. Most of the survivors were returned to their old home, though some were allowed to settle with local tribes allied to Rome.

THE CONFLICT BROADENS

Whilst still in Gaul, Caesar received requests for aid from allied tribes. A Germanic army numbering some 120,000 had invaded Gaul. Despite some trepidation in the ranks, Caesar led his legions against this new foe and, after a fierce fight, defeated them.

Having beaten two major enemies in a single year, Caesar had won great fame and glory, but he was not yet satisfied. He had under his hand a powerful and well-honed tool in the form of his army, and he was determined to use it to best effect. Thus in the following year he marched against the Belgae and, despite some reverses, defeated them. He then divided his command to undertake several minor campaigns all over Gaul in 56 BC.

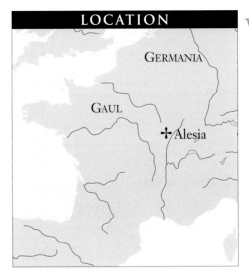

The town of Alesia is now called Alise-Ste.-Reine, on Mount Auxois, near the source of the Seine river. It was in Central Gaul, a province that Caesar himself had added to Rome's empire.

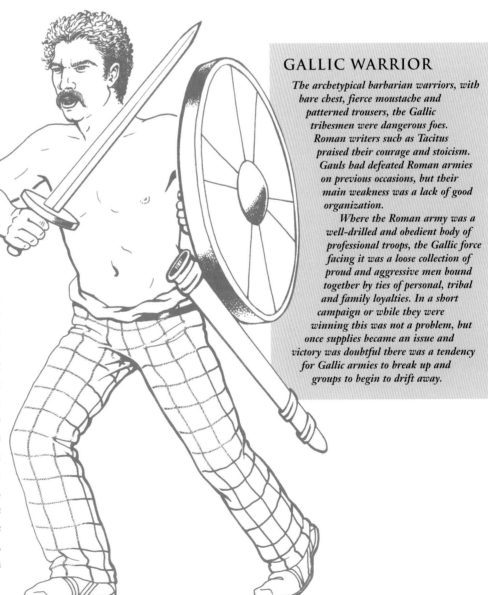

GALLIC WARRIOR

The archetypical barbarian warriors, with bare chest, fierce moustache and patterned trousers, the Gallic tribesmen were dangerous foes. Roman writers such as Tacitus praised their courage and stoicism. Gauls had defeated Roman armies on previous occasions, but their main weakness was a lack of good organization.

Where the Roman army was a well-drilled and obedient body of professional troops, the Gallic force facing it was a loose collection of proud and aggressive men bound together by ties of personal, tribal and family loyalties. In a short campaign or while they were winning this was not a problem, but once supplies became an issue and victory was doubtful there was a tendency for Gallic armies to break up and groups to begin to drift away.

ALESIA

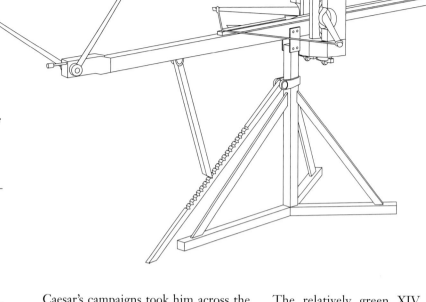

A torsion oxybeles of the first century BC. Modern reconstructions have shown that the wooden frames of such catapults sustained extensive damage with prolonged use from the violent forward movement of the arms. Later versions featured iron around the head for reinforcement. The catapult's bolt could penetrate shield and armour at ranges of more than 400m (437yd).

The ballista. In the third century BC, the Romans began adopting Greek siege warfare technology. The ballista was a new version of the stone-throwing lithobolos. The frame and base were now sturdier, the holes through which the rope was inserted and the washers by which it was secured went from being square in earlier models to an oval shape. This allowed more rope to be used in the springs and these were also twisted tighter. The springs were now exclusively made of sinew, much stronger than the old horsehair versions. All of this gave the machine much greater range and accuracy.

Caesar's campaigns took him across the Rhine in 55 BC, and even to Britain in the same year and in 54 BC, and it seemed that he was unstoppable. All the while his stock was rising in Roman politics, and much of what he did was planned to increase his wealth and standing. Inevitably, however, the Gauls were provoked into a more serious response, and in the winter of 54–53 BC, Caesar discovered that he had a fight on his hands.

The Belgae rose up against Rome and inflicted some defeats on Caesar's army.

The relatively green XIV Legion, with some additional troops attached, was caught by surprise in winter quarters. After some fighting its commander negotiated a withdrawal. However, in an ambush that foreshadowed events in the Teutoberger Wald half a century later, the legion was set upon in forest where it could not form up properly and was massacred.

A similar attack on another legion was fended off long enough for Caesar to march to its relief, and early in the new year Caesar launched a series of punitive expeditions to put down what was becoming a widespread revolt. This quietened things for a while, but the following winter (53–52 BC), the Gauls rose up again. This time they were acting together, though it could not be said that they were entirely in concert. Many important figures led the war against Rome, but Vercingetorix, a chieftain of the Arverni, emerged as the overall leader.

THE OPPOSED FORCES

ROMANS (estimated)
  12 Roman legions, with auxiliaries
  Total: **60,000**

GAULS (estimated)
  Besieged warriors: 80,000
  Relief forces: 150–200,000
  Total: **230–280,000**

VERCINGETORIX MAKES WAR

The Gauls were fierce fighters, with a military system based upon duty to tribal leaders. The Gauls were mainly organized in warbands around their nobles, who tended to be ferocious warriors and courageous leaders. The bulk of Gallic soldiery were armed with spear and shield, though well-made swords were prized possessions as well as deadly weapons. The Gauls were nothing like as well organized as the Roman invaders, who had well-established practices for logistics and line of supply. However, Vercingetorix and his followers did seek to establish adequate supplies for their army and were consequently able to take the field with more men than the Gauls had previously been able to manage, and keep them concentrated.

At first the Gauls were successful. Raids were launched against Roman and pro-Roman Gallic settlements. Traders were massacred and troops in winter quarters came under attack. Caesar was at this time in Cisalpine Gaul, attending to his duties as governor, and had to make a choice between calling his legions to him, which might look like a withdrawal as well as leaving them open to attack and defeat in detail, or establishing local defence with minor forces and going to the legions himself.

Caesar chose the latter course, and even managed to lead an attack into Arvernian lands which caused dismay among the rebel chieftains. As Vercingetorix marched to meet this threat, which was actually fairly minor but reported as a major Roman army by panicked local leaders, Caesar rejoined his legions and concentrated them for a decisive battle. His supply situation was not good as it was very early in the year, but with Vercingetorix on the march he had to act. Delay would make matters worse as the

Modern-day Alesia in the Burgundy region of France. The site of the battle is seen here from Caesar's position. The hill offered Vercingetorix obvious defensive advantages, but once surrounded it became a deathtrap.

Gauls won minor successes which might persuade more chiefs to join their cause. Caesar had to act, and quickly.

The usual Roman response to an uprising was aggressive, and Caesar followed this course. Demanding grain from allied tribes to supply his army, he advanced towards where Vercingetorix was besieging Gorgobina, seizing supplies on the march and destroying targets of opportunity such as minor rebel strongholds along the way. Caesar's approach caused Vercingetorix to break off his siege and go to meet the Romans. After a cavalry action around Noviodunum,

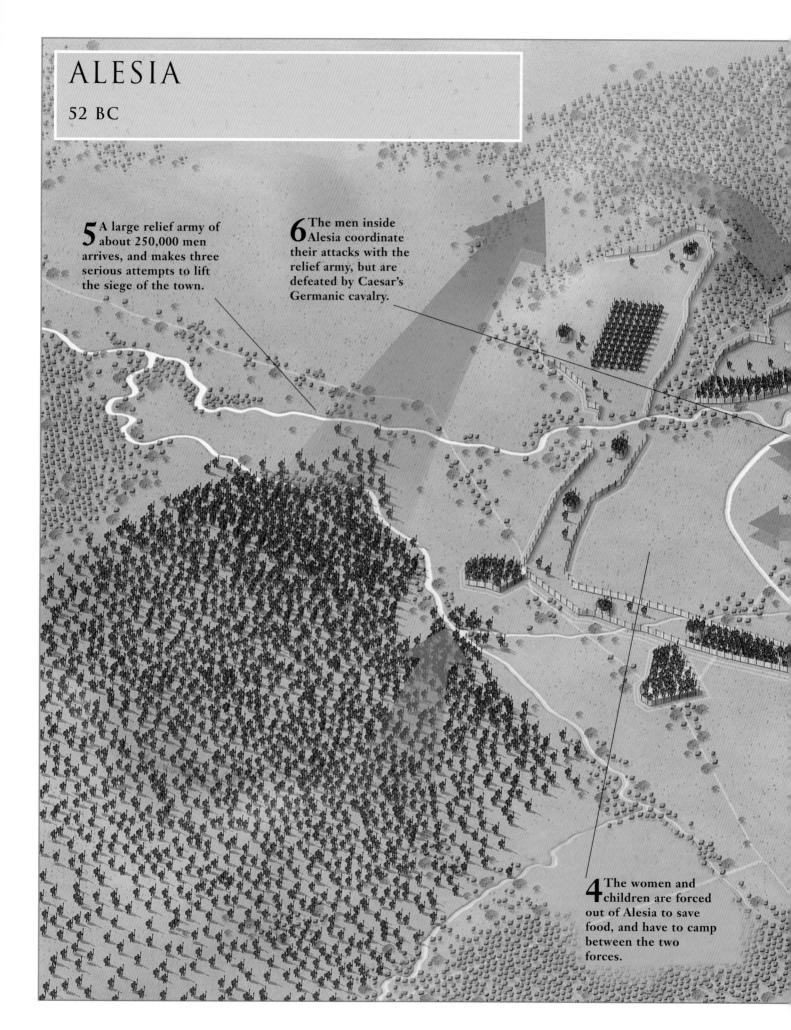

ALESIA
52 BC

5 A large relief army of about 250,000 men arrives, and makes three serious attempts to lift the siege of the town.

6 The men inside Alesia coordinate their attacks with the relief army, but are defeated by Caesar's Germanic cavalry.

4 The women and children are forced out of Alesia to save food, and have to camp between the two forces.

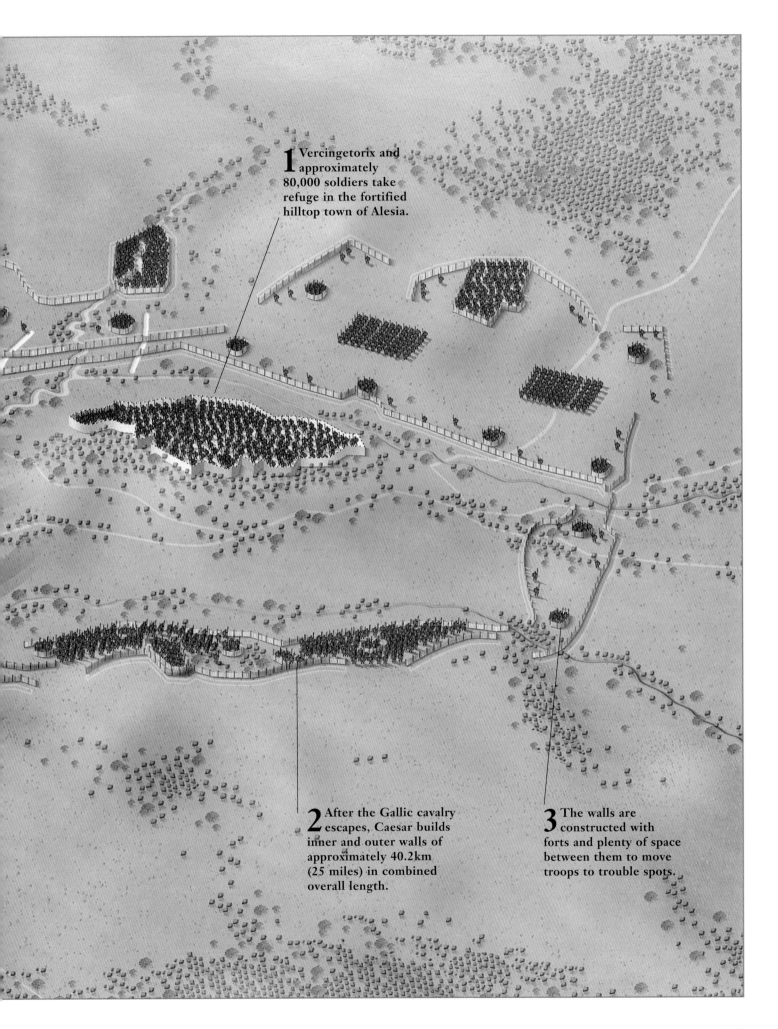

1 Vercingetorix and approximately 80,000 soldiers take refuge in the fortified hilltop town of Alesia.

2 After the Gallic cavalry escapes, Caesar builds inner and outer walls of approximately 40.2km (25 miles) in combined overall length.

3 The walls are constructed with forts and plenty of space between them to move troops to trouble spots.

ALESIA

which went in the Romans' favour, Caesar advanced on Avaricum.

Instead of allowing himself to be drawn into a decisive battle, Vercingetorix settled down to play a long game, choking the Roman army by cutting off its supplies whilst wearing down its strength by ambushes and small actions. The struggle went on like this for some time, with Caesar's forces besieging Avaricum whilst the Gallic army effectively tried to besiege the Roman field army. Supplies were getting short in both armies, and Caesar was having trouble obtaining more. Some allies had nothing more to send, and others were reconsidering their position. However, the Gauls were also running short of supplies and in general lacked the patience for such a protracted action.

CAESAR'S INITIATIVE

With the Romans steadily reducing Avaricum and his commanders becoming restless, Vercingetorix allowed himself to be talked into taking more direct action. Moving up closer to the town, he offered battle from a strong position but Caesar refused to sanction what would have been a costly assault. The siege continued, with the Romans gradually gaining the upper hand. The warriors Vercingetorix had sent into the town now attempted to fight their way out, but were contained. Shortly afterwards the legions stormed the town and put the defenders to the sword, capturing large stocks of grain into the bargain.

Caesar now went on the offensive, launching attacks against other rebel towns in rapid succession. His legions and auxiliaries were being worn down by the constant fighting and rapid marching, but there was no time to be lost.

In the meantime, the fall of Avaricum had actually strengthened Vercingetorix's political position as he had argued against defending it in the first place. More tribes came to join him, and rebellion broke out

Legionaries construct defensive works around the perimeter of Alesia. The Roman army were unparalleled in the Ancient world as builders of small fortresses for siege warfare.

ALESIA

In this illustration by artist Henri Paul (1846–1922), Roman soldiers are depicted operating an onager at the siege of Alesia. The weapon and its crew are protected from counter-fire by simple but effective fortifications.

Fearing that he had lost the initiative and that more Gauls would be encouraged to join the rising, Caesar launched a counter-offensive and called in his detached forces. He also raised more auxiliaries and hired mercenaries from the German tribes. Vercingetorix had also been reinforced, and a fierce running battle developed, mainly between the cavalry of both armies, along the line of march.

After a long and hard fight, Caesar's army drove off the Gauls and pursued them for the remainder of that day. The Gallic army rallied and re-formed on a hill outside the town of Alesia and the Romans, who now had more than sufficient supplies, decided to besiege it.

THE SIEGE BEGINS

The Romans were not great originators of siege technology. Indeed, much of what was available to them was copied from foreign powers, mainly the Greeks. What the Romans were very good at was what might today be called combat engineering. Experts at erecting field fortifications, the Romans were able to quickly throw up an entire ring of defences – a line of circumvallation – around the Gallic camp, making it difficult for Vercingetorix to sally out and for supplies to get in.

However, the Roman army was deep within hostile territory, and it faced attack from outside the town, so a second line of defences – a line of contravallation – facing outwards was also built. The inner line, containing the defenders, was 17.7km (11 miles) long. The outer line, protecting the besiegers, was 22.5km (14 miles) long.

The defences were formidable. Initially a makeshift set-up with a ditch and a wall no more than 1.8m (6ft) in height, the fortifications were rapidly developed into a very impressive set of works. A 6m (20ft) wide ditch ran right around the Gallic position to slow down any advance by Vercingetorix and buy time for reserves to assemble to meet an assault. The main belt consisted of a 3.6m (12ft) earth-and-timber wall fronted by two 4.6m (15ft) wide ditches to break up an attack.

In some places these ditches were flooded and in others they were reinforced with sharp stakes and small pits. Wooden

even among tribes previously staunch allies of Rome. Caesar brought the situation under control and inflicted defeats on the Gauls, but matters remained serious.

THE DECISIVE PHASE

After a surprise attack on a Gallic force near Gergovia, the aggression of the legions got out of control. This led to a disorganized and chaotic attempt to storm the city. Despite early successes, the assault was broken and the Romans suffered heavy casualties, including no less than 46 centurions. Caesar withdrew from the town to deal with other problems including further uprisings and the massacre of Roman garrisons along his supply route.

frameworks from which iron spikes projected were buried in some areas as well. Alone, these obstacles would not contain the Gauls, but this was not their purpose. They were intended to inflict some casualties but above all impose delay on a force assaulting the Roman besiegers. Every moment longer taken to reach the defenders meant another hail of missiles from the wall, another maniple of reserves rushed up to the endangered section, and an ever smaller chance of success. The outward-facing line of contravallation was equally formidable, and both lines were strengthened by the inclusion of towers every 24m (80ft) along the line as well as independent strongpoints.

According to Caesar's own account of events, around 80,000 Gauls were trapped within the fortifications. This figure is suspect, since the besiegers can only have numbered around 40,000–70,000, but whatever the exact figure, what is certain is that Vercingetorix commanded a very substantial force within the camp. He also enjoyed massive support all across Gaul. It has been estimated that as many as 250,000 Gallic warriors were available to come to the assistance of the besieged army. However, supplying such a huge force was beyond the means of the tribes; there was no chance of a quarter of a million warriors all turning up at once.

The Gauls were not idle during the construction of the siegeworks, but despite launching many raids and spoiling attacks were not able to prevent the ring from closing on them. Cut off from additional supplies, Vercingetorix had to hope that relief would reach him, and to extend the time he could hold out, he expelled all non-combatants from the town. Already Vercingetorix's cavalry (numbering some 15,000 according to Caesar) had been sent out to join the relief force. It forced its way through the defences at the second attempt, though with heavy losses. Now women, children and anyone else who could not fight were sent out of the town and the Gallic camp, but Caesar would not allow them through his lines. Thus these innocents were left to starve between the two armies. The campaign had entered its final, desperate phase.

RELIEF ARRIVES

The Gallic relief army reached Alesia soon after the expulsion of non-combatants. While Caesar's figure of 250,000 infantry and 8000 cavalry seems excessive, nonetheless this force was probably very large. Caesar was now forced to defend his positions from attack from outside, while Vercingetorix was leading an attack from within. As the besieged Gauls worked to fill in parts of the ditch, a cavalry melee developed on the plains outside. This was eventually won by the Roman heavy horse, who routed the Gallic cavalry and massacred their supporting light infantry.

The following day was quiet, but at midnight that night, the relief army launched its attack and Vercingetorix responded by attacking from within the circle of fortifications. A confused and bloody battle erupted with Roman troops

A statue of Julius Caesar in Vienna. Caesar literally changed the world, converting Rome from a republic to an empire, and casts a long shadow over world history. Some later words for 'emperor' (Kaiser, Tsar) are derived from his name.

ALESIA

Vercingetorix led the Gauls rather than commanded them, which limited his options. He was successful in fighting a guerrilla war and wearing down the Romans, but when forced into open battle his forces were outmatched by better tactics and superior equipment.

defending their positions using javelins and light siege engines called scorpions, and hurling stones that had been readied for just such an occasion. A hail of missile fire – arrows, javelins and slingstones – was sent against the Roman positions as Gallic infantry tried to gain a foothold on the fortifications. Matters were in doubt for some time, but Roman reinforcements led by Mark Antony and another of Caesar's legates were able to stabilize the situation and drive the assaults back.

CRISIS POINT

At midday the next day, a force some 60,000 strong (according to Caesar) made an assault on one of the Roman forts while other forces made diversionary attacks at various points along the line. There was no way to inform Vercingetorix of what was planned, but when he heard the noise of battle he again led his forces out to assault the Roman positions.

The Romans were hard-pressed, but they were tough, tenacious and highly disciplined. They stood and fought stubbornly wherever they were attacked, and this bought time for Caesar to make use of the Romans' other great advantage, the ability to manoeuvre quickly. Time and again Caesar called up reserves from elsewhere in the line and fed them into a crisis point. He also sent the legate Labienus with five cohorts to reinforce the beleaguered fort. Labienus had complete latitude to do as he had to. He could deploy his cohorts and the two legions already in the fort as he saw fit, and had permission to abandon the position and fight his way out if need be.

THE LAST HURRAH

Knowing that this was the best and perhaps the last chance he would be offered, Vercingetorix launched an all-out assault on the Roman positions. A massive hail of missiles swept the defenders from the wall, and under its cover the Gauls made their final assault.

The attack was a success. Gallic warriors began destroying the defences and some gained the ramparts. Caesar ordered Decimus Brutus to throw them back, and Brutus led several cohorts into a counter-attack. The fighting was still desperate, so

Caesar ordered the legate Gaius Fabius to Brutus' aid with virtually all the available troops. Between them they were able to retake the defences. Vercingetorix's assault faltered and with it any hope of linking up with the relief army was gone.

Meanwhile, Caesar himself gathered a final reserve from lightly engaged sectors and led it to the assistance of Labienus, whose troops had been forced off the ramparts but were holding out inside the fort. Supported by a force of cavalry, Caesar's troops threw back the Gauls, who broke and were vigorously pursued by the cavalry. This disheartened the relief force, which gradually melted away leaving the siege unbroken.

AFTERMATH

The following day, the starving defenders of Alesia agreed to Caesar's demand for their unconditional surrender. Vercingetorix, dressed in his most impressive armour and riding a fine horse, laid down his weapons before Caesar and was taken away as a prisoner.

The surrender of Vercingetorix was not quite the end of the rebellion. A smaller uprising took place in 51 BC but was quickly put down. Treatment of the vanquished varied. Some tribes were treated leniently in the hope of winning them back over to Roman allegiance. Some were punished very harshly as an example to others. Vercingetorix himself was kept captive in Rome for six years before being publicly executed by strangulation.

So many prisoners were taken in the campaign that every man in Caesar's army was given one to sell as a slave. Caesar himself became fabulously wealthy from the campaign, even after paying off the huge debts he had started out with.

Caesar's reputation was made in the Gallic campaign – in Rome, but more importantly with the Roman army. It was this army that was at his back when he crossed the Rubicon and entered Italy, and this army that defeated Pompey in the civil war that followed. In Rome, political and military power were inextricably mixed. Caesar knew this, and exploited it to the full.

Entitled 'Vercingetorix Throwing His Weapon's at the Feet Of Caesar', Lionel-Noël Royer's (1852–1926) depiction of Vercingetorix offers a romanticized view of the Gallic leader's surrender. Caesar is portrayed dressed as a political figure rather than a soldier. To Rome, the two were often the same thing.

ACTIUM
31 BC

THE GREAT NAVAL BATTLE OF ACTIUM, AN ATTEMPTED FLIGHT THAT TURNED INTO DISASTER FOR MARK ANTONY AND CLEOPATRA, WAS THE LAST BLOW THAT DESTROYED THE ROMAN REPUBLIC. THE WINNER, AUGUSTUS CAESAR, IS REGARDED AS THE FIRST ROMAN EMPEROR.

WHY DID IT HAPPEN?

WHO A Roman/Egyptian fleet, under the command of Mark Antony (82–30 BC), opposed a Roman fleet, commanded by Marcus Vipsanius Agrippa (63–12 BC).

WHAT Mark Antony's fleet tried to break out of the Gulf of Ambricia, where Agrippa's fleet had been blockading him for months. The fleets engaged closely, the combat taking the form of marines shooting and hurling missiles, plus efforts at boarding.

WHERE The Ionian Sea off the west coast of Greece. The modern town of Preveza, Greece, is nearby.

WHEN 2 September 31 BC.

WHY Mark Antony and Octavian, later Augustus Caesar (63 BC – AD 14), were locked in a mortal struggle for control of the Roman state, the last phase of a series of civil wars that began with Julius Caesar's assassination in 44 BC.

OUTCOME Octavian's fleet won a partial victory. Two-thirds of Mark Antony's fleet was sunk or captured, but Antony escaped to attempt a final resistance in Egypt.

The Roman Republic was no longer a viable political entity by the second half of the first century BC, and its final years were marked by a relentless military and political contest for absolute control, waged by a number of ambitious men to whom traditional Roman moralities meant little. Gaius Julius Caesar (100–44 BC) won the position of dictator for life, only to be assassinated by reactionary senators. Caesar's troops were outraged and their two natural leaders – Marcus Antonius (Mark Antony), his second in command, and Gaius Julius Caesar Octavianus (Octavian), his great-nephew and adopted son – took advantage of their loyalty to defeat the assassins and claim control of the state.

At first the youthful Octavian and the experienced Mark Antony worked well together, Octavian taking charge of Rome's western provinces and Antony the eastern. To seal their alliance, Antony even married Octavian's sister, Octavia. Over the next few years, though, their relations rapidly soured, especially when Antony abandoned his Roman wife and first had an affair with and then married Cleopatra VII (69–30 BC), queen of Egypt.

Besides the personal insult to his family, Octavian and many others were deeply troubled by the foreign woman's influence over Antony – Rome was traditionally suspicious both of the East and of women engaged in politics. In 32 BC matters came to a head. Octavian arranged for the Roman Senate to declare war, not on the Roman

This nineteenth-century engraving of the battle of Actium reminds us that both Antony's and Octavian's land armies were close at hand and would have witnessed Antony's attempt to break out of the Gulf of Ambricia by sea.

Antony, but on Cleopatra of Egypt, knowing that Antony's fate was by that time entwined with that of the queen.

INVASION PLANS

For much of the year 32 BC, both Antony and Octavian raised forces for a final confrontation by both land and sea. By late in the year, Antony had assembled his troops and fleet in central Greece, poised to invade Italy at the beginning of the next year's sailing season. He and Cleopatra had assembled an army 100,000 strong, with a backbone of seasoned Roman legions but also many troops that were less well trained. They had also assembled a fleet of 500 warships (of which Cleopatra supplied 200), along with 300 merchantmen that had been forced into service to transport the army across the Ionian Sea. Most of the eastern

fleet wintered in the harbour just within the promontory of Actium, with other detachments in smaller harbours along the Greek coast.

Meanwhile, Octavian mustered an army and fleet in Italy, ready to attack Greece as soon as possible. His army was smaller, about 80,000 men, but mostly consisted of trained legions. Octavian's fleet was probably about equal in number to Antony and Cleopatra's. His ships, however, were on the average smaller. Octavian had most of the standing Roman fleet, which consisted for the most part of quinqueremes (rowed by five men per bay of the ship) and perhaps even small swift liburnians with their single bank of oars. Antony's ships, collected from Rome's subject allies in the East, were heavier, taller ships built to Hellenistic standards. They were rowed by six to ten men per bay, in staggered ranks, making them higher in the water, heavier, and also more powerful.

Octavian, although one of the most influential men in world history, was not much of a general. He was, however, fortunate in his loyal followers and friends. His close friend Marcus Vipsanius Agrippa, of too humble birth to challenge him for power, was a naval genius who had already proved his worth against pro-republican forces at the battle of Naulochus in 36 BC. In 31 BC Agrippa stole a march on Mark Antony, setting out at the very beginning of

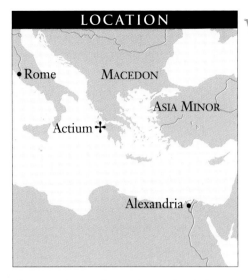

Actium was between Octavian's power base in Rome and Antony and Cleopatra's in Egypt. The battle was to be Antony's last throw in his challenge to Octavian's rule.

BALLISTAE

The Romans experimented with shipboard ballistae, small torsion catapults. The type shown would have been operated by winching back the shooting cord, pulling against the tension created by the wound rope spools in the foreground. It would fire a lead shot or heavy bolt, aiming against personnel rather than hoping to pierce the ships themselves. Such machines were difficult to operate at sea, because the damp affected the tension and rendered them inaccurate. It is not clear from extant accounts whether ballistae were used on the ships engaged in battle at Actium.

ACTIUM

Right: This anonymous English print showing the battle of Actium presents the Augustan propagandists' view of events, suggesting that Cleopatra deserted Antony's fully engaged ships at the height of the battle.

THE OPPOSED FORCES

OCTAVIAN

Ships, mostly quinqueremes:	*c.* 400
Rowers:	*c.* 120,000
Marines:	*c.* 12,000
Total:	**c. 132,000**

ANTONY AND CLEOPATRA

Ships, quinqueremes, etc:	*c.* 230
Rowers:	*c.* 69,000
Marines:	*c.* 9200
Legionaries:	*c.* 20,000
Auxiliary archers:	*c.* 2000
Total:	**c. 100,200**

the sailing season and travelling well south of the usual route from Italy to Greece, so Antony's patrolling ships never spotted him. Agrippa struck Antony's strong garrison at Methone, then sailed northward, attacking other Antonian outposts as he went. Then, while Antony's attention was diverted, Octavian ferried his entire land army from Brundisium (Brindisi) to Greece. The speed of the invasion unnerved Antony's soldiers

and oarsmen, who were already deeply divided. Many strongly disapproved of Antony's liaison with Cleopatra, especially since Cleopatra was in the camp with them, taking part in councils and behaving in a way regarded as unsuitable for Roman women.

Besides, Octavian had launched a highly effective propaganda campaign that left many of Antony's men doubting his loyalty

to Rome and even his ability to make independent decisions. Desertion rapidly became a serious problem.

Most of Antony and Cleopatra's ships were safely at anchor in their harbour at Actium when Agrippa's fleet arrived. Agrippa could not attack them, since Antony had built towers to guard the entrance to the Gulf of Ambricia. So Agrippa called on Antony to join him in

battle in the open waters of the Ionian Sea, an offer that Antony refused, since his oarsmen had been struck down by an epidemic, probably dysentery or malaria, and he would have been forced to fight against the odds.

Besides, Antony's army was still dispersed in its winter camps, and he needed two to three weeks to call his forces together.

THE STAND-OFF

Since Antony's fleet could have wreaked havoc if it were left unattended to sail away at will, Agrippa commenced a blockade of the harbour, while Octavian established his headquarters on a hill some 8km (5 miles) north of the gulf's entrance. There he constructed a mole to provide some protection for his ships. And there he proceeded to wait.

ACTIUM

31 BC

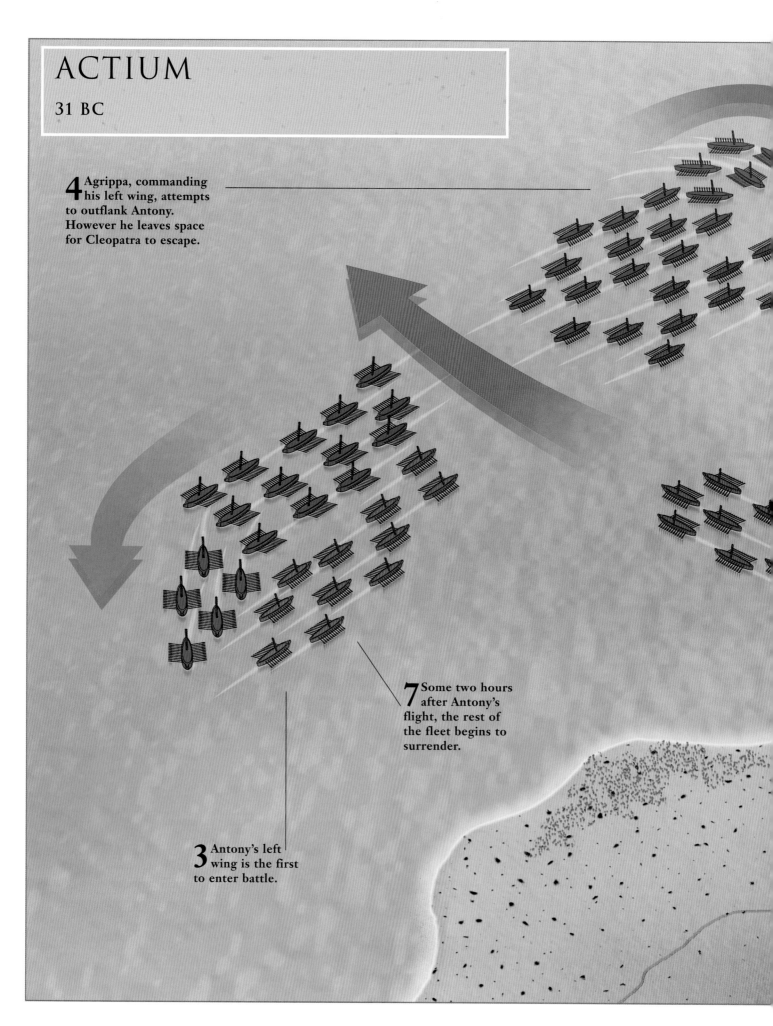

4 Agrippa, commanding his left wing, attempts to outflank Antony. However he leaves space for Cleopatra to escape.

7 Some two hours after Antony's flight, the rest of the fleet begins to surrender.

3 Antony's left wing is the first to enter battle.

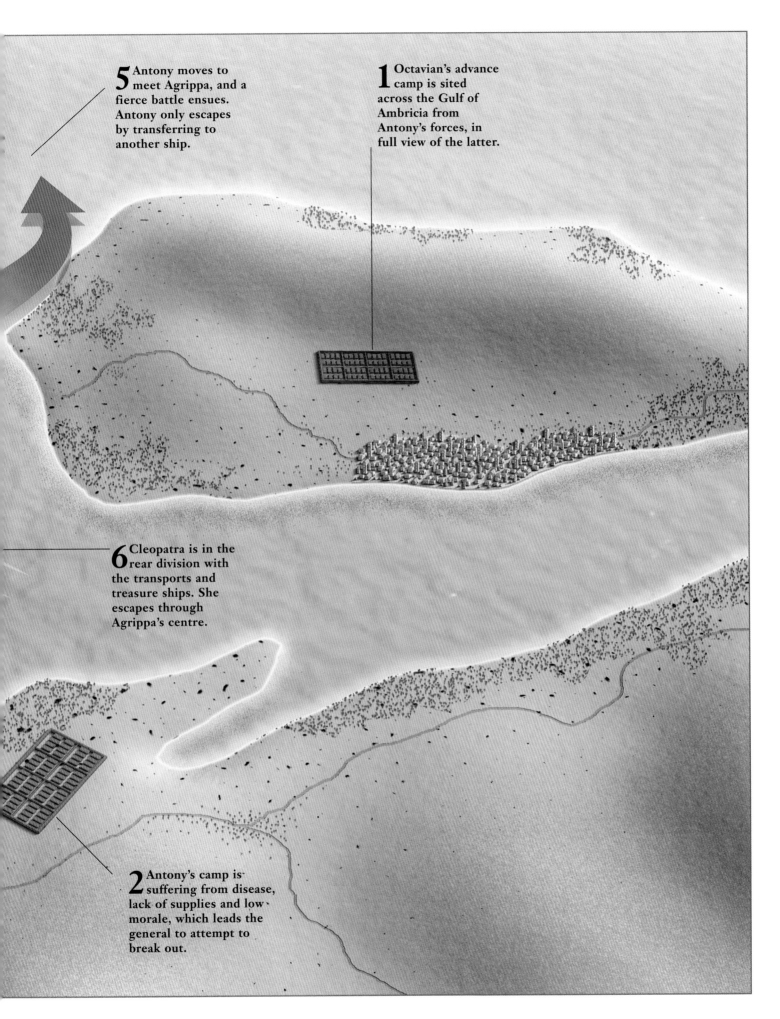

5 Antony moves to meet Agrippa, and a fierce battle ensues. Antony only escapes by transferring to another ship.

1 Octavian's advance camp is sited across the Gulf of Ambricia from Antony's forces, in full view of the latter.

6 Cleopatra is in the rear division with the transports and treasure ships. She escapes through Agrippa's centre.

2 Antony's camp is suffering from disease, lack of supplies and low morale, which leads the general to attempt to break out.

ACTIUM

A highly romanticized rendering of Cleopatra aboard her flagship at Actium. Like her husband Mark Antony, she succeeded in escaping with her life and returning to Egypt.

forces and formally offered battle. But Octavian refused, and since his men were by that time dug into a strongly fortified camp, there was no way to force an engagement.

With control of the sea, Octavian was in a better position to harm Antony than vice versa. In late April and May, Octavian's admiral Agrippa won a series of small victories along the Greek coast, taking bases that had been protecting Antony's supply route. He began intercepting the eastern supply ships, and soon Antony's camp was short of food, while many continued to die in the epidemic.

By midsummer, Antony was clearly growing desperate. He kept trying to force a land battle, but Octavian kept his men in tight check. Morale in Antony's army plunged, especially as more and more of his officers defected to Octavian. Since a land battle was increasingly unlikely, Antony also sent press gangs far inland to find replacement oarsmen, men who were both unwilling and untrained for the job.

PREPARATIONS FOR BATTLE

Under these circumstances, it is far from clear why Antony waited so long before attempting to break the western blockade with his fleet; Antony's indecisiveness through the summer lent force to Octavian's taunt that he had become a spoiled easterner. By the end of August, Antony was almost out of supplies. He had only two choices before him: he could retreat with his army into Greece, abandoning the fleet, or he could break out with the fleet (there seems to have been no thought of winning a fleet action) and leave his army to its fate.

Antony chose to make his escape by sea. He planned the withdrawal with care, only to have an old friend and lieutenant defect and carry his battle plans to Octavian. There was no chance of escaping by stealth under any circumstances. Antony's camp was in full view of Octavian's scouts, who would have reported every move as he made it. Antony redistributed his diminished ship crews, then burned all the spare ships, including almost all the transports. He could not take his army, since the transport vessels would have been too slow to evade Agrippa's fleet. Antony did, however, take 20,000 legionaries and 2000 archers as

Although he had a weaker fleet than Octavian's, Antony possessed the stronger land forces, so he resolved on an attack against Octavian's army, after which he could easily have driven the fleet away by attacking its base. By late April Antony's army had assembled, so he paraded his marines aboard his diminished fleet of about 230 ships – which had to face Agrippa's 400 vessels.

Everything was prepared by 29 August, but yet again Antony had to sit and wait; this time thanks to a series of storms that swept through the area. He was finally able to put to sea on 2 September.

THE BATTLE

Antony did not plan a battle but an escape, although he would certainly have expected to have to fight his way to the open sea. His plans are clear from his ships' equipment: the warships under his command kept their masts and sails aboard. The universal custom of the Ancient World was to leave both ashore when setting out for battle. Not only did they clutter the decks far too much for marines to operate effectively; in an age that liked to throw firepots at enemy vessels, flammable sails were an invitation to disaster. Indeed, on that day a battle of any duration would be disastrous, since Antony's ships were heavily outnumbered and his crews were sick, hungry, undertrained, and deeply discouraged.

As the eastern fleet finally left its harbour, it divided into four squadrons. Three squadrons led, forming a crescent with Antony in command of the right wing. Behind them came the fourth squadron, 60 ships commanded by Cleopatra. She had in her charge the remaining merchant ships and all the valuables, including the war treasury. Even more tellingly, few of the marines were posted to this squadron, so it seems clear that it was not intended to fight, but rather to escape while the other squadrons cleared the way.

Seeing Antony's ships at the mouth of the gulf, Agrippa took a position about 1.6km (1 mile) out to sea. He clearly wanted Antony's larger ships in the open water, where his own larger numbers could overwhelm them on all sides. Antony, though, stayed close to the shore, where his ships could not be encircled. So there was one last stand-off between the forces, in this summer of stand-offs and stalemates.

There was more to Antony's plan than simple desperation, however. Off the promontory of Actium the winds are very predictable in fair weather, and Antony

knew he could expect a stiff breeze from the southwest by about noon. He merely had to gauge his time correctly and row out to open water just as the breeze came up, and before his ships could be too badly mauled by Agrippa's superior force. Once they caught the breeze, Antony's ships would have a great advantage – they had their sails ready for use, while the sails of Agrippa's ships were on land. With sails up, Antony could hope to get out of range quickly, perhaps making a clean getaway.

Antony and Cleopatra might indeed have escaped with little damage, if Agrippa

A bust of Marcus Vipsanius Agrippa (63-12 BC), Roman general and statesman. Agrippa was responsible for the defeats of Sextus Pompeius in the battle of Mylae (36 BC) and Mark Antony in the battle of Actium, allowing Augustus Caesar to become sole ruler of Rome.

Right: In this 1887 painting, French artist Alexandre Cabanel (1823–1889) presents a sultry, decadent Cleopatra testing poisons on condemned prisoners while pondering the best way to commit suicide.

A C T I U M

had not been an outstanding admiral. Antony appears to have judged his moment well, and to have headed for the open sea just as the wind rose. Two things went wrong, however. First, Agrippa's right wing was not thrown off station by the rising wind, nor had his captains been lulled from their watchfulness by the hours of inaction. Instead, they surged forward to engage Antony's left wing, which was soon deeply committed to battle and unable to extricate itself. Second, Antony's right wing edged to the north as the ships rowed out to sea, hoping to pass beyond Agrippa's left wing before it could react. However, Agrippa himself commanded that wing. As Antony began his manoeuvre, Agrippa extended his own line to outflank Antony's ships.

Antony's right wing, which he himself commanded, had to move even further northward to counter Agrippa's flanking manoeuvre. Antony's squadron became detached from his central squadron, and engaged in a lively fight with the ships of Agrippa's left flank. A period of confused fighting ensued, during which Cleopatra's squadron, which had been hanging behind, fled through the centre of Agrippa's line and won the open sea.

Some ships of Antony's right wing were also able to get away to safety. Those escaping from the right included Mark Antony himself. His flagship was so heavily engaged that he could not break loose, but he used a rowboat to reach another vessel, and from there sailed in pursuit of Cleopatra. This squadron and a half, perhaps as much as one-

third of Antony's fleet, did indeed make good their escape.

Contemporary historians, writing from the perspective of the winners, made of this flight a dastardly tale of female duplicity and besotted lust. At their hands, Actium became a battle that only turned into a flight when Cleopatra seized an opportunity to turn tail and run. Antony, the story goes, was so deeply enslaved by the queen that he abandoned his own fleet to accompany her. The story, for the reasons given above, is very unlikely, however, and should be credited to Octavian's impressive command of propaganda rather than to actual events during the battle.

Few details survive about the rest of the battle. Although the ships on both sides were equipped with heavy bronze rams, they appear to have seen little use that day.

The ram came into use on warships some time in the sixth century BC. It only became possible to use it as ships' hulls became stronger, with solid frameworks giving the attacking vessel the strength to withstand the impact. This example probably dates from around the first half of the second century BC.

It seems likely that Agrippa, with his lighter and smaller ships, did not think the likelihood of damaging the eastern ships, with their reinforced bows and heavier planking, worth the risk of ramming. Instead, he relied on his greater numbers and manoeuvrability, which would have been particularly striking since so many of Antony's rowers were raw recruits. It became a struggle between marines, a fight of projectile weapons at close range, succeeded by attempts to board enemy vessels and fight it out hand to hand. Perhaps, as at the battle of Naulochus in 36 BC, Agrippa fired grapnels into enemy ships and then hauled them in reach of his marines; if so, the sources fail to mention it.

The majority of Antony's fleet, hemmed in and cut off from open water where they could escape, kept up the fight for about two hours, but started to surrender by about 4.00 p.m. Those who surrendered were well treated by the victors.

THE AFTERMATH

After the battle of Actium, Antony's land army began its withdrawal, and Octavian's army soon caught up. But Antony's men, whose leader had run for his life and abandoned them, refused to fight. A week of intense negotiation ensued, at the end of which the whole eastern army surrendered, on the promise that the soldiers would be treated equally with the winners of this last civil war of the Roman Republic.

Antony and Cleopatra fled to Egypt, hoping for time to raise fresh troops and continue the fight. Octavian pursued, however, and their support melted away. Antony committed suicide in 30 BC rather

than fall into his enemy's hands. At first Cleopatra tried to negotiate, but when it became clear that Octavian wished to humiliate her and strip her of her kingdom, she too killed herself.

Thus, although the battle of Actium was only a partial victory, it was the last serious military action in Octavian's path to absolute power. He returned from the campaign in triumph, and as the uncrowned ruler of Rome. The Senate, thoroughly cowed by this point, soon voted Octavian a near divine title, and as Augustus Caesar he proceeded to shape Rome into an empire with himself at its head. By the time he died in AD 14, the Republic was only a distant memory. Augustus' propaganda machine had transformed Actium into a battle against decadent and untrustworthy Egypt, rather than the last gasp of the Republic.

TEUTOBERGER WALD
AD 9

TEUTOBERGER WALD WAS A SHOCKING DEFEAT FOR THE ROMAN EMPIRE, AND ONE THAT ENSURED THAT THE GERMANIC FRONTIER WAS NEVER FULLY PACIFIED. THE BATTLE HAD CONSEQUENCES THAT CHANGED THE COURSE OF EUROPEAN HISTORY.

WHY DID IT HAPPEN?

WHO Three Roman legions under Publius Quinctilius Varus (d. AD 9), with supporting cavalry, versus Germanic troops of the Cherusci tribe under their chief Arminius (?18 BC– AD 19), who was supposedly a Roman ally.

WHAT The Roman forces were betrayed, ambushed and massacred by the Cherusci in the forests of the Teutoberger Wald.

WHERE Along the line of march towards winter quarters in the deep forest, near Osnabrück in northwest Germany. There were many actions and the exact locations are hard to place.

WHEN September–October AD 9

WHY Tiring of Roman policies, the Cherusci turned on their allies and used guerrilla tactics to destroy them in the forests where standard legionary formations were ineffective.

OUTCOME Three Roman legions and supporting troops were annihilated. The Roman Empire never regained control of the Germanic frontier.

In AD 6, when Publius Quinctilius Varus was appointed governor of the province of Germania, the Roman army was apparently an unstoppable war machine. Formed around a professional core of long-service regulars backed up by auxiliary troops where necessary, the Roman army was years ahead of its time in terms of organization and fighting power.

The Romans enjoyed many advantages over their enemies. Individual soldiers were well equipped, thoroughly trained and physically tough. Fighting with their short stabbing swords (*gladii*) while protected by shields and good armour, individual Roman soldiers were deadly combatants. Yet for all this the main strength of the empire was not its individual soldiers. Many barbarian tribes and foreign nations produced fighting men every bit as physically powerful as the Roman solider. Often bigger, stronger and every bit as motivated and aggressive, these warriors fell before the swords of the legions and were assimilated into the empire. The reason was not individual skill or courage, but organization.

In battle, the Roman soldier did not fight in closely packed ranks but had sufficient space to manoeuvre as he needed to. However, he did fight as part of a unit. Part of his training involved being aware of the men on each side of him. A legionary who got into trouble could expect prompt assistance from his companions in the front

The Roman general Publius Quinctilius Varus prepares to commit suicide as his legions are slaughtered around him in the Teutoberger forest. Varus imposed harsh financial penalties on colonized peoples which lost him much local support.

rank, or replacement by a fresh man from the rear. Roman policy was that no man could fight effectively for more than 15 minutes at a time, and troops were rotated out of the front line as they tired. This was trained for and well practised; where a barbarian warrior would battle on until he dropped, a Roman soldier would fight for a period, then retire to catch his breath before returning to the fray. This took place on a larger scale too. Manoeuvre and drill were an important part of the Roman army's training, so gaps in the line could be quickly plugged, maniples wheeled to face a new threat on the flanks, and tiring units replaced in the front line – all without confusion or loss of cohesion.

Thus the Roman legion was composed of formidable fighters but was more than the sum of its parts. Advancing confidently to contact with the enemy, releasing a hail of *pila* (heavy javelins) just before impact, then entering hand-to-hand combat as a coherent and mutually supporting whole, it was impressive. But what made the Roman army really stand head and shoulders above its foes was the fact that it could maintain its cohesion and combat capability through a long engagement. As its foes tired, the legion simply kept on going.

This was the war machine that Varus had at his disposal when he took over from Augustus' stepson (and future successor) Tiberius in AD 6, and its capabilities were enhanced by allied and auxiliary troops which provided specialist functions (skirmishers, scouts, and so forth) and raw numbers to cover ground.

FAILURES OF POLICY

Despite the fact that Varus had over 15,000 Roman troops at his disposal, this was not sufficient to pacify such a large region if the inhabitants rose up together against Rome. A conquered or occupied region only stays that way if the inhabitants consent to remain pacified. So long as the local tribes were divided, the frontier was safe. And so it was in AD 6. Some tribes were allied to Rome; some were hostile but cowed by the threat of force or by the example that had been made of others that opposed Rome; some were neutral so long as Roman interference was minimal.

GERMANIC CHIEFTAIN

The chieftain was as bound to his people as they were to him, by ties of family, kinship and language. He was expected to be generous with gifts as well as to receive his due from others. In battle he was expected to lead as well as to command. His place was at the forefront of the action, surrounded by the warriors of his household. He might have body armour of mail or, as here, fight only in a decorated tunic and a helmet. His sword was as much a badge of office as it was his sidearm, but most of all he was expected to wield it with courage and skill. Much depended on the battle deeds of a chieftain: an action might be won or lost by his heroic example.

Varus' mission was to continue the work of Tiberius in making the Germanic frontier safe and secure. The key to this was cooperation of the local tribes such as the Cherusci, which could field large numbers of highly capable fighting men. While revolts and local opposition could be put down easily enough, it was important that Varus built long-term relationships with the tribal leaders, playing them off against one another and gradually creating a 'natural order' of things on the frontier whereby Rome was the master but the tribes were respected allies and 'Friends of Rome'.

But Varus instead undertook policies that alienated the tribal leaders and their people. Heavy taxation and lack of respect for Germanic culture, coupled with

LOCATION

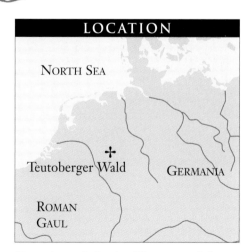

Germania was the frontier of Roman-controlled territory. But for the events of AD 9, Germania might have eventually been absorbed into the empire. After Teutoberger Wald there was little chance that would ever happen.

cross across the sun, a phenomenon that does, in fact, naturally occur under proper atmospheric conditions. Having seen the amazing sight, Constantine later told a biographer of a dream in which the God of the long-persecuted Christians had shown him a 'rho' [ρ] crossed with a 'chi' [χ], and commanded '*In hoc signo, vincere*' (In this sign, conquer). If for no other reason than their remarkable persistence in the face of extensive persecution, the Christians were a moral force in the empire, and Constantine's soldiers accepted their general's vision and painted the emblem

upon their shields. Constantine's army had victory and vision on their side, and quickly moved south along the old Via Flaminia of Punic War fame.

DISPOSITIONS

What doomed Maxentius was a fatal attack of vacillation. The king being the cause in a war for political supremacy, a moment's uncertainty meant ultimate defeat. The general account is that the wide stone bridge over the Tiber, the *Pons Milvius*, had been cut in order to delay Constantine's attack and hinder his supply lines during the

The confusion and disaster of Maxentius' retreat across the Tiber finds expression in this detail from Raphael's c. 1517–1524 depiction of the battle. The precise order needed to move large numbers of men and mounts safely across the river perished immediately as hundreds of Maxentius' troops and the emperor himself fled to drowning and disaster in the face of Constantine's well-coordinated onslaught.

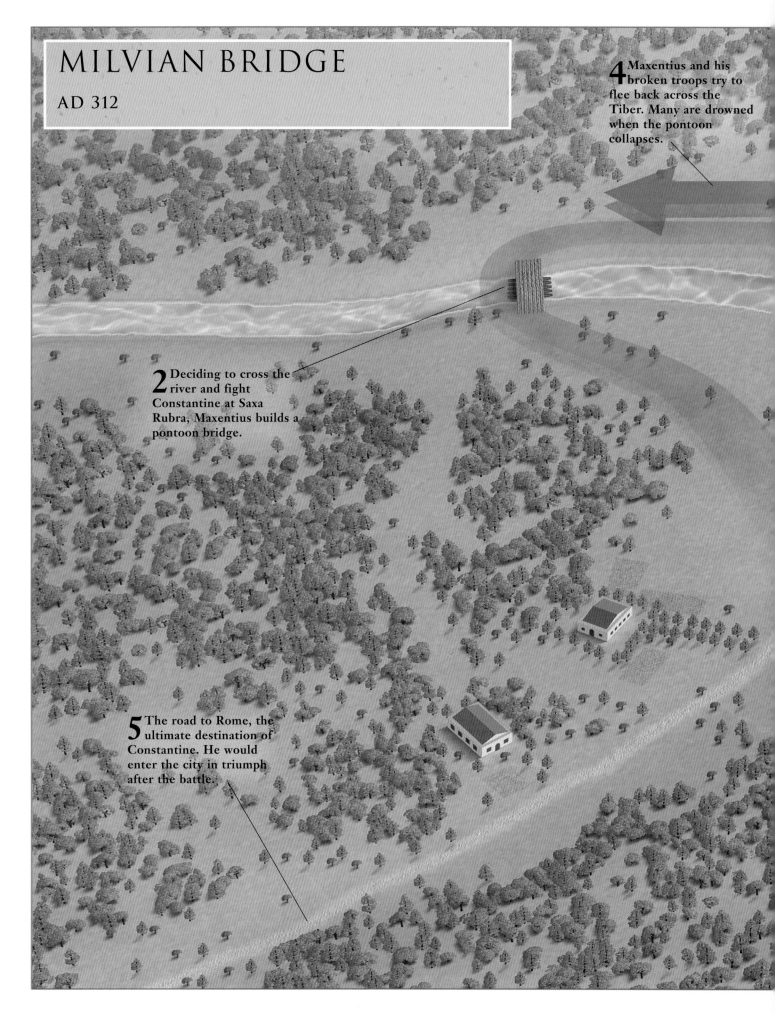

MILVIAN BRIDGE

AD 312

4 Maxentius and his broken troops try to flee back across the Tiber. Many are drowned when the pontoon collapses.

2 Deciding to cross the river and fight Constantine at Saxa Rubra, Maxentius builds a pontoon bridge.

5 The road to Rome, the ultimate destination of Constantine. He would enter the city in triumph after the battle.

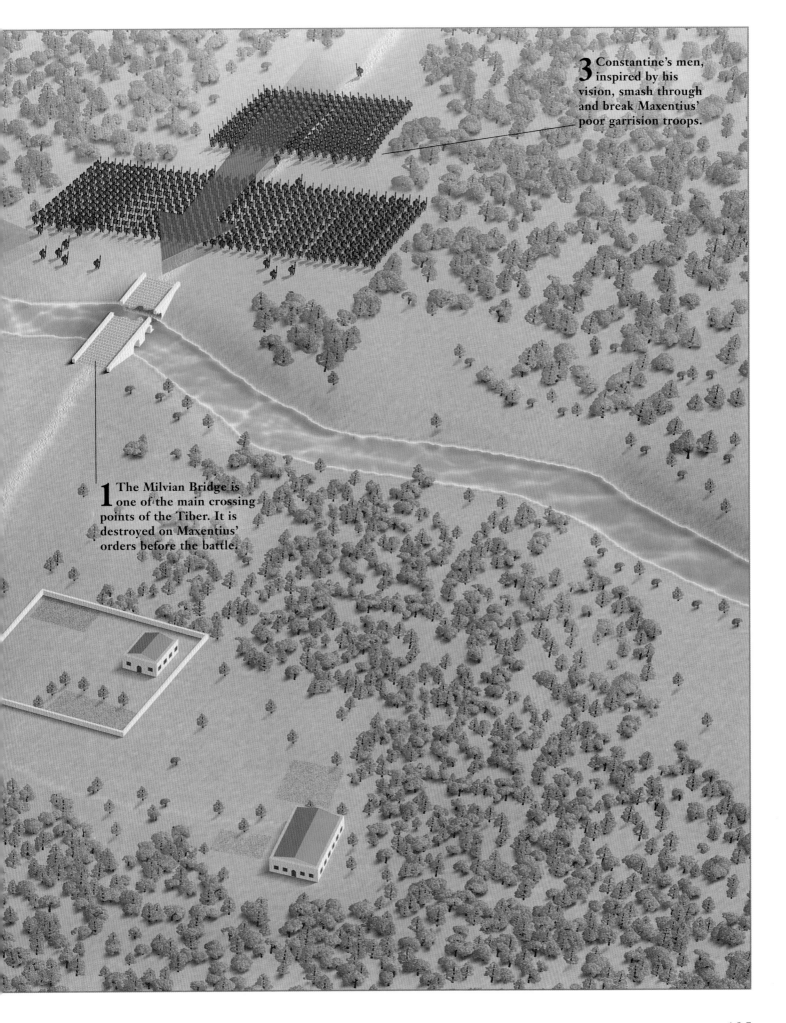

3 Constantine's men, inspired by his vision, smash through and break Maxentius' poor garrision troops.

1 The Milvian Bridge is one of the main crossing points of the Tiber. It is destroyed on Maxentius' orders before the battle.

Whether through divine inspiration or an atmospheric anomaly, the morale of Constantine and his troops surged after Constantine's announcement that he had seen a vision in the sky of the Greek letter 'rho' (ρ) crossed with a 'chi' (χ) – not the cross shown here – and heard a voice telling him 'In this sign, conquer'. The Christian device figured henceforth on the shields of Constantine's army and on his personal emblems.

expected siege of Rome. That destruction would have made sense if Maxentius had chosen to stay where he was and await his enemy within the fairly formidable fortifications of Rome itself.

Rome's weakness on her frontiers had prompted Aurelian (*c.* AD 215–275), one of Maxentius' predecessors as emperor, to construct the wall named after him in the second half of the previous century. Walls of volcanic concrete and brick facing stretched for a total of 20km (12 miles) around the central area of the city, with fortified gates and towers spaced at 30m (100 foot) intervals along the circuit. Despite the speed of Constantine's advance, there should have been stores enough in Rome for Maxentius to wear down the smaller, if more aggressive, forces of his opponent and hope for relief, a failure of Constantine's nerve, or at the very least a change in his fortunes. The demolition of the stone *Pons Milvius* committed Maxentius to taking the chance of a siege.

Instead of the course dictated by prudence and preparation, however, Maxentius decided to offer battle on the far side of the Tiber at a place called Saxa Rubra. As an immediate consequence, his engineers had to construct a wooden pontoon bridge to move his forces across the Tiber in order to form his line of battle, and such construction under hasty and desperate conditions was no more sound than Maxentius' strategic volte-face. Their commander's nervousness and sudden reversal of plans could not have been lost on Maxentius' soldiers.

On 28 October AD 312, the two would-be emperors confronted each other over the best arrangement of their forces that they and their command staffs could arrange. Maxentius still enjoyed some advantages, even in the final struggle. Foremost was the elite unit of the Roman Empire, the celebrated and notorious Praetorian Guard, officered by Maxentius' favourites within the military establishment. The empire itself had grown out of the Roman Empire when the relationship between an army and its commander had superseded all loyalties to the Senate and Roman people. For centuries, the Praetorians had functioned to coerce the population of Rome into at least physical loyalty to the emperor. They owed their fortunes and their perquisites to Maxentius, and those were at stake in the impending struggle, with disgrace and death the likely consequences of defeat. From his actions, Maxentius put more faith in these seasoned, if rear-echelon, soldiers than in the new walls of Rome.

What resources of the empire Maxentius controlled also provided him with what should have been a potent advantage and what became a severe liability. Maxentius had sufficient confidence in his cavalry to send it out into combat across that improvised wooden bridge, and in the hands of a competent commander its heterogeneous nature could have been a strong asset. Arrayed against Constantine were what the previous battles had left of Maxentius' heavy armoured troopers, alongside a number of light North African skirmishers who could have harried Constantine's forces while the heavy horse shattered the challenger's strength.

THE BATTLE

Maxentius arranged the Praetorians and raw Italian levies in the centre of his line with the cavalry disposed upon the flanks as a covering force. Constantine recognized that threat and countered it in the same way Alexander had at the Granicus some six centuries before, by personally leading his own proven cavalry in a headlong attack, seizing the initiative and testing the coordination of Maxentius' ill-assorted forces in the face of a threat that the cataphract cavalry, at least, had failed to surmount in previous encounters. There were no sub-commanders capable of meeting the challenge, and Constantine's cavalry soon had their counterparts in headlong retreat towards the wooden bridge over which they had crossed to Saxa Rubra. The troopers' swift retreat into panic and the Tiber river left the flanks of Maxentius' infantry fatally exposed.

The Praetorians justified Maxentius' faith in them by standing their ground in the face of the advance of Constantine's seasoned infantry, but they were the only Italian forces to hold their positions.

Maxentius had augmented his forces with levies from an Italy demilitarized for centuries, and these, who had taken up arms under duress, took to their heels at the first opportunity and fled in complete disorder towards the dubious safety of the wooden bridge. The Praetorians remained until they were engulfed and slaughtered where they stood, their bodies still in the ranks that had not been enough to preserve Maxentius' claim to empire.

The resulting chaos of the collapse of Maxentius' army extends into the historical record, for the exact means by which the final outcome of the struggle occurred remain somewhat unclear. Flight was still possible over the remaining stones of the severed *Pons Milvius* or by way of the wooden pontoon structure.

Crossing a pontoon bridge under even the most tranquil of circumstances requires discipline – armies customarily break step, for example, so that the oscillation that would result from a measured march does not weaken the structure of the bridge. Frightened mobs are notoriously hard on wooden structures. With the complete

collapse of his army's discipline came the complete collapse of either the remnants of the *Pons Milvius*, or the wooden bridge itself, and among those thrown into the hungry waters of the Tiber was the Emperor Maxentius himself.

AFTERMATH

Maxentius drowned in his armour, but the truth of his fate was not to be left uncertain to any remaining supporters beyond the opened gates of Rome. Constantine had the river dredged. Maxentius' head alone returned to Rome the following day, Constantine ostentatiously exhibiting it impaled on a lance in testimony to a complete and decisive end to the struggle for the empire.

Lavish larceny from earlier monuments put an elegant face on the irreversible decay of Constantine's new empire. Roundels from the time of Hadrian on Constantine's triumphal arch joined pilfered images from the time of Trajan and Aurelian to decorate the symbol of Constantine's triumph, here depicting an emperor hunting and sacrificing on a pagan altar.

ADRIANOPLE
AD 378

THE BATTLE OF ADRIANOPLE WAS THE ONLY GREAT VICTORY IN A PITCHED BATTLE OF THE GERMANS WHO OVERRAN THE WESTERN EMPIRE. THE GOTHIC VICTORY DEMONSTRATED ROMAN WEAKNESSES AND EXPOSED THE EMPIRE TO FURTHER ATTACK, BEGINNING A DOMINO EFFECT THAT ENDED IMPERIAL RULE IN THE WEST.

WHY DID IT HAPPEN?

WHO The field army of the Eastern Roman Empire, commanded by the Emperor Flavius Valens (AD 328–378), met a mixed Gothic army, with a core consisting of the Tervingi tribe under Fritigern, supported by Greuthungi led by Alatheus and Saphrax, as well as other tribes.

WHAT The battle took place between the rebellious Goths and a Roman army that had been called together to suppress the rebellion.

WHERE About 13km (8 miles) from Adrianople, modern Edirne in European Turkey.

WHEN 9 August AD 378.

WHY Having made a treaty with the Romans in AD 376 that allowed them to settle within the empire, the Goths rebelled against the ill-treatment they received. Valens intended to end this Gothic threat but attacked based on a mistaken report of Gothic strength, without waiting for the Western Roman army under Emperor Gratian (AD 359–383) to arrive.

OUTCOME The Roman army was completely defeated. Two-thirds of the Roman forces, perhaps 10,000 men, were killed, including Valens.

A gold coin of Roman emperor Valens (reigned AD 364–378), later converted into a necklace. Valens was one of the last Roman emperors to appear on coins in civilian garb.

The Goths were not a distinct group, but rather shifting alliances of eastern Germanic tribes, with little sense of ethnic identity. Nineteenth-century historians oversimplified them, dividing them into 'Visigoths' and 'Ostrogoths'. The reality was more complex. Both major Gothic divisions, the Tervingi and the Greuthungi, fought at Adrianople. In the year AD 376 the Tervingi received permission to settle in Roman territory to escape attacks by the Huns. They crossed the Danube, only to suffer systematic abuse from the Roman authorities placed over them. The Romans had promised provisions and land for settlement, in return for which the Goths would fight for the Romans. But Roman policy-makers were increasingly alarmed by the presence of a Germanic tribe within the empire, and local officials made matters much worse by making outrageous demands on the refugees. The contemporary Roman author Ammianus Marcellinus tells that they demanded Gothic children as slaves, in return providing dead dogs for food. Faced with starvation, the Goths attempted to force the Romans to honour their treaty by applying increasing pressure. They broke into full rebellion after the local Roman commander attempted to assassinate their leaders, Fritigern and Alavivus. Fritigern survived the attempt and led his followers to raid Roman territory.

The Goths travelled from place to place with their families, slaves, and all their goods in wagons, hoping to receive or take a place they could settle. They defeated a regional Roman army at Marcianople in AD 376 and fought another, indecisive, battle with the Romans at Ad Salices in AD 377. Thanks to these two engagements, the Goths at Adrianople would mostly have been using Roman arms and armour. Their position, however, remained desperate.

THE CAMPAIGN

By AD 378, continuing Gothic rampages were proving to be a major embarrassment to the Eastern Roman emperor, Valens. He was an unpopular ruler, especially because of his religious policy, which favoured Arian Christians over both Catholics and non-Christians. Valens was, however, an experienced and successful commander, who had spent much of his reign in the field. About 50 years old at the time of the battle of Adrianople, he had won several noteworthy battles against Goths in the 360s. Valens was cautious, though. He arranged for the Western emperor, his

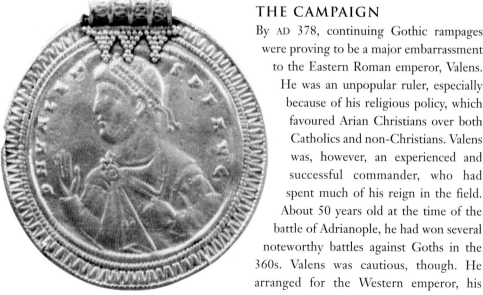

nephew Gratian, to join forces with the Eastern field army in a joint attack against the Goths. It is clear from this level of preparation that the Roman emperors regarded the Goths as a major threat.

Valens assembled the Eastern field army outside Constantinople, in a temporary camp, and joined them there on 12 June. And then he waited for the Western army, while Gratian was delayed by a campaign in the West. By the time Valens and his army had sat doing nothing for two months, morale had plummeted. Moreover, Valens had received word that his co-emperor was bringing only a small force, not the major field army anticipated. According to Ammianus Marcellinus, Valens was also jealous of his nephew's military successes, and wanted all the glory of victory for himself.

Valens' opportunity appeared to have arrived when scouts reported that the Gothic force that was approaching contained only about 10,000 fighting men. In response to this news, Valens moved his force the short distance to Adrianople, close to which the Goths had been sighted. He then decided to wait no longer for his co-emperor, Gratian, both because he believed his Eastern army outnumbered that of the Goths and because the Gothic force was trying to manoeuvre between Valens and Constantinople in a bid to cut the Roman supply lines. Thus Valens decided to join battle on 9 August.

THE SIZE OF THE ARMIES

Valens' decision to fight brings to the forefront the question of how many Gothic and Roman warriors fought at Adrianople. Historians have credited the Goths with up to an impossible 200,000 fighting men, but recent scholarship has reconsidered the issue. The key to number estimates is the report given to Valens shortly before the battle that only about 10,000 Goths were in the opposing force.

It is interesting to note that Valens did not immediately decide to attack when he heard this but rather had his military council debate the next step to take, which suggests that the Roman army was not a great deal larger than the 10,000 reported

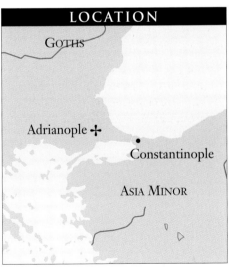

ALAN HEAVY CAVALRYMAN

It is likely that the Roman and Gothic forces at Adrianople both contained at least some heavy cavalry, sometimes known as cataphracts. Mounted on heavy horses that could bear the weight of their own body armour (27–36kg/60–80lb) as well as the weight of their armoured riders (an additional c. 18kg/40lb of metal), such horsemen could break up an enemy line by their sheer weight on impact. Since their armoured horses were less susceptible to crippling injuries, such troops were also more willing to close with the enemy, where their weapon of choice – the thrusting spear – could be devastatingly effective.

Goths. The number now most commonly accepted for the Roman army is about 15,000. While the entire Roman military in AD 378 consisted of about 500,000 men, the vast majority of these were permanently stationed on Rome's enormous frontier, while others were committed to ongoing wars against the Persians in the East and the Alamanni in the West.

The truth of the matter is that the Goths had more than 10,000 men; the remainder, perhaps as many as another 10,000, joined the battle at a key moment. So instead of the numerical superiority Valens had expected, the Romans were outnumbered, but not by a great deal. The Gothic leader Fritigern's eagerness to negotiate a peace with Valens bears out this argument in favour of roughly equal forces. On the night before the battle,

LOCATION

Goths

Adrianople ✝

Constantinople

Asia Minor

Adrianople guarded the European land approach to Constantinople, one of the Roman Empire's great metropolitan centres. Valens met the Goths there to prevent their move into more heavily populated lands.

ADRIANOPLE

Emperor Valens concludes a treaty with the leader of the Goths in AD 376, just two years before the massacre at Adrianople.

Fritigern sent a priest to try to make peace. Just before the battle, as the Romans deployed, he sent two more sets of envoys. It has been suggested that Fritigern was just stalling, waiting for the other Gothic group, the Greuthungi, to join him. Since his envoys declared that Fritigern himself was willing to go to the Roman positions to speak directly to the emperor (in return for hostages), though, it appears much more likely that he was not willing to commit his troops to a near equal battle, even if he knew how close his reinforcements were. Similarly, Valens did in fact listen to the final envoys and began to arrange an exchange of hostages, a step that would have been highly unlikely if his numerical superiority had been so great that he felt completely confident of victory.

THE OPPOSED FORCES

GOTHS (estimated)
Cavalry:	10,000
Infantry:	10,000
Total:	**20,000**

ROMANS (estimated)
Cavalry:	5000
Infantry:	10,000
Total:	**15,000**

THE BATTLE

On the morning of 9 August AD 378 the Roman army marched about 13km (8 miles) from its camp outside Adrianople to where the Gothic army had been sighted north of the city. They reached the site at about 2.00 p.m. to discover that the Goths had assumed a defensive position. They had created a wagon circle, within which their women, children, elderly, slaves and goods were placed for safety. While some warriors would have been posted to defend the wagons, most of Fritigern's force was lined up along a ridge, from which they could charge the Roman army at full speed. Most of these Gothic fighters were probably infantry; it became clear at a decisive point in the battle that the cavalry had been off foraging in the neighbourhood.

When the Romans arrived, they began to deploy in a traditional formation: two lines of heavy infantry formed the centre with a screen of skirmishers thrown out before them, and cavalry on both flanks. Ammianus describes the Roman army as 'mixed', which probably means that it included many veterans and that the units were more diversified than usual. It is almost certain that the cavalry included both regular heavy cavalry and horse archers. Most of the heavy infantry would have been equipped with chain mail, round or oval shields, and the longer swords favoured by the late Roman military, and there were also archers. The Roman army then waited, without food or water in the August sun, while their emperor proceeded to negotiate with the Goths. Probably at this point, the Goths lit grassfires upwind of the Romans, so the Roman troops also had to cope with added smoke and heat.

At this stage, everything was shaping up for a classic late Roman battle, one that would rely mostly on infantry. The only essential difference from an earlier imperial army was that the number of cavalry had grown in the course of the fourth century, and formed perhaps one quarter of the Roman force at Adrianople. While the parley was still in progress, though, things started going wrong.

The fault appears to have lain with the badly disciplined Roman cavalry, which had never been fully integrated into Roman warfare and had for decades been unpredictable on the battlefield. The Roman right-wing cavalry advanced while the negotiations continued, probably to probe for weak points in the Gothic line. Without orders, two cavalry units, probably a mix of elite cavalry and horse archers, proceeded to attack the Goths. It seems likely that the ill-disciplined troopers had seriously underestimated the 'barbarians' and regarded them with a very risky contempt. The Roman cavalry attack, unplanned and unsupported, was soon driven back.

The engagement became general. The Romans were still not fully deployed from their march; the cavalry of the left wing in particular had been at the rear of the column and were not fully formed up.

Gothic cavalry charging. Unlike the nomadic peoples of the steppe, who relied on mounted archers, Gothic cavalry fought in Greco-Roman style, with short thrusting spears and swords.

ADRIANOPLE

AD 378

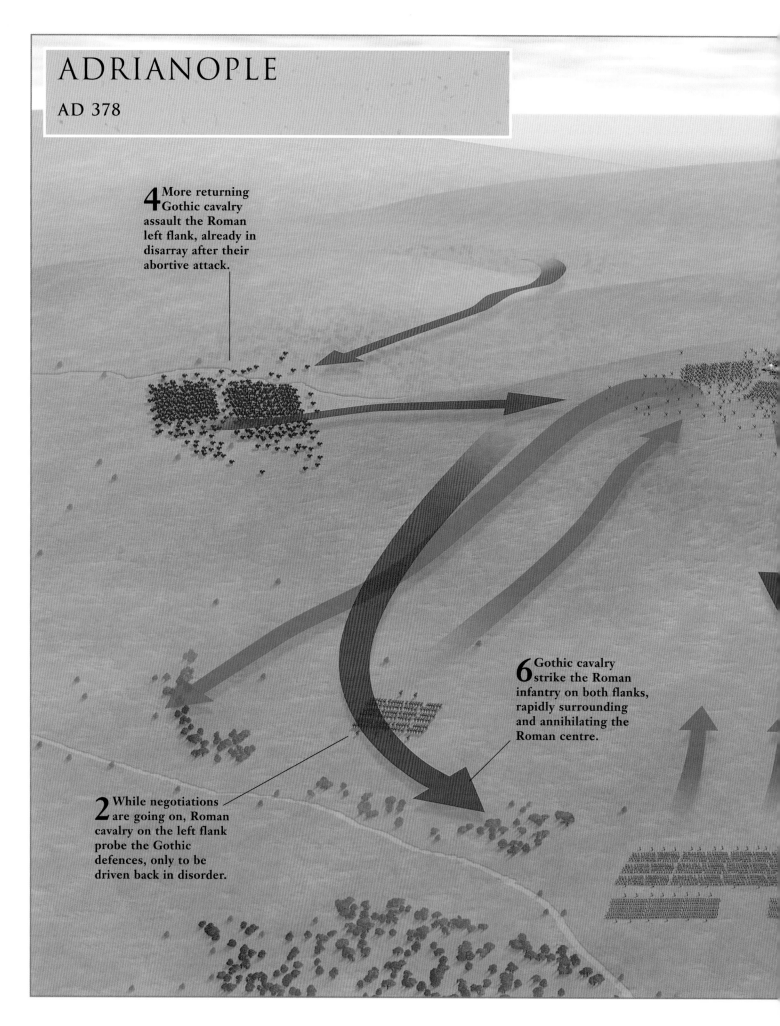

4 More returning Gothic cavalry assault the Roman left flank, already in disarray after their abortive attack.

6 Gothic cavalry strike the Roman infantry on both flanks, rapidly surrounding and annihilating the Roman centre.

2 While negotiations are going on, Roman cavalry on the left flank probe the Gothic defences, only to be driven back in disorder.

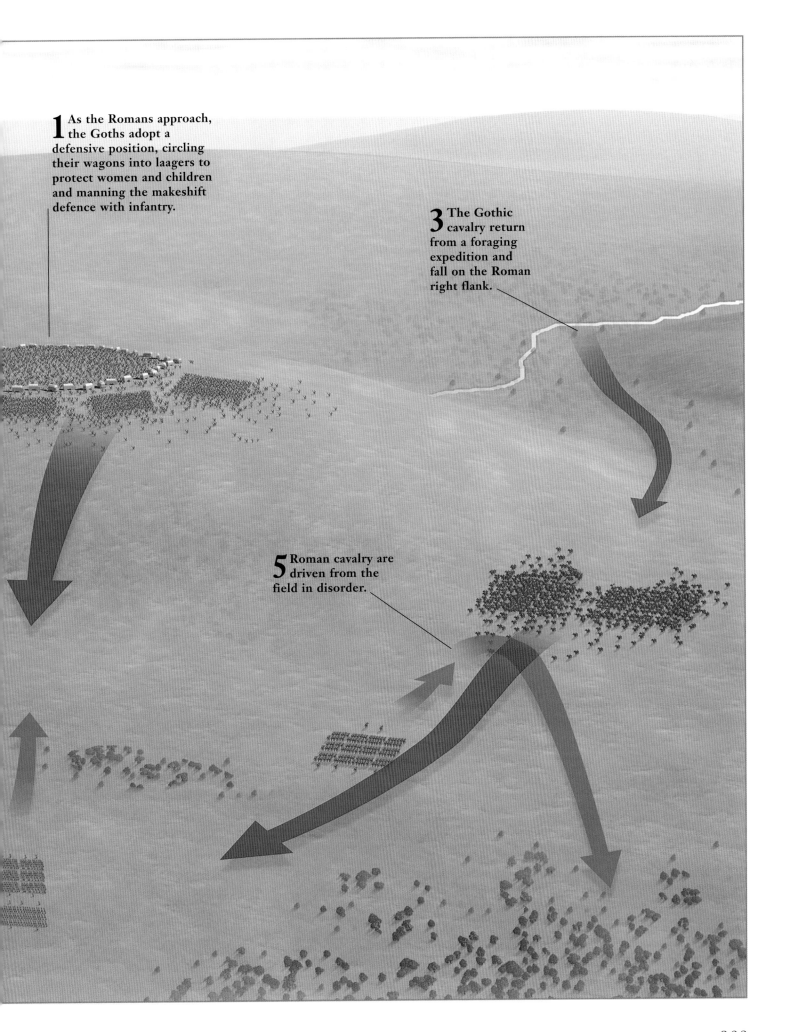

1 As the Romans approach, the Goths adopt a defensive position, circling their wagons into laagers to protect women and children and manning the makeshift defence with infantry.

3 The Gothic cavalry return from a foraging expedition and fall on the Roman right flank.

5 Roman cavalry are driven from the field in disorder.

Detail from the huge Ludovisi Sarcophagus (c. AD 250–260), showing Roman troops in battle against Germans. The sarcophagus is housed in the National Museum of Rome.

At this point, catastrophe struck the Romans. While the emperor's scouts had probably been accurate in reporting about 10,000 Goths in their camp, they had completely overlooked another large Gothic force, which had been foraging in the neighbourhood. This second group, Greuthungi under the command of Alatheus and Saphrax, also included Huns and Alans, and appears to have been mostly mounted. They appeared on the battlefield just as the Roman left wing's attack stalled and was certainly in need of reinforcement from their still unprepared comrades. The newly arrived Greuthungi achieved a complete tactical surprise. They fell on this Roman force and shattered it while the rest of the Roman left wing was still forming up to come to their support. The surviving Romans of the left wing fled for their lives, completely abandoning the battlefield.

While the Roman left wing was being routed, the Tervingi, who until then had held their position on the ridge, deployed all along the Roman infantry line. This action alone would not have caused serious worry – after all, Roman infantry had frequently defeated much larger Germanic armies in the recent past, relying on discipline and teamwork. But in this case, the Roman infantrymen were close to exhaustion from heat, hunger, and thirst before they began fighting. Much worse, the flight of the Roman cavalry had left the infantry flank fully exposed.

By the later fourth century, Roman infantry typically fought in very close order. When the Greuthungi cavalry, having driven their Roman counterparts from the field, returned and smashed into the open Roman left flank, few of the hapless infantrymen could even turn to respond effectively. Under heavy attack from both the front and the flank, the Romans were rapidly compressed still further, until they could not manoeuvre or even draw their swords to defend themselves. They soon found themselves mostly surrounded, Gothic archers adding to the confusion and panic by shooting deep into the Roman ranks.

Nonetheless, a part of the wing was sent in to attack, perhaps to draw the Goths' attention from inflicting further damage on the Roman right wing. At first this second cavalry group made good progress. They pushed the Goths back to their wagon circle, and nearly took the wagon laager itself in a spirited assault.

Most of the Roman soldiers soon broke and fled, to be cut down by Gothic cavalrymen as they tried to escape. Only two elite legions, maybe 1500 men (a fourth-century legion was only 1000 men at full strength), held firm in a desperate last stand. Emperor Valens was apparently with them. One account tells that he ordered two commanders to bring up the Roman reserves – only to find that the reserves had been among the first to flee, at the same time that the cavalry left the field. It is unlikely that any of these men survived; the emperor himself certainly did not. There are two alternative stories of Valens' death. According to one, he was killed by an arrow, and his body was never found in the carnage. A more detailed report tells that Valens was wounded, then taken to a nearby farmhouse by a few members of his bodyguard. A group of Goths attacked and, meeting resistance, burned the place down without realizing that such a valuable potential captive was inside. In all, Ammianus Marcellinus tells that two-thirds of the Roman army was left dead on the battlefield, probably amounting to some 10,000 men.

WHAT WENT WRONG?

Historians used to credit the Gothic victory to their supposed use of the stirrup, an invention that did not in fact reach Europe for several more centuries. In reality, the Roman and Gothic armies, both cavalry and infantry, would have had quite similar equipment. Nor did a vast horde of barbarians simply overwhelm a much smaller Roman force; if the Goths enjoyed numerical superiority, it was not too great. Instead, one must look to failures in the Roman army at Adrianople when seeking reasons for this military disaster. Three problems in particular stand out: 1) Low morale. The Roman army that fought at Adrianople was tired, hungry and thirsty. Moreover, their ranks were torn by religious controversy between Arian Christians, Catholic Christians and non-Christians. Many soldiers must have seen the defeat, as contemporary Catholic churchmen did, as a divine judgment against Emperor Valens for supporting the Arians. 2) Poor scouting. A traditional Roman weakness, in this case the misinformation provided by inadequate or untrained scouts was catastrophic. 3) Poorly trained and disciplined cavalry. While the Roman army employed increasing numbers of cavalry in the fourth century, during this period of transition to the largely cavalry forces of the Byzantine Empire this branch of the army appears to have been badly officered and was several times an embarrassment on the battlefield.

AFTERMATH

On 10 August, the day after the battle, the Gothic army tried to take Adrianople by assault, aiming in particular for the imperial treasury that had been left there. They failed, having no experience of attacking walled cities, and probably suffered greater losses there than they had in the main battle. So they went on to loot Thrace.

Emperor Theodosius I (c. AD 346–395) replaced the dead Valens, and both he and the Western emperor Gratian devoted their energies to defeating the Goths. They could not do so, nor could the Goths achieve another significant victory over the new Roman armies that came against them. Finally, after four years of warfare, in AD 382 the two sides made another treaty. The terms were essentially the same as the treaty of AD 376: the Goths were to receive land for settlement and autonomous status within the Roman Empire, in return for which they would provide warriors for Rome's armies.

Things appeared to be back where they had started, as if the battle of Adrianople were only a bad dream. In reality, though, much had changed. The Romans who fell at Adrianople included a high proportion of veterans, who would have been an inestimable help in ongoing battles against the Goths and Rome's other enemies. More importantly, the Roman authorities were forced to accept, once and for all, the presence of Germanic tribes on Roman soil. The Goths had proven to themselves and to the world that they could meet and defeat a Roman emperor in the field, which emboldened them in their demands. If it had not been for Adrianople, the Goths would surely never have dreamed of the course that led them, in AD 410, to sack the city of Rome itself.

Emperor Theodosius I (reigned AD 379–395). A successful general before being named Eastern emperor, Theodosius later reigned as sole ruler of a reunited empire, the last emperor to do so.

CATALAUNIAN FIELDS
AD 451

IN AD 451, THE ROMAN GENERAL AETIUS MET THE HITHERTO INVINCIBLE HUNNIC HORDES, LED BY THE 'SCOURGE OF GOD' HIMSELF, ATTILA. THE HUNS' DEFEAT HERE WAS ONE OF THE TURNING POINTS IN WESTERN HISTORY, WHEN THE WESTERN ROMAN EMPIRE WAS SAVED.

WHY DID IT HAPPEN?

WHO The army of the Huns under Attila (d. AD 453) was checked by an army of Romans, Visigoths and Alans commanded by Flavius Aetius (d. AD 454).

WHAT Aetius' army occupied the high ground at the start of the battle, from which the Huns were unable to drive them despite hard fighting. After a few days' stalemate, the Huns withdrew but the Romans did not pursue them.

WHERE The Catalaunian Fields, somewhere between Troyes and Châlons-sur-Marne in what is now the Champagne region of France.

WHEN June AD 451.

WHY Aetius sought to halt the Huns' invasion of Gaul.

OUTCOME Attila withdrew with his army and loot intact, but his reputation was damaged and the conquest of Gaul was prevented.

Very little is actually known about the infamous Attila the Hun. There are no Hunnic chroniclers, nor did the Huns have Romans write their history, like other Germanic tribes, most notably the Goths, Lombards and Franks. Thus it is only through non-Hunnic sources that anything is known about Attila, and these are always critical of him. Interestingly, and perhaps because Attila was so successful against Christians, although pagan himself he is described in these chronicles as the 'Scourge of God'. He was the Christian God's instrument of punishment against a wicked people.

Attila the Hun was certainly the dominant character of his age. Christians even called him the 'Scourge of God'. Although there is no contemporary description of Attila, artists throughout history have tried to depict him, as in this interesting portrayal.

THE HUNS

Historians are not sure when or where the Huns originated or even why they chose when they did to move out of their homelands to attack their neighbours. The best theory is that the Huns originated in the steppe regions of Siberia and Mongolia, and that in the fourth century AD they were pushed out of these regions by those who would later be called the Mongols. Evidence for this is found not only in their attack westward against the Germanic tribes and eventually the Roman Empire, but also in their move into China at the same time. It is further thought that in the West, among the Germanic tribes living north of the Danube river, the attacks of the Huns caused a 'domino effect' as they pushed one tribe fleeing from their lands into another in the wake of their invasions.

By the third quarter of the fourth century AD, the Huns began invading the territory of the Visigoths, who by AD 376 had nowhere to go but into the Roman Empire. Two years later, at the battle of Adrianople, these Visigoths crushed a Roman imperial force led by Emperor Valens, the emperor being slain during the fighting. In the view of many historians it is with this defeat that the fall of the Roman Empire began.

A more direct influence on the fall of Rome came less than 20 years later. In AD 395 the Huns began attacking the Roman Empire itself, launching a large raid into the Eastern Empire around the Black Sea and through the Caucasus. However, this proved to be a unique military expedition, as the Huns' main campaign continued into Eastern Europe until by the 420s they had established their main base on the Middle Danubian (now known as the Great Hungarian) Plain west of the Carpathian Mountains. From there the Huns conducted frequent raids over the Danube against nearby Roman settlements.

Even before they were led by their most famous leader, Attila, the Huns had made an impression on the Roman people. Ammianus Marcellinus' contemporary description is often repeated:

'… they are not well suited to infantry battles, but are nearly always on horseback, their horses being ill-shaped, but hardy; and sometimes they even sit upon them like women if they want to do anything more conveniently. There is not a person in the whole nation who cannot remain on his horse day and night. On horseback they buy and sell, they take their meat and drink, and there they recline on the narrow neck of their steed, and yield to sleep so deep as to indulge in every variety of dream … Sometimes, when provoked, they fight; and when they go into battle, they form in a solid body, and utter all kinds of terrific yells. They are very quick in their operations, of exceeding speed, and fond of surprising their enemies. With a view to this, they suddenly disperse, then reunite, and again, after having inflicted vast loss upon the enemy, scatter themselves over the whole plain in irregular formations.'

This form of combat seems to have been quite novel to imperial forces more used to fighting battles against less mobile troops, and this is perhaps why the Romans were unable to keep them from continuing to invade the empire.

ATTILA

Attila came to power sometime between AD 435 and 440 when he and his brother, Bleda, inherited leadership over the Huns from their uncle, Rua (or Ruga). Although it is not known how old or how militarily experienced they were at their inheritance, it is thought that Attila and Bleda had been raised to take over their uncle's throne and thus were probably well trained in Hunnic strategy and tactics. This was witnessed quite quickly after the brothers' ascension. In the summer of AD 441, the Huns crossed

the Danube and attacked Roman forts and villages. Clearly showing that they were undaunted by any Roman opposition, the brothers continued their invasions into the Balkan peninsula until finally stopped, not by military force but by a treaty with the Eastern Emperor, Constantine VII, that promised substantial annual subsidies of at least 1400 pounds of gold.

In AD 444 or 445, Attila had Bleda murdered and assumed complete control over the Huns. By this time Eastern Roman subsidies had fallen into arrears. In response, in AD 447 Attila sent to Constantinople to ask for payment. When his request failed to bring the desired result, he launched a campaign that led all the way to the city. En route the Huns defeated two large Roman armies, but despite

The location of the Catalaunian Fields has never been conclusively determined, although sources agree that the battle took place in June or July in northeastern France, not far from the town of Chalôns.

HUNNIC HORSE ARCHER

The Huns primarily used light cavalry, all carrying composite bows, and some also carrying spears and swords. They operated as mounted archers, which rode around their enemy, firing as they passed. These soldiers were capable of shooting their bows with great accuracy from either side of their horses at full gallop. They could also fire across the rear of their horses, in order to protect themselves when withdrawing or retreating. Their bows were not very powerful, and could not deliver an arrow able to penetrate armour worn by their opponents, although against unarmoured enemies or unprotected parts of armoured soldiers their barbed arrows could be lethal.

CATALAUNIAN FIELDS

Despite Attila's reputation as a successful general, the battle of the Catalaunian Fields was a defeat from which he could not recover. This illustration, from a nineteenth-century English magazine, shows an obvious Wagnerian influence – note the wings on Attila's helmet.

THE OPPOSED FORCES

ROMANS & ALLIES (estimated)

Total: 30–50,000

HUNS & OSTROGOTHS (estimated)

Total: 30–50,000

Constantinople's walls having been damaged by an earthquake earlier that year, they were unable to gain entrance into the city. Nevertheless, their destruction of the Eastern Roman Empire was immense, with one contemporary writer claiming the capture and sacking of more than 100 cities. Eventually the Romans were again forced to seek a peace treaty.

THE CAMPAIGN

For four years Attila was at peace with the Roman Empire. But in spring AD 451 Attila once more went on the warpath, not however against the Eastern Empire – which really had little more to offer him – but against the Western Roman Empire. Very little is known about Attila's 451 campaign prior to the battle of the Catalaunian Fields, as the main source, Jordanes, gives only the most meagre

details. It is known that Attila followed but did not cross the Upper Danube river until he reached the Rhine river, which he crossed near Coblenz. He may have captured and sacked Metz and Trier and may have reached Paris, but there is only slim evidence to substantiate this. What is certain is that in June, Attila laid siege to Orléans, a rich Roman city that was garrisoned by a large number of Alan allies of the Romans, under their king, Sangibanus.

Why Orléans was the target is not known. Contemporary sources do not mention and modern historians cannot agree on Attila's motive in selecting such a site for conquest that was so deep in Roman Gaul, especially if Metz and Trier were not attacked first. One suggestion is that Attila was looking to entice the Alans to turn against the Romans and join his army, but as he had not sought such allies in the past, this seems unlikely. The simplest answer may be that his army – described as very large, maybe half a million strong if one can trust Jordanes – ranged throughout Gaul with only Orléans (and perhaps Paris) proving to put up any opposition.

Orléans was also surrounded by a tall, thick wall further strengthened by a large number of towers. A part of this wall and a tower which have recently been excavated near the medieval Cathedral of the Holy Cross attest to this strength. Attila's siege of Orléans did not last long: by 14 June, hearing of the approach of a large Roman army, and seemingly not wanting to be caught encamped around Orléans – or perhaps not wanting to fight a battle at all – the Huns raised their siege and began to march out of Gaul.

No doubt slowed by the amount of booty they had taken, the Huns were caught up with by the Romans between Troyes and Châlons on the Catalaunian Fields.

FLAVIUS AETIUS

The Roman army that marched towards the Huns in June 451 was commanded by the experienced general Flavius Aetius. In a world where it must have seemed that all the great Roman generals were gone, Aetius' skills stood out. A contemporary, Renatus Frigiderus, left the following portrait:

'Aetius was of medium height, manly in his habits and well-proportioned. He had no bodily infirmity and was spare in physique. His intelligence was keen; he was full of energy, a superb horseman, a fine shot with an arrow and tireless with the lance. He was extremely able as a soldier and he was skilled in the arts of peace. There was no avarice in him and even less cupidity. He was magnanimous in his behaviour and never swayed in his judgement by the advice of unworthy counsellors. He bore adversity with great patience, and was ready for any exacting enterprise; he scorned danger and was able to endure hunger, thirst and loss of sleep.'

Procopius' description is more succinct: Aetius 'was the last true Roman of the West'. Of course, these qualities made him the ideal selection to lead any defence of the empire, but they also often engendered jealousy in lesser men (and women) whose political power Aetius was also forced to deal with. Eventually this would bring his demise, by an assassin employed by one of

This magazine illustration of the battle of the Catalaunian Fields attempts to portray the clash of battle. What it does not show, however, is the fatigue of the soldiers on both sides, who fought for most of a whole day.

CATALAUNIAN FIELDS

AD 451

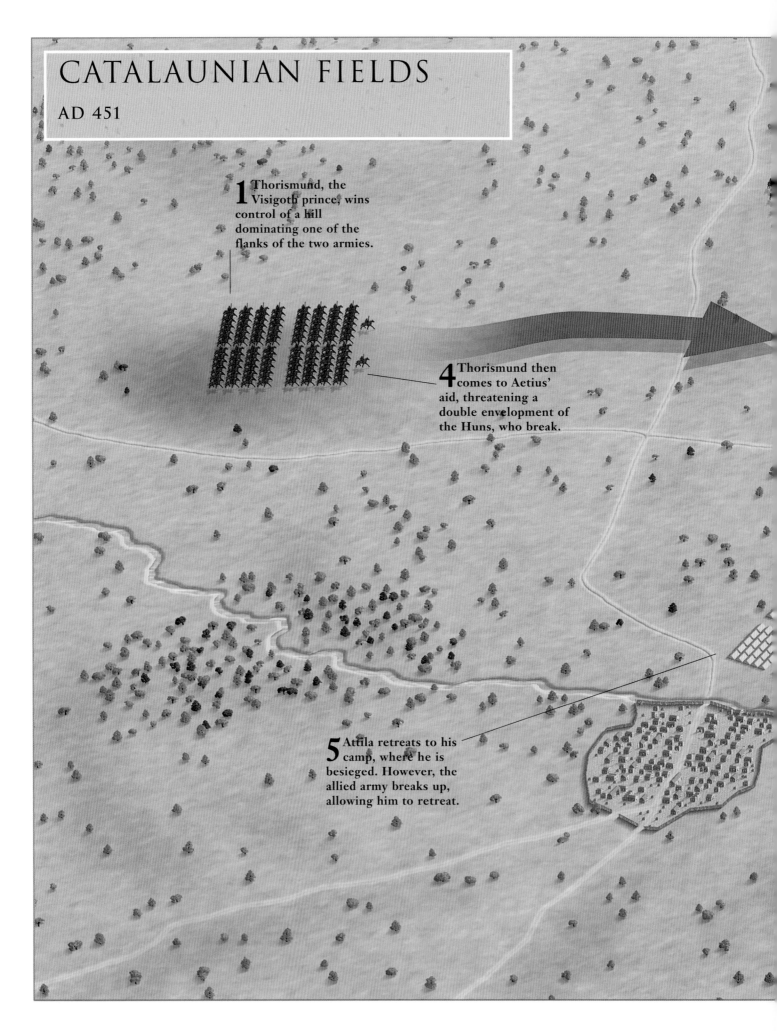

1 Thorismund, the Visigoth prince, wins control of a hill dominating one of the flanks of the two armies.

4 Thorismund then comes to Aetius' aid, threatening a double envelopment of the Huns, who break.

5 Attila retreats to his camp, where he is besieged. However, the allied army breaks up, allowing him to retreat.

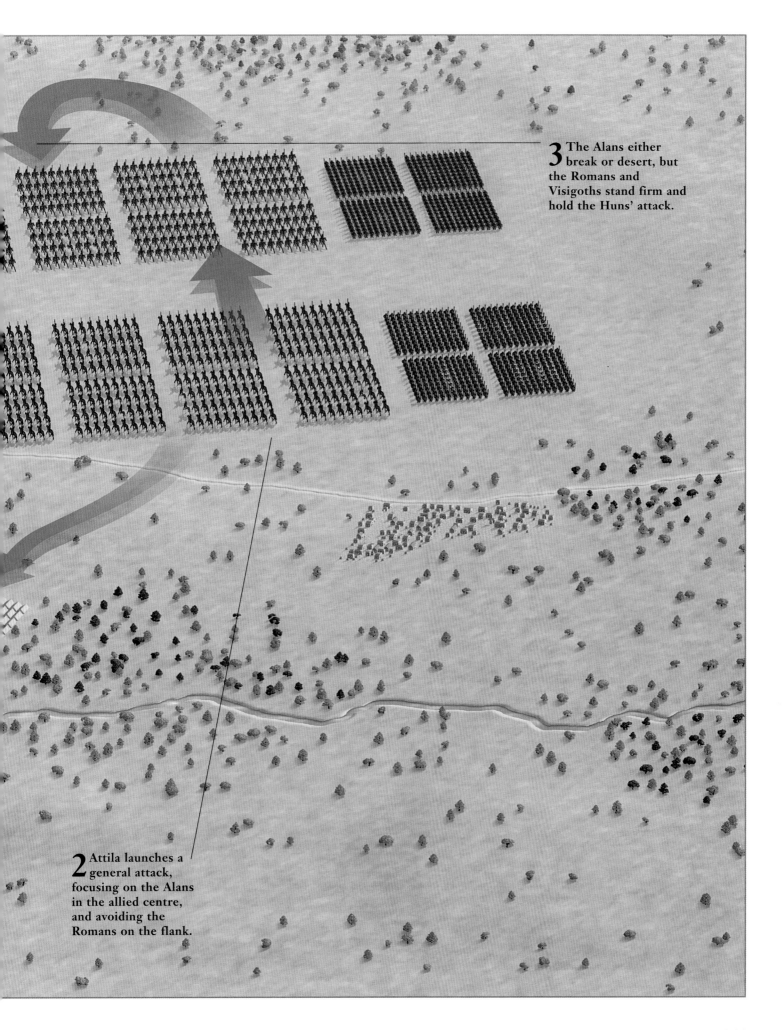

3 The Alans either break or desert, but the Romans and Visigoths stand firm and hold the Huns' attack.

2 Attila launches a general attack, focusing on the Alans in the allied centre, and avoiding the Romans on the flank.

CATALAUNIAN FIELDS

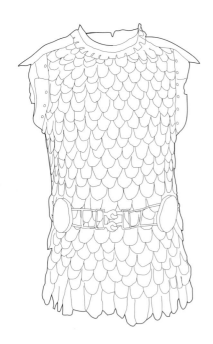

By the fourth century AD, Roman lorica squamata *(scale mail) was the most common body armour for Roman soldiers. Most scales that have been found are bronze and are 20–29mm by 10–15mm (0.9–1.14in by 0.39–0.59in), but larger iron examples exist.*

the emperors whom Aetius had protected, Valentinian III.

In AD 451, however, his assassination was still three years off. His immediate task was the halting of Attila the Hun's conquest of Gaul. Aetius knew the Huns well. As a young man he had served as a hostage, given first to Alaric the Visigoth, and then to Rua, king of the Huns and uncle of Attila. Hostages in the Ancient World were always treated to the lifestyle that they were accustomed to, and there is no doubt that during his time with the Huns Aetius had come to know their fighting style, tactics and strategy. He also had led Hunnic contingents on campaign and in battle in service of the Romans during the 430s when his generalship was required in conflicts in southern France against Visigoths and Franks, in northern Africa against Vandals and Alans, and in Italy against the imperial usurper, Boniface. And on the occasions when he fell out of favour at the Roman court, Aetius also sought refuge in the Hunnic camp.

Between AD 436 and 451 Aetius took a special interest in Gaul. The reality of Roman control there had long since passed, but Aetius still wished to sort out the problems that existed between the various tribes in the province despite the dissolution of Roman governance. Among the most historically significant of the crises that Aetius intervened in there were the expansion of the Burgundians, which was stopped when the Huns massacred more than 20,000 of them in AD 437 – an event made mythic in the Germanic Nibelungenlied – and the forced settlement of the remainder in Savoy, and the settlement of Alans in the lands and cities around Valence and Brittany to keep the peace there. Perhaps it was because of this connection to the Alans that Aetius decided to march against the Huns in AD 451, although some historians have also suggested a personal conflict between Attila and Aetius as the cause.

THE ARMIES

By the time of the battle of the Catalaunian Fields, the Roman army had ceased to be effectively 'Roman', at least in ethnic make-up. Because of the lack of imperial citizens

to fill their armies, for a long time the Romans had sought outside recruitment. In AD 212 Emperor Caracalla granted universal citizenship to all within the boundaries of the Roman Empire, thus removing one of the biggest incentives for military service. The answer was to recruit soldiers among German tribes, both those who had settled within the empire's boundaries as *foederati* (or confederates), and, increasingly, also from outside. By the time of the Visigothic invasion in AD 376 the Roman army had, in the minds of many contemporaries, become 'barbarized'.

Did this 'barbarization' change the Roman army? Vegetius, the famous late antique military strategist, although not specifically blaming recruitment policies, saw a laziness that had crept into the training practices that denoted a lack of military discipline. Soldiers refused to perform drills and complained about the weight of their armour. Vegetius' conclusion was that the Romans, when faced with troops like the Huns, would lose.

But they did not lose on the Catalaunian Fields. In fact, Aetius had increased the number of barbarians in his forces rather than decreasing them. Expecting a Hunnic assault since at least AD 443, Aetius had built alliances with German tribes which also feared the Huns. The Alans were on board, as were the Burgundians, who blamed the Huns rather than Aetius for the massacre of their people. Yet Aetius felt that this still left him with too few troops, so he approached the Aquitainian Visigothic king, Theodoric, for further assistance. Why Theodoric agreed to provide assistance is one of the mysteries of the battle of the Catalaunian Fields, as all the sources are silent on what must have been an intricate set of negotiations. The result, though, was that Theodoric joined his army with Aetius', providing especially needed heavy cavalry and infantry. These were added to the primarily heavy Roman infantry and lighter infantry, cavalry and missile troops supplied by the other allies.

The traditionally dominant arm of the Hunnic army was its mounted archers. These soldiers were capable of shooting their bows with great accuracy from either side of their horses at full gallop. They could also fire across their horses' rear, to protect themselves as they withdrew from an attack. Previous Roman and Germanic armies were unable to keep up with the speed and dexterity of the Huns' mounted archers and had often fallen victim to their tactics. However, by the time of the battle of the Catalaunian Fields Attila's army was no longer so reliant on mounted archers. Indeed, it is clear from contemporary accounts that the majority of his soldiers fought as infantry, using close-combat weapons: spears, swords and axes. This may have been a simple tactical evolution brought about by the greater contact with and against Western armies, although some historians have suggested that it may have been more indicative of the lack of European grazing lands leading to a decline in the numbers of horses contained in the Huns' herds.

THE BATTLE

Where exactly the battle of the Catalaunian Fields was contested is not known. Contemporary sources never name the site – except as the Catalaunian Fields or the *campus Mauriacus* – and are vague in their descriptions of it. Nor have archaeologists found the battlefield, and local historical memory does not remember it either. Jordanes, the best source on the battle, only mentions that 'the battlefield was a plain rising by a sharp slope to a ridge'. This high ground was obviously advantageous to the side which held it, and Jordanes makes the point that both sides sought to begin the battle from this ground. The Huns approached from the right and the Romans from the left.

Aetius had placed his own troops on his left wing and the Visigoths on his right. In the centre he positioned his Alan allies, with Jordanes insisting that Aetius did this as a 'military caution to surround by a host of faithful troops the man [Sangibanus] in whose loyalty [he] had little confidence'. Most modern historians have accepted this, but Jordanes, a Goth, seems to hold a bias against the Alans, and his statement could merely be evidence of that, especially as the Alans had recently held Orléans with such tenacity against the Huns. Besides, placing a weaker unit in between two stronger ones

was a widely used tactic and had proven effective at Marathon, Cannae and elsewhere. Attila ordered his army in an exactly opposite formation, placing his own troops in the centre with his weaker allies on his flanks, the Ostrogoths facing the Visigoths and the Gepids the Romans.

Aetius' army was the first to reach the summit of the ridge, pushing Attila's troops back as they did so. The Huns retreated in confusion, and Attila had to harangue them

Huns, under the command of Attila, have the reputation of ruthlessness and brutality. This depiction, by Alphonse de Neuville (1835–1885), has rampaging Huns riding over women and children.

CATALAUNIAN FIELDS

Hunnic military activities consisted mostly of raiding poorly protected Roman and German settlements. Battles – because of their risk – and sieges – because of the length of time – were avoided, despite the preference of later artists to depict them in such engagements.

to return to the fight with words such as these:

'Here you stand, after conquering mighty nations and subduing the world … What is war but your usual custom? … Let us then attack the foe eagerly … You know how slight a matter the Roman attack is. While they are still gathering in order and forming in one line with locked shields, they are checked, I will not say by the first wound, but even by the dust of battle … Attack the Alans, smite the Visigoths! Seek swift victory in that spot where the battle rages … Let your courage rise and your own fury burst forth! Now show your cunning, Huns, now your deeds of arms!'

The Huns responded by rushing into battle, and hand-to-hand fighting ensued for the rest of what seems to have been a rather lengthy battle. Jordanes notes the uniqueness, calling it a battle that 'grew fierce, confused, monstrous, unrelenting – a fight whose like no ancient time has ever recorded'. The fighting was also extremely

violent, as he repeats the 'old elders'' story that the brook flowing through the battlefield was 'greatly increased' by blood from the wounded soldiers flowing into it. In the midst of the battle King Theodoric of the Visigoths was killed, according to Jordanes either by being knocked off his horse and trampled under the feet of his soldiers and their horses or by the spear of an Ostrogoth warrior named Andag. (Theodoric's son, Thorismund, was also killed.) But rather than discouraging the rest of the Visigoths, their king's death enraged them and they fought with such spirit that the Huns were driven back to their camp as night fell.

ENCAMPED

Aetius expected that battle would begin again in the morning, but the Huns refused to attack. Attila assembled his troops and marched up and down in front of them, as if he was planning to lead them again up the hill. Jordanes characterizes him as 'a lion pierced by hunting spears, who paces to and fro before the mouth of his den and dares not spring, but ceases not to terrify the neighbourhood by his roaring'. But no attack followed. It may have been that by this Attila was trying to draw the Romans down from the high ground, but this is not the conclusion of the contemporary sources, who nonetheless never question the bravery of the Hunnic king.

For several days the Huns did not move from their encampment. In a sense they were being besieged, especially as they could not get supplies. Yet, they did not weaken. Instead, eventually the Visigoths became restless at the inactivity. According to Jordanes, they petitioned Aetius to allow them to attack the Hun camp, but the Roman general refused. Aetius was worried that a victory of the Huns over the Visigoths

would give them too much power and lead to the eventual fall of the empire. Instead, he advised the Visigoths to return to southern Gaul, which they did. This story makes little sense, however, as by sending them away Aetius essentially broke his battlefield unity. Thus one cannot help but wonder if the pro-Goth Jordanes contrived it to explain the Visigoths' abandonment of their alliance with the Romans. Their desertion – whatever its cause – did allow Attila to withdraw his own army from the battlefield without further loss of life, and with his wagons of booty intact. The Romans did not pursue him.

AFTERMATH

After his defeat at the battle of the Catalaunian Fields, Attila's star began quickly to wane. This most feared of all barbarian leaders had been forced to turn back from an invasion of foreign lands, virtually the first time that this had happened to a Hun army since AD 405. Attila tried to regroup at his Hungarian headquarters, but in AD 452 when he turned his army south into Italy on another campaign, he found that he could not regain his former military status. His army, hampered more by disease than by enemy action, was forced again to turn back.

Attila did not live much longer, dying in AD 453 according to contemporary sources after a night of drinking and carousing. Thus Attila was a man whose excesses in life more than any military activity brought his premature death. A Hunnic civil war followed Attila's demise, fought between his two sons over leadership of the tribe. Those previously subjected to the Huns, both barbarians and Romans, quickly took advantage of this turmoil and the extremely weakened Hun army could do nothing in response. By the end of the next decade, most of the Huns had begun retreating from Europe back towards the steppes.

Original sources have Attila the Hun dying in his mid-forties of a nosebleed after a night of drinking and carousing, which to the Christian authors of these sources would have been one of the most dishonourable of deaths. Later writers have Attila's new wife murder him.

BIBLIOGRAPHY

Adcock, Frank E. *The Greek and Macedonian Art of War.* Berkeley, University of California Press, 1957.

Anderson, J.K. *Military Theory and Practice in the Age of Xenophon.* Berkeley, University of California Press.

Banks, A. *A World Atlas of Military History.* London, Seeley Service & Co, 1973.

Barker, P. *Armies and Enemies of Imperial Rome.* Worthing, Wargames Research Group, 1981.

Caesar, Julius. *Commentaries.* (Ed. and trans. John Warrington), London, 1953.

Carter, John M., *The Battle of Actium.* London, Hamish Hamilton, 1970.

Casson, Lionel. *The Ancient Mariners, Seafarers and Sea Fighters of the Mediterranean in Ancient Times.* 2nd ed., Princeton, Princeton University Press, 1991.

Connolly, P. *Greece and Rome at War.* London, Macdonald Phoebus, 1981; American ed. Englewood Cliffs, Prentice-Hall Incorporated, 1981.

Ducrey, Pierre. *Warfare in Ancient Greece.* (trans. Janet Lloyd), New York, Schocken Books, 1986.

Ellis, John. *Cavalry: The History of Mounted Warfare.* New York, G. P. Putnam's Sons, 1978.

Ferrill, Arther. *The Origins of War: from the Stone Age to Alexander the Great.* New York, Thames and Hudson, 1985.

Fuller, J.F.C. *Julius Caesar.* New Brunswick, 1965.

Fuller, J.F.C. *The Generalship of Alexander the Great.* Wordsworth Military Library, Cambridge, Wordsworth Editions Ltd., 1998.

Gardiner, Robert, ed. *The Age of the Galley.* London, Conway Maritime Press, 1995.

Garlan, Yvon. *War in the Ancient World.* (trans. Janet Lloyd), London, Chatto & Windus, 1975.

Gibbon, Edward. *The Decline and Fall of the Roman Empire,* two vols., Everyman's Library Series, New York, Knopf, 1993.

Gilliver, C. M. *The Roman Art of War.* Stroud, Gloucestershire, Tempus, 1999.

Goldsworthy, Adrian. *Roman Warfare.* London, Cassell, 2000.

Goldsworthy, Adrian. *The Punic Wars.* London, Cassell, 2000.

Goodfellow, D., ed. *Atlas of Military History.* London, Collins, 2004.

Grant, M. *Romans.* Edinburgh, Thomas Nelson & Sons Ltd, 1960.

Grayson, A.K. 'Assyrian Civilisation' in J. Boardman et al. (eds), Cambridge Ancient History 2 3.2., Cambridge, Cambridge University Press, 1991, p.194–228.

Green, Peter. *The Year of Salamis, 480–479 BC.* London, Weidenfeld and Nicolson, 1970.

Green, Peter. *The Greco–Persian Wars.* Berkeley, University of California Press, 1996.

Greer, J. *The Armies and Enemies of Ancient China.* Worthing, Wargames Research Group, 1975.

Gurval, Robert A. *Actium and Augustus.* Ann Arbor, University of Michigan Press, 1995.

Hackett, J. (ed.) *Warfare in the Ancient World.* London, Sidgwick and Jackson, 1989.

Hanson, Victor Davis, ed. *Hoplites: the Classical Greek Battle Experience.* London, Routledge, 1991.

Hanson, Victor Davis. *The Wars of the Ancient Greeks.* London, Cassell, 1999.

Head D. *Armies of the Macedonian and Punic Wars, 359BC–146BC.* Worthing, Wargames Research Group, 1982.

Heather, Peter J. *The Fall of the Roman Empire: A New History of Rome and the Barbarians.* New York, Oxford University Press, 2006.

Holmes, R. *The World Atlas of Warfare.* London, Mitchell Beazley, 1988.

Hopkins, C. 'The Siege of Dura' in *Classical Journal,* 42, 1947, p.251–259.

Humble, Richard. *Warfare in the Ancient World.* London, Cassell, 1980.

Hyland, Ann. *Equus: The Horse in the Roman World.* London and New Haven, Yale University Press, 1990.

Josephus. *The Jewish War.* London, Penguin Classics, 1981.

Keegan, John. *A History of Warfare*. London, Hutchinson, 1993.

Kern, P.B. *Ancient Siege Warfare*. London, Souvenir, 1999.

Lazenby, J. F. *The First Punic War*. Stanford, Stanford University Press, 1996.

Leach, John. *Pompey the Great*. London, Croom Helm, 1978.

Livy. *History of Rome*. (trans. B. O. Foster, E. T. Sage, and A. C.Schlesinger), Loeb Series. 14 vols. Cambridge, Mass., 1919–1957.

Livy, *The War with Hannibal*. London, Penguin Classics, 1970.

Marsden, E.W. *Greek and Roman Artillery*. Oxford, Clarendon Press, 1971.

May, Elmer C., Gerald P. Stadler, and John F. Votaw. *Ancient and Medieval Warfare*. The West Point Military History series, Wayne, N.J., Avery Pub. Group, 1984.

McCartney, Eugene S. *Warfare by Land and Sea*. New York, Cooper Square Publishers, 1963.

Morrison, J.S., J.F. Coates and N.B. Rankov. *The Athenian Trireme*. 2nd ed., Cambridge, Cambridge University Press, 2000.

Perrett, B. *The Battle Book*. London, Arms and Armour Press, 1992.

Plutarch. *The Fall of the Roman Republic*. London, Penguin Classics, 2005.

Plutarch. *Lives*. New York, Penguin, 1987.

Polybius. *Histories*. (trans. W. R. Paton), Loeb Series. Cambridge, Mass., 1922–1927.

Pritchett, W.K. *Ancient Greek Military Practices*. Part I, University of California Publications, Classical Studies, vol. 7, Berkeley, University of California Press, 1971.

Pritchett, W.K. *The Greek State at War*. Part II, Berkeley, The University of California Press, 1974.

Pritchett, W.K. *The Greek State at War*. Part V, Chapter 1, 'Stone Throwers and Slingers in Ancient Greek Warfare', Berkeley & Los Angeles, University of California Press, 1991, pp.1–67.

Richmond, I.A. 'The Roman Siege-works at Masàda, Israel', *Journal of Roman Studies*, 1962, p.142–155.

Rodgers, William Ledyard. *Greek and Roman Naval Warfare*. Annapolis, US Naval Institute, 1964.

Sage, Michael M. *Warfare in Ancient Greece: a Sourcebook*. London, Routledge, 1996.

Shipley, G. *The Greek World after Alexander, 323–30 BC*. London, Routledge.

Stark, F. *Rome on the Euphrates*. London, John Murray, 1966.

Starr, Chester G. *The Influence of Sea Power on Ancient History*. New York, Oxford University Press, 1989.

Sun Tzu. *The Art of War* (trans.Samuel B. Griffith). Penguin, New York, 1963.

Tacitus. *The Histories*. London, Penguin Classics, 1975.

Thucydides. *History of the Peloponnesian War*. London, 1954.

Warry, John G. *Warfare in the Classical World: An Illustrated Encyclopedia of Weapons, Warriors, and Warfare in the Ancient Civilisations of Greece and Rome*. Norman, University of Oklahoma Press, 1995.

Webster, G. *The Roman Imperial Army*. London, Adam and Charles Black, 1974.

Whitby, Michael. *Rome at War, A.D. 293–696*. Oxford, Osprey, 2002.

Vegetius. 'The Military Institutions of the Romans.' In T. R. Phillips (ed.) *Roots of Strategy*. Harrisburg, 1940.

Xenophon. *Anabasis*. (trans. W. Miller, et al.), Loeb Series. Cambridge, Mass., 1914–1925.

Yadin, Y. *The Art of Warfare in Biblical Lands*. London, McGraw Hill, 1963.

Yadin, Y. *Masada, Herod's Fortress and the Zealot's Last Stand*. London, Weidenfeld and Nicolson, 1966.

INDEX

Page numbers in *italics* refer to illustrations; those in **bold** type refer to map illustrations with text. Abbreviations are as follows: (B) – battle; (NB) – naval battle; (S) – siege.

PICTURE AND ILLUSTRATION CREDITS

All maps produced by **JB Illustrations** © Amber Books

Unless credited below all illustrations are © Amber Books

AKG-Images: 10, 53, 58, 63, 148, 172, 188

AKG-Images/Peter Connolly: 9, 14–15, 85, 92–93, 108, 126–127, 142, 146–147, 156–157, 178–179

Ancient Art and Architecture Collection: 16, 31, 36, 57, 110–111, 150, 159, 160, 189, 192, 197, 198, 214

Art Archive: 30, 96, 158

Corbis: 7, 8, 13, 18, 20, 24, 27, 28, 35, 37, 62, 66, 67, 69, 71, 88, 90, 100, 103, 106 (top), 120, 123, 132, 149, 153, 164–165, 169, 170–171, 175, 182, 185, 190, 204, 205, 206, 215

Mary Evans Picture Library: 25, 26, 38, 44, 45, 47, 48, 49, 52, 59, 68, 72, 74, 78, 93, 99, 102, 117, 118–119, 128, 129, 138, 139, 162, 168, 196, 200, 208, 209

Getty Images: 81, 82, 89, 106 (bottom), 107, 114, 115, 137, 140, 181, 213

Heritage Image Partnership: 12, 46, 98, 192–193

Photos 12: 161

TopFoto: 178